A SHORT COMMENTARY ON
KANT'S *CRITIQUE OF PURE REASON*

A SHORT COMMENTARY
ON KANT'S
CRITIQUE OF PURE REASON

by-

A. C. EWING

Reader in Philosophy in Cambridge University and
Fellow of British Academy

METHUEN & CO. LTD., LONDON
36 *Essex Street, Strand, W.C.* 2

First published . . November 3rd 1938
Second edition . . 1950
Reprinted . . 1961

CATALOGUE NO. 2/5322/10

PRINTED IN GREAT BRITAIN
BY BRADFORD & DICKENS
LONDON WCI

PREFACE

It is a very surprising fact that in all the flood of literature which has been called forth by the study of Kant there is not to be found a single English commentary on his chief work which is adapted to the needs of the ordinary honours student, who so often has to tackle the *Critique of Pure Reason* as a set book. Existing books on Kant seem to me, however admirable in themselves, either somewhat too detailed and lengthy for such students, or are outlines of the whole of Kant's philosophy and do not attempt a systematic exposition and examination of the first Critique chapter by chapter, so that they are not detailed enough. The present work is an attempt to supply this deficiency by giving the honours student what he needs by way of comment in the modest compass of 270 pages. Not that it is intended for honours students alone: I cannot help feeling that the treatment is sufficiently original to be also some contribution to Kantian scholarship,—how much it is not for me to assess—, and that it should be of some value to professional philosophers and more advanced students also. Students of all classes, however, must remember that it is essentially a commentary to be read in conjunction with the text and aims at exegesis and that amount of criticism which is inseparable from exegesis rather than at an independent decision concerning the problems of philosophy discussed by Kant. The author's standpoint on many of these may be found in *Idealism*.[1] It must not be assumed that, where I make no criticism, I necessarily adopt a doctrine of Kant's.

[1] Methuen, 1934.

Since this book is a putting together of results derived from a reading and teaching of Kant spread over many years, it is impossible to give a full account of my obligations. The books that have helped me most by far are Professor Kemp Smith's *Commentary* and Professor Paton's *Kant's Metaphysic of Experience*, but their influence often operates in reverse directions. My perusal of the latter has in fact changed a good many opinions about Kant which I had adopted under the influence of the former, but the influence of both can be traced throughout.

I am also under considerable personal obligation to Professor Kemp Smith himself and Professor Stout for having been kind enough to look through most of my MSS and suggest improvements, and to my mother for having carried out the laborious task of proof-reading. I have also enjoyed the help in interpreting certain passages of Dr. Werner Brock. Finally I must thank the Faculty Board of Moral Science at Cambridge for having consented to set Kant's work as special subject for the Moral Sciences Tripos some years before it was due, so that I had the opportunity of giving a course of lectures on the Critique earlier than would otherwise have been the case, thus facilitating the speedier writing of the book.

A. C. EWING

Trinity Hall, Cambridge
June, 1938

CONTENTS

PAGE

CHAPTER

I. Introductory   1

II. The Transcendental Æsthetic   28

III. The Transcendental Deduction of the Categories   66

IV. The Individual Categories and Their Proofs   132

V. Kant's Attitude to Material Idealism. The Thing-in-Itself   176

VI. The Paralogisms and the Antinomies   199

VII. Theology and the Ideas of Reason   241

Index   271

Index of Comments on Particular Passages   277

NOTE CONCERNING REFERENCES

I have used Professor Kemp Smith's translation of the *Critique of Pure Reason* throughout. I am responsible myself for any translations of passages from other works, except that I have, with some alterations, made use of Abbott where the latter's translations were available.

A and B stand for the original pagings of the first and second editions respectively of the Critique. Berl. = Berlin edition of Kant's work. References to Kemp Smith are to his *Commentary*, and references to Paton to his book entitled *Kant's Metaphysic of Experience*, unless otherwise stated. References to Abbott are to the book called *Kant's Theory of Ethics* in which he translates selections from Kant's ethical works.

CHAPTER I

INTRODUCTORY

KANT was born in 1724 and died in 1804. From 1755 onwards he lectured at the university of Königsberg in East Prussia, till 1770 as an ill-paid *Privatdozent* and after that as a Professor, and all his life never travelled outside this part of Germany. The Critique of Pure Reason (*Kritik der reinen Vernunft*) was published in 1781, and was his first extremely important work. Had Kant died the year before at the age of 56 without it being published his name would probably be unknown now even to the ordinary English student of philosophy. The second edition of the Critique was published in 1787.

The scope of the present book does not allow for any more than the briefest summary of Kant's development up to the Critique of Pure Reason.[1] He was brought up in the Leibnizian, "rationalist" school, the leader of which after Leibniz's death was Wolff, whom Kant described even in the Critique of Pure Reason as "the greatest of all the dogmatic philosophers."[2] The form Kant gave to his work and his *a priori* approach to problems always shows very strongly the influence of this school, which no doubt agreed with his own temperament: in so far as he was an empiricist at all he was probably an empiricist against his

[1] For a short account of Kant's earlier works *v*. Lindsay, *Kant*, ch. 2, and Ewing, *Kant's Treatment of Causality*, ch. 2. A much fuller account is given by Caird in *The Critical Philosophy of Kant*. For a very interesting brief sketch of Kant's life and personality *v*. Lindsay, ch. 1.

[2] B XXXVI.

I

will. Up to 1760 he would no doubt have called himself a member of the school, though attacking it at some points. About 1763 he definitely broke with it, probably partly under the influence of Hume, and wrote various works assailing its main doctrines.[1] The principal points where he joined issue with it then are these, (a) he thought the mathematical method totally unsuitable for philosophy; (b) he rejected the rationalist view that cause was a species of logical ground and the consequent assimilation of reality to an intelligible system; (c) he criticised the current proofs of God. He was at that time perhaps nearer to empiricism than he ever was later, since he did not yet realise the necessity of the categories for science and for consciousness of objects, but though he despaired of all existing metaphysics he still hoped that one would be written and even thought this the most important task of the human intellect.[2] Only he thought that such a metaphysics must be preceded by an investigation of the human faculties of knowledge in order to determine what we could hope to know and what we could not. *The Critique of Pure Reason* was intended originally as this preliminary investigation, to be followed by a real metaphysics, but he concluded later that it left no scope for any metaphysics beyond itself.

In the Latin dissertation of 1770, *On the Forms and Principles of the Sensible and of the Intelligible World*, with which he inaugurated his professorship at Königsberg, Kant first took the drastic step of making space and time and everything that was in them only appearance, but he

---

[1] *The Only Possible Proof of the Existence of God, Enquiry into the Evidence of the Principles of Natural Theology and Morals, Treatise on Negative Quantity, The Dreams of a Ghost-Seer as illustrated by the dreams of Metaphysics.*

[2] e.g. *Berl.* I, 6, 7.

still held that we could attain *a priori* knowledge of the real world. This confidence was soon shattered, perhaps by reading extracts from Hume's *Treatise* quoted by an opponent, Beattie. (The *Enquiry* was translated into German in 1754-6 and Beattie's book in 1772; Kant's rejection (about 1763) of the then prevalent view that cause is a species of logical ground has been connected with the former, his realisation (about 1772) of the difficulties connected with the general principle that every change has a cause and so of the general problem of synthetic *a priori* judgments with the latter. It is very doubtful whether Kant ever read the *Treatise* itself, which was not translated into German, and he shows ignorance of Hume's view of mathematics there. Kant gave to Hume the credit of having first aroused him from his " dogmatic slumbers,"[1] but to which of the two periods he is referring is not certain, though it is more probably the later.)

In a letter of 1772 Kant first raises the difficulty how we can be justified in applying *a priori* categories to objects. This problem soon resolved itself into two : (1) How can we be justified in applying them even to appearances in advance of experience, as we must do if we are to have science? (2) Can there be any justification at all for applying them to reality? The Critique of Pure Reason is, very roughly, an answer to these two problems, but this abstract formulation must not blind one to the deeper issues behind them.

In February 1772 Kant expressed the hope that he would complete the Critique in three months; in fact he took about nine years longer, eleven years in all, and then finished in a hurry because he was afraid that he might die before he had completed his great work. In view of this it seems

[1] *Prolegomena, Berl.* IV, 260.

almost certain that the work contains parts written at very different times, and this, since he changed his opinions a good deal during the eleven years in which he was engaged on the book, is very likely to have given rise to inconsistencies. On this basis complicated theories have been developed purporting to show how certain parts of the Critique were constructed by the combination of notes which were written at different times and therefore were often quite inconsistent with each other. But we do not know how far Kant may not have revised his earlier notes, and I am very sceptical as to our ability to discover in detail which parts of the work are early and which late, and so, like Prof. Vaihinger and Kemp Smith,[1] to divide it into an elaborate series of " strata."

Further, as the advocates of the theory would no doubt mostly themselves admit, we ought to start with the assumption that a great philosopher is not likely to be always contradicting himself, and consequently, wherever there are two interpretations, one of which will make Kant consistent and the other inconsistent, prefer the former to the latter, if reasonably possible. Now proceeding on these lines I seem to find that of verbal contradictions there are a good many, and this is no doubt due partly to the haste with which the work was composed; but I think that, if we understand the words sympathetically in the light of their context, we can generally arrive at a consistent doctrine which will reconcile the apparently conflicting passages. Whether I am right or not on this is a matter which can only be decided in connection with my detailed exegesis. If and in so far as I am

---

[1] *v.* Vaihinger, *Die Transzendentale Deduktion*, Kemp Smith, *Comm.*, XX-XXIV, 202-34. For a searching criticism of the theory *v.* Paton, *Proceedings of Aristotelian Society*, 1929-30, p. 143 ff.

right, it removes the only ground for distinguishing between different strata in the Critique. But in any case and whatever the commentator's personal views, it is certainly desirable not to confuse the student in an outline commentary with constant discussions as to the composition of the text but rather to concentrate on explaining the doctrines expounded, and this I shall do with only a short note on the multiple theory, as I shall call it, in connection with the *Transcendental Deduction of the Categories*, where it has been carried to the greatest extremes,[1] and with a quotation from Kant here.

The quotation refers to his version of the *Critique* for the second edition in 1787.[2] " In the propositions themselves and their proofs, and also in the form and completeness of the plan, I have found nothing to alter. This is due partly to the long examination to which I had subjected them before offering them to the public " (*i.e.,* before the first edition came out), " partly to the nature of the subject-matter with which we are dealing. For pure speculative reason has a structure wherein everything is an *organ*, the whole being for the sake of every part, and every part for the sake of all the others, so that even the smallest imperfection, be it a fault (error) or a deficiency, must inevitably betray itself in use. This system will, as I hope, maintain, throughout the future, this unchangeableness. It is not self-conceit which justifies me in this confidence, but the evidence experimentally obtained through the parity of the result, whether we proceed from the smallest elements to the whole of pure reason or reverse-wise from the whole to each part. Any attempt to change even the smallest part at once gives rise to contradictions, not merely in the system, but in

[1] *v.* below, p. 95 ff.   [2] B XXXVII–XXXVIII.

human reason in general."[1] I do not claim to refute the multiple theory here : this could only be done by detailed exegesis removing the inconsistencies, but the quotation seems to me to rule out the only possibility that could provide at all a plausible basis for it. Kant might possibly in his anxiety to finish the Critique have strung together a number of notes written at different times and either not realised their inconsistency just because he had not time to revise them or said to himself : " This is the best I can produce in the time; no doubt there are inconsistencies, but on the whole it will do." But if this had been the case he would hardly *after* the revision required for the second edition have had such complete confidence that he had made no mistakes in the doctrine set forth (as opposed to the mode of exposition, which he did amend), and that the work constituted not merely a consistent whole but a system so organic that one could not alter any part without destroying the whole. While there are no doubt some inconsistencies to be found in every philosopher, it seems to me incredible that any philosopher with a reasonable claim to greatness should both have thought his work to form such a completely coherent system and yet have been in fact guilty of so many inconsistencies as are attributed to him by the holders of the multiple theory. I cannot agree with Professor Kemp Smith in holding that the passage quoted refers mainly to Kant's " architectonic " (classification of knowledge). A careful reading of the passage seems to make it quite clear to me that it is intended to refer unambiguously to the whole content of Kant's work. The alterations added in the second edition are expressly said to be merely changes in the method of exposition.[2]

[1] B XXXVIII.   [2] *Methode des Vortrags* (B XLII).

It is indeed important to realise, as Professor Kemp Smith insists, that there is a sense in which inconsistency may sometimes be a mark of greatness rather than of the reverse. Where a smaller mind might be consistent at the expense of breadth a great philosopher may, just because he sees further, be faced with two conflicting principles which he cannot wholly reconcile and yet neither of which he can abandon. But, if Kant really carried this so far that he "flatly contradicts himself in almost every chapter,"[1] or, worse still, the Critique "is the merest patchwork or mosaic of scraps, specimens of which have been collected by hundreds,"[2] this does seem to me to detract considerably from his greatness. It is only fair to say that the multiple theory has been applied mainly to the first edition transcendental deduction, which Kant himself discarded in the second edition, and not to the Critique as a whole; but, when Kant rewrote the transcendental deduction in the second edition, he did not, according to his own account, do it because he thought the original version self-contradictory or in parts fundamentally inconsistent with his present opinions, but because he wished to alter merely the method of exposition, as we can see from the passage just quoted and B XLII; and Professor Kemp Smith in his *Commentary* is always pointing out contradictions not only in the transcendental deduction but throughout the Critique and ascribing them to an inconsistency between earlier and later notes. I am certainly not prepared to go to the other extreme and admit that the Critique was the completely coherent system which Kant fancied it to be, but the reader will see when he goes through this book that I am very moderate in my ascription of con-

---

[1] Kemp Smith, *Commentary*, p. XX.
[2] Ward, *A Study of Kant*, p. 41.

tradictions to Kant, though perhaps not quite as moderate in this respect as is Professor Paton.

Some of Kant's letters and private notes throw a valuable light on his method of composition, and, more than that, on the method which any philosopher ought to pursue, and I shall accordingly quote them here. " You know that I do not approach reasonable objections with the intention merely of refuting them, but that in thinking them over I always weave them into my judgments, and afford them the opportunity of overturning all my most cherished beliefs. I entertain the hope that by thus viewing my judgments impartially from the standpoint of others some third view that will improve upon my previous insight may be obtainable."[1] " Relaxations and diversions must maintain its (the mind's) powers in freedom and mobility, so that it may be enabled to view the object afresh from every side, and so to enlarge its point of view from a microscopic to a universal outlook that it adopts in turn every conceivable standpoint, verifying the observations of each by means of all the others."[2] " We must consider propositions in all their various applications; even when they may not seem to require a special proof, we must make trial of their opposites, and in this way fight for delay, until the truth becomes in all respects evident."[3] These are admirable precepts as to the method a philosopher should follow in arriving at his views and in seeking to revise them afterwards, but to consider different inconsistent standpoints while writing a book is very different from incorporating them all in the text of the book as if they were

---

[1] *Berl.* X, 116-7. These quotations are taken from Kemp Smith, *Comm.*, XXII-III.

[2] *Berl.* X, 127.

[3] Erdmann, *Reflexionen*, II, 5.

all held by the author to be true, and I am unable to agree with Professor Kemp Smith that the passages quoted make the multiple theory more plausible.

Whether we accept some form of the multiple theory or not, it is hardly possible to avoid making some distinction on occasion between passages which seem to be fully in accord with Kant's mature standpoint and passages which, at least in their phraseology, suggest a point of view divergent from the characteristic Kantian doctrine and reminiscent of positions held earlier by Kant. Such passages are commonly described as " pre-critical " by commentators. But as to which the pre-critical passages are there is a great deal of difference of opinion, and it is a matter in which the judgment of commentators seems to depend very largely on their personal opinion as to what are the best and truest parts of Kant's philosophy and therefore on their own philosophical views.

To pass on to the content of the work itself, the *Critique* may be said to have had two main aims, (1) in the *Æsthetic* and the *Analytic*, to provide a philosophical basis for physical science, which assumed an *a priori* knowledge that was necessary for its very existence, yet hard to defend, (2) chiefly in the *Dialectic*, " to deny knowledge in order to make room for faith."[1] The second purpose, which was for Kant even more important than the first, may seem obscurantist, but faith does not for Kant mean belief on authority or belief without grounds, but believing what we have adequate grounds for believing but cannot absolutely prove. The grounds for the belief in God and immortality, however, being ethical, are not given here in detail but, chiefly, in the *Critique of Practical Reason.* What Kant maintains on this

[1] B XXX.

subject in the *Critique of Pure Reason* is only that (1) we cannot settle religious questions either positively or negatively by using the categories which we use in thinking about objects of science, and therefore cannot prove God and immortality by means of premises which are scientific or metaphysical but not ethical in character; (2) neither can we ever disprove God and immortality; (3) science can recognise no limits in the sphere of Nature, its categories, and its categories alone, are to be recognised there. This left it open for him to use ethical arguments in another work to establish the existence of God and immortality, not indeed as something proved with conclusive certainty, but as a reasonable belief. Further, Kant claimed in the *Critique of Pure Reason* to have solved the problem of freedom, which was a necessary presupposition of ethics and yet hard to reconcile with causality, and to have solved it without denying the unbroken reign of law in the natural world.

The importance of the ethical and religious motive for the *Critique of Pure Reason* in Kant's mind has often been overlooked. But Kant, under the influence of Rousseau, had rejected the Leibnizian view, which found the chief good in thought, and had come to the conclusion that the chief good was the moral will, something which we could have without cleverness or education, and that thought and knowledge were of value only as a means, so that he said "I should regard myself as much more useless than a common labourer if I did not believe that my work could accomplish something of worth to all in restoring the rights of humanity."[1] The main thing which Kant thought his work accomplished was to make religion and ethics for ever secure against the sceptic, and he no doubt regarded even the com-

[1] Hartenstein's edition, VIII, p. 624.

plicated analysis of the *Æsthetic* and the *Analytic* as a means without which that end could not be adequately attained. However the ultimate end which Kant thought that he served is kept far enough away from the means, so that many have been greatly influenced by the *Critique* who had little sympathy with the purpose I have just mentioned, at least as envisaged by Kant.

As I have said, the *Critique* had another main purpose, namely the provision of a philosophical basis for science. It is this purpose that is predominant in the *Æsthetic* and *Analytic*. In this connection we should remember that Kant was deeply interested and well versed in the physical sciences, and that in his early years he made original contributions to theoretical physics as well as to philosophy, e.g. he suggested a nebular theory as to the origin of the planets,[1] in which he anticipated to a large extent the work of the great physicist, Laplace. When thinking of science, the science which he had most in mind was Newtonian physics. This presupposed the validity for the physical world of mathematics, the law of conservation of matter, the law of universal causality and the principle that every particle of matter interacted with every other. The problem for Kant was that these principles seemed necessary for the very existence of science, but could not be justified empirically, and had not yet been successfully justified *a priori* by any philosopher. The main aim of the *Æsthetic* and *Analytic* is to explain the occurrence of this *a priori* knowledge and provide its justification. This account must not be taken as contradicting the fact that there are a vast number of important points in the *Critique* which cannot be brought under the two primary aims I have

[1] *General Natural History and Theory of the Heavens*, 1755.

mentioned. The Critique contains points of importance for practically all philosophical questions.

Further, the two main purposes react on each other. The belief that God, freedom and immortality can either be proved or disproved by metaphysics rests on the assumption that we can apply indiscriminately to reality the categories, such as causality, which we apply to the objects of science. It is natural to think that we can extend beyond these objects principles which we know *a priori* to apply to these objects, but Kant thinks that in the very act of proving the scientific categories he can show that the proof is valid only for objects of actual or possible human experience and cannot therefore be used to justify their application in metaphysics. According to Kant, as long as we have not seen exactly what the justification of these is and that the only justification is of a sort which will make it impossible to extend them beyond the bounds of experience, we shall be liable to oscillate between a scepticism which doubts science because of the failure of metaphysics and a dogmatism which finds in the successful application of our *a priori* categories in science a justification for their application in a region where they cannot be applied successfully. The two evils can be permanently removed only by a " critical " philosophy, which will show that the categories can be proved, but only for the kind of objects which we encounter in science and ordinary experience.

The idea of a preliminary investigation of our cognitive faculties in order to determine what we can and what we cannot know was far from being peculiar to Kant. The current objection that we must in order to examine our cognitive faculties use the very instrument which we are examining would be admitted by Kant, but he holds that we can still examine them in their working. When he criticises our knowledge or alleged knowledge he is not criticising it from outside, so to speak, but criticising part of it in the light of the higher standard set by the other parts. He is not putting us in the position of men who tried to test their vision by looking at their own eyes, but in the position of men who compared the objects which they saw clearly with those they saw only dimly, made generalisations as to the kinds of objects which fall into the two classes and explained the difference by a theory of vision.

I shall now turn to the actual text and devote the rest of this chapter to saying what I have to say about Kant's prefaces and introduction. I must again warn the reader that my commentary requires to be read side by side with the Critique, at least in Professor Kemp Smith's abridged edition, and is not intended to be read straight through by itself. Any student who uses it as a *substitute* for reading the Critique will find it both very uninteresting and very unhelpful. It is intended to fall midway between the detailed commentaries of Caird, Kemp Smith and Paton and the abbreviated outline accounts of Adamson, Lindsay and Clarke, and thus to provide a book which will be neither too short nor too long for the average honours student, whose needs I have most in mind. It seems to me that the lack of such a book is much felt, and I have therefore restricted myself to less than 300 pages. This necessity for comparative brevity has made it impossible to discuss in detail a great many points on which I might perhaps have profitably enlarged, but I still hope that my book may be of some value also to more advanced students of Kant. I must add that this is a work of exegesis and not of criticism, except where this is necessary for the exegesis, or where I am " sorely tempted," and that the fact that I have not objected to a given view or argument of Kant mentioned here is not to be taken as evidence that I necessarily agree with it. The criticisms that I have made are enclosed in square brackets in order to separate them from the exegesis. Nor is even my exegesis intended to provide an adequate summary of Kant's argument. Except in the more difficult passages this task of making a summary is best left to the student, and he must not expect me to mention all important points in the argument, but only those where I think he needs help.

The Preface to the First Edition is clearly written, and there is only one point in connection with it on which I wish to comment at the present stage. This is Kant's audacious claim to completeness and certainty for his philosophy,[1] a claim which he never withdraws. He thought completeness possible, because by definition pure reason covers only those elements in knowledge which arise from our nature independently of experience, and these we should be able to know if we know anything, and can know further that they could from the nature of the case never be contradicted or even enlarged by experience, and secondly, because its knowledge, being *a priori,* must constitute a system such that each part is entailed by the rest and the omission of any part would therefore lead to difficulties in the rest.[2] Certainty he opposes to opinion and declares that there can be no room whatever for opinions in philosophy, because it is *a priori.* For Kant a person who said that a philosophical conclusion had been shown to be probable would be like a

---

[1] A XIII-XVI, XX, *cf.* B XXIII-IV.
[2] This at least is Kant's view here. Professor Kemp Smith would say he changed it later (*v.* B 145-6).

schoolboy who said he saw that " 5 plus 7 was *very likely* equal to 12."[1]

[We may grant that an *a priori* conclusion cannot be merely probable in the same sense as that in which a conclusion based on induction is probable, and that any uncertainty in *a priori* reasoning must be due merely to the risk of our having committed some error. But modern philosophers will realise better than Kant that even the greatest thinker cannot be sure that he has not committed some error in handling these difficult subjects. Nor can we say even that, while we may be uncertain about an *a priori* argument, the argument itself must either be logically certain or a mere fallacy, for an argument, especially in philosophy, may be invalid in the sense that it has not succeeded in establishing what it set out to prove, and may yet really prove something *like* the conclusion put forward, and so improve our knowledge by bringing those who accept it at least nearer the truth, though nobody may succeed for centuries in analysing exactly what could be proved. As regards his claim to completeness in this section, it would not be admitted by any modern critic, and the argument for it seems to be founded on a separation between *a priori* reason and experience which is far too sharp to be in accord with the principles of Kant's own philosophy.]

The reader should note specially Kant's remarks concerning the obscurity or clearness of his work.[2] The *Metaphysics of Nature* projected in A XXI was never written.

The *Preface to the Second Edition* is important and should

---

[1] *cf.* B 803. Even the beliefs in God, freedom and immortality are not said to be probable, but "certain for practical reason," *v.* below, p. 249.

[2] A XVIII-XIX.

be carefully read but, unless we anticipate our comments on subsequent parts of the book, there is again only one point that calls acutely for discussion in a commentary of this size, i.e. Kant's alleged " Copernican revolution."[1] It may seem that Kant's revolution was opposite rather than analogous to that of Copernicus since, while Copernicus put an end to the anthropocentric character of astronomy, Kant rather made philosophy anthropocentric. But Kant means that he resembles Copernicus in attributing to ourselves and so classing as appearance what his predecessors had attributed to reality. Just as Copernicus taught that the movement round the earth which men had ascribed to the sun was only an appearance due to our own movement, so Kant taught that space and time which men had ascribed to reality were only appearances due to ourselves. The parallel is therefore correct. Kant would, like Copernicus, say that this view was not more anthropocentric than that of his predecessors but less so, since it no longer, like their views, attributed to independent reality what belonged to men.

Introduction. § 1. Kant here lays down his famous principle that all our knowledge begins with experience but does not all arise out of experience, i.e. there is no knowledge temporally before experience but it is not all either causally due to or logically based on experience. Kant is here using experience to mean sense-experience.[2] Towards the end of the second edition version of the section Kant distinguishes between relatively *a priori* and absolutely *a priori* know-

---

[1] B XVI-XVII.

[2] " Throughout the *Introduction* the term *experience* has (even at times in one and the same sentence) two quite distinct meanings, (1) as product of sense and understanding acting co-operatively, and (2) as the raw material (the impressions) of sense." (Kemp Smith, *Commentary*, p. 52.)

ledge, the latter being not merely "independent of this or that experience but absolutely independent of all experience," and gives as an example of the latter the principle that every alteration has a cause (though he declines to regard it as "pure"). This is verbally inconsistent with his fundamental view that the categories can only be proved by reference to experience, but he is here thinking of dependence on experience in the sense in which empirical generalisations depend on experience. In that sense he never held that the categories could be derived from experience. Again we must not assume that the narrowing of the meaning of "pure" which we find here represents his common usage. More commonly *pure* and *a priori* are used as synonymous, as in the title of the book.

The first edition version of this section is much more rationalistic and less empirical than the second edition.

§ 2. Kant here gives as the two criteria of *a priori* knowledge universality and necessity. He held rightly that the two entail each other, for, if B follows necessarily from A, B must be present whenever A occurs, and unless B follows from A we have not genuine universality because exceptions are always at least possible. He further assumes (rightly) that no proposition which has these two characteristics can be derived simply from experience (observation, including sense-perception and introspection). [Whether the notion of the *a priori* as developed later in the Critique really provides us with universality and necessity in *this* sense is another question.]

§ 3. The term *Anschauung* which occurs in B 8 and in a vast number of other passages in the Critique is usually translated "intuition," but it has no connection with the sense in which this word is most commonly employed in

English to-day as meaning *a priori* insight not based on reasoning. By derivation it is really " a looking at," and, though this is also what " intuition " should mean by derivation (intueor), *Anschauung* in Kant keeps much more closely to its etymological meaning, though intended to cover other senses besides sight. It means for Kant *awareness of individual entities*. In human beings this awareness can only occur in sense-perception (including introspection), but we cannot know it to be impossible that there might be other beings who enjoyed it without sense-perception or anything analogous. *Anschauung* is sometimes translated perception, but as Kant has another word which must be translated in this way, *Wahrnehmung*, it is better to keep to " intuition " for *Anschauung*. *Wahrnehmung* is slightly narrower since, as I said above, there might be beings, though not human beings, who had *Anschauung* otherwise than by *Wahrnehmung*.

§ 4. *The Distinction between Analytic and Synthetic Judgments*. The distinction is invented by Kant and was not familiar to his predecessors.[1] Judgments here = propositions as the term is used now in philosophy. That is, it does not refer to the act of judging but to what is judged. The terms, analytic and synthetic, as thus applied to judgments are treated by Kant as logical contradictories, i.e. all judgments are either analytic or synthetic and no judgment can be both. The definitions given presuppose that the judgments concerned are reducible to subject-predicate form, but they could be amended to fit relational judgments. Kant thinks analytic judgments to be useful as clarifying

[1] But *cf*. Locke's account of " trifling propositions " (*Essay on the Human Understanding*, Bk. IV, ch. 8), which in some ways is superior to Kant's treatment here.

what we already know, though incapable of yielding any fresh knowledge. He accordingly would not exclude them from science or philosophy or deny their title to be judgments, but merely points out that for science we also need synthetic *a priori* judgments.

An analytic judgment is one which is true by the definition of its subject-term, but we must not therefore confuse it with a definition, which is usually a synthetic and empirical judgment expressing the way in which people actually use words or the writer's intention to use a word in a certain way, or sometimes hortative—" let us use the words to mean this "—and so not a judgment at all. This is shown by the fact that there is always a verbal contradiction in denying an analytic proposition, but there is certainly never a contradiction in asserting that the established meaning of a word is different from what it really is, i.e. in denying a definition. Granted that " rational animal " is the meaning of man and " sentient material being " the meaning of animal, that man is material is an analytic proposition true by definition, but to assert either of the definitions is to assert that certain beings (Englishmen) generally use the sound " man " on certain occasions, which is as contingent as any fact could be. Kant does not anticipate his as yet unproved doctrine that all judgments, even those we call empirical, have an *a priori* element, but speaks here as though some judgments were purely empirical.

It has been objected against Kant that the same judgment may be synthetic for one person and analytic for another who has more knowledge. But the question is one of the ultimate justification of a judgment, i.e. is the judgment true because the predicate is part of the meaning of the subject-term or for some other reason? Consequently a judgment cannot be analytic on one occasion and synthetic on another, if we are really dealing with the same judgment on the two occasions and not merely with the same form of words. Nor must we be disturbed by Kant's insistence later on that even analytic judgments involve a synthesis, for " synthesis " as thus used is not synonymous with the noun of " synthetic " as used here.

[The problem whether there are synthetic *a priori* judgments, which Kant now raises, is really a question about inference—can I by inference pass with logical necessity from one fact to another, different fact, or is the conclusion of any inference (excepting only the empirical generalisation or argument from analogy which constitutes problematic induction) always merely part (or all) of the premises restated in different language? " 5 plus 7 = 12 " or " every change has a cause " are single propositions not arguments, but the question about them can still be adequately represented as a question about inference—how is it that we can infer that *a* is 12 from " *a* is 5 plus 7 " and that " *a* has a cause" from " *a* is a change "? The question is one of the most important in the whole of philosophy. If there are no synthetic *a priori* judgments in this sense, thought can never give us new truth but only the same truth as we had before but expressed in different words; all deductive inferences and self-evident propositions will be a matter of arbitrary verbal convention; there will be no philosophy beyond the ordering and clarification of propositions known, if known at all, in some other way; mathematics will be merely a game with symbols; there will be no relation of entailment or necessary connection in the objective world but merely a set of brute facts any of which might perfectly well exist without the others existing also.

Unfortunately, however, many philosophers seem to have confused "analytic propositions" as meaning (a) propositions which, though true, give no new knowledge with (b) propositions which cannot be denied without self-contradiction. We thus often come across the statement that the rationalists prior to Kant held that all *a priori* propositions were analytic. Now, provided we do not interpret it as meaning that they recognised the distinction between analytic and synthetic explicitly in Kant's form, this is a true statement about these philosophers if we are using analytic in the second sense but not if we are using it in the first. Descartes, Spinoza, Leibniz and Wolff certainly held that they could by *a priori* reasoning arrive at startling new truths about e.g. God which were not merely part of their premises expressed in a different way, though they did think that *a priori* propositions and inferences could not be denied without self-contradiction. Whatever the merits or demerits of the conclusion, e.g. that monads do not interact but that there is a pre-established harmony, it is certainly a new fact that Leibniz was intending to assert and not part of a received definition expressed in different language.

Now, even if we distinguish the two senses, many people will think it obvious that a proposition which is analytic in the second sense must be analytic in the first although the two do not mean the same thing, and this seems to have been what Kant thought. It is indeed one of the chief reasons which have led people to deny that *a priori* propositions and reasoning could give new truth, since it is hard to avoid holding that all *a priori* propositions are ana-

lytic at least in the second sense, but that it must be fallacious can easily be seen as follows. Once we have
distinguished the two meanings it is clear that the proposition that what is analytic in the second sense must be
analytic in the first sense is itself synthetic (i.e. not analytic)
in the first sense. Therefore anybody who holds that there
cannot in that sense be synthetic *a priori* propositions on
these grounds is using a synthetic *a priori* proposition to
prove that no synthetic *a priori* propositions are possible,
and anybody who, like Kant, holds that there can be synthetic *a priori* propositions, but only if they are justified by
a quite special mode of proof by reference to experience, is
holding this on the ground of a synthetic *a priori* proposition which he has certainly not justified by this special
mode of proof. The fallacy may be due to a confusion
between saying that it is self-contradictory to assert S and
deny P and saying that it is self-contradictory to assert S
and not assert P; the latter statement can only be true if P
is part of S, but it does not follow that the former cannot
be so.[1]]

Now, because Kant held that a proposition which is
analytic in the second sense must be analytic in the first, he
supposed that pure thought as such must be analytic in the
first sense, i.e. it cannot give new knowledge but only
analyse what is given from another source. But, since he
could not escape admitting that some *a priori* propositions
are not analytic in this first sense, he had to account for the
fact that, while being necessary and universal, they yet
gave new knowledge by reference, not to thought, but to
our other main cognitive faculty, sense-perception. This is
part of the basis of his view that it is impossible to go be-

[1] For a fuller account of this subject *v.* my *Idealism*, ch. V, § 5.

yond the realm of sense-experience, so the effects of the confusion, if, as I think, it is a confusion, are very far-reaching. Kant's view is that, because there are some *a priori* propositions which are not analytic in the first sense, these propositions are not analytic in the second sense either; and this seems to be the reason which makes him think a proof by reference to experience necessary for them as opposed to a proof by concepts. He also thinks that there are some propositions which are analytic in both senses, and that these are the only propositions, outside Ethics at least, which can be established without reference to sense-perception. His problem now is to explain how we can have judgments which are *a priori* and yet based on sense-perception.

§ 5. The section points out that synthetic *a priori* judgments occur in some sciences, leaving it to the rest of the Critique to explain and, where possible, justify their occurrence. The first sentence seems to contradict what Kant himself says in B 16-7 and does not express his usual view, which is that most, but not all, propositions in mathematics are synthetic (or does he mean that the analytic propositions mentioned in B 17 are not *mathematical* propositions at all, being only " links in the chain of method "?).

In showing that arithmetical judgments such as " 5 plus 7 = 12 " are synthetic he points out that 5 plus 7 is only the concept that 5 and 7 are to be united in one number and does not include the concept of what that number is. To put it in another way, the two concepts cannot be the same, since to say that some things are 12 in number is not to say anything about two different groups, 5 and 7, and to say that they are 5 plus 7 is not to say what happens when the two groups in question are combined. We must not be confused by the sign of equality and take for identity of concept equality in quantity or identity of the number to which the two concepts refer. Kant points out that this contention becomes clearer if we take the case of large numbers. His reference to the use of fingers in counting may suggest that arithmetic depends on empirical perceptions; this is not his view, he thinks it depends on " pure intuition "[1] and that the use of fingers etc. is merely an illustration.

The last three sentences of the part of the section on mathematics in the German text (B 17) have apparently been displaced and should follow immediately the end of the previous paragraph, where Professor Kemp Smith in his translation has in fact placed them.

The examples which Kant gives of synthetic *a priori* propositions in natural science are not categories (or even schemata), but principles which he supposed to be deducible from the categories. The second one, which must be distinguished from the category of community, does not occur again in the Critique, but an attempt is made to prove it *a priori* in the *Metaphysical First Principles of Natural Science*.[2]

§ 6. The *Æsthetic* answers the question—how are synthetic *a priori* judgments possible in mathematics? The *Analytic* answers the question—how are they possible in natural science? The *Dialectic* shows that they are not possible in metaphysics and explains how they came to be wrongly thought possible there. Such judgments are of course few in natural science, but they are very important as seeming to be necessary presuppositions of science.

[1] *v.* below, p. 58.   [2] *Berl.* IV, 544.

Metaphysics. By metaphysics, in the sense in which he rejects it, Kant means alleged knowledge about the general nature of reality as it is in itself as opposed to knowledge of it as it appears to us. He assumes that this metaphysics must be *a priori*, since from the nature of the case it goes beyond our experience. In rejecting metaphysics he wishes to exclude both any theology based on non-ethical premisses and philosophical realism. But he also uses the term metaphysics in a sense in which he admits its possibility, as a science which deals with general concepts valid in the realm of experience. Where a metaphysical argument is contrasted with a transcendental argument he means by the former an argument which proceeds by analysing concepts.

§ 7. *Meaning of "Transcendental."*[1] It is important to distinguish the terms transcendental and transcendent. *Transcendent* refers to what is not a possible object of experience, hence for Kant transcendent knowledge is impossible. *Transcendental* refers to the necessary conditions of our experience. Transcendental knowledge is therefore certainly possible for Kant and in fact constitutes the chief part of the Critique. In particular Kant claims to give transcendental proofs, meaning proofs which proceed by showing that if the principle he proved were not true of an object we could not "experience" that object. Unfortunately, however, Kant sometimes, especially in the *Dialectic*, uses the term transcendental where we should expect transcendent, especially in the phrase "transcendental use of concepts."

Kant's General Answer to the Question how Synthetic A Priori Propositions are Possible. Kant assumes that a

[1] B 25.

perceptual element is necessary in order to make a proposition synthetic.[1] But a proposition derived from particular
sense-perceptions, he was equally clear, could not be *a
priori*, for it would be lacking in universality and necessity.
Therefore he had to find some way of connecting synthetic
a priori propositions with sense-perception which did not
involve their derivation from particular perceptions. So he
bases these propositions on general conditions admittedly
common to all sense-perception of the kind we have. These
conditions are, with outer objects, space and, with all objects, time. For anything to be perceived in space or time,
he argues, it must conform to certain principles and these
are therefore themselves necessary conditions of experience
and so *a priori*. E.g. all objects given in sense-experience
except those of introspection are perceived as in Euclidean
space, therefore the axioms and theorems of Euclidean
space must be valid of all outer objects of experience (outer
here =, I think, other than oneself); everything that we
experience is in time, nothing can be experienced in time
which is not caused, therefore causation is valid for all objects of experience. In this way the principles in question can be synthetic because they are connected with
experience, and also *a priori* because they are necessary
and therefore universal conditions of human experience.
The synthetic *a priori* propositions are proved by reference
to the conditions of all human experience; they are proved
by showing that, if they were not true of objects, these
objects could not be experienced by us. This would not
matter to the objects if they were things-in-themselves, but
they are only appearances, and therefore could not exist
without being objects of experience to us, so they must

[1] *v.* above, p. 22.

conform to any conditions which are necessary if they are to be objects of experience to us. But for this very reason the synthetic *a priori* principles cannot be shown to apply to independent reality (things-in-themselves), but only to actual or possible objects of experience (" phenomena " or " appearances ").

CHAPTER II

THE TRANSCENDENTAL ÆSTHETIC

Æsthetic must be understood strictly in its etymological sense as derived from the Greek word αἴσθησις (sense-perception). It has nothing to do with the theory of beauty but should rather be understood as " theory of perception,"[1] though it does not deal with the problems with which we are familiar under that heading to-day.

Too much attention must not be paid to Kant's definitions of terms in § 1.[2] The meaning of the various terms as used by him cannot be adequately understood from the definitions given here, and I prefer to explain them, in so far as necessary, as the question arises in the context of Kant's philosophy. The reader is reminded that *intuition* as used in the Æsthetic has nothing in common with the sense of intuition as immediate *a priori* insight but means *the awareness of individual existents*.[3] The definition given of it in the first sentences of the section is unsatisfactory since it would exclude pure intuition. The very general term *representation* (*Vorstellung*) covers all images and ideas.

What does Kant mean by calling space and time pure or a priori intuitions? Since intuition is, for human beings at least, sense-perception, and the *a priori* is most commonly defined as that which is not derived from sense-perception, *a priori intuition* seems very much like a contradiction in terms, and certainly calls for some explanation. Unfor-

[1] *v.* B 35 and note.
[2] *v.* Kemp Smith, *Commentary*, pp. 79-80.
[3] *v.* above, pp. 17-8.

28

tunately the term *a priori* as used by Kant has several meanings, by which I do not mean so much that he used it inconsistently as that he included under it various characteristics of which it is by no means clear that they all necessarily go together.

1. As applied to judgments it signifies *logical necessity*. Kant certainly does not hold the intuitions of space and time to be themselves *a priori* in this sense, but when he speaks of them as *a priori* he often has in mind the fact that, though not themselves logically necessary, they are the source of logically necessary and thus *a priori* propositions, especially in geometry. They can only be so because as wholes they determine their own parts *a priori* and therefore everything which falls within them, though only as regards its spatial and temporal characteristics.[1]

2. *A priori* also bears the meaning of *not derivable from particular sensations* (including sensation of the inner sense, i.e. introspection).

3. *A priori* also signifies *what is presupposed in all our experience*.

4. Finally the *a priori* is *what is contributed by ourselves*.

These four notions are not clearly separated, and Kant in

---

[1] "It seems reasonable to hold that space and time are ultimate and necessary elements in human experience—we can conceive no human experience without them. But this might be said equally of sensation. What is the special kind of necessity which belongs to space and time, and not to sensation? . . . Space and time are such that we can say what their parts must be. They are, so to speak, necessary through and through, and there is nothing in them which is not necessary. We know not only *that* they must be in all experience, but what they must be in all experience. . . . Space and time are known *a priori*, firstly as wholes which necessarily determine the character of their parts, and secondly as necessary conditions of experience. If they were not *a priori* ideas in the first sense, they would not be *a priori* ideas in the second sense." (Paton I, pp. 153-4.)

fact seems to think that, if space and time are *a priori* in any of the first three senses, they must be *a priori* in the fourth also. He holds that the fourth follows from the first, since it is only because we ourselves make what we know that we can have synthetic *a priori* knowledge at all; he assumes that, if space and time are not due to sensations, there is no other alternative but that they should be contributed by ourselves; and he holds that the fact that they are presupposed in all our experience can only be explained by supposing that they are so contributed. (I have said "contributed by ourselves" rather than "contributed by the mind" because the latter phrase suggests that they are the work of thought, whereas Kant insisted that they are on the contrary to be ascribed to our nature as sentient beings and not as thinkers. He probably regards their source as lying in the real counterpart of the phenomenal objects which we call our sense-organs, whatever that counterpart may be.)

Space and time are thus sensible and yet *a priori* because they are derived not from particular sensations but from the general constitution of our nature in so far as we are adapted to receive sensations. They are those factors in our sense-experience which are due to ourselves and not to things-in-themselves acting on us. Because they are contributed by ourselves we can tell *a priori* that all objects which we experience will conform to them, just as when we use blue spectacles we can tell *a priori* that everything we see will look blue. This account of the *a priori* carries with it the implication that we can have *a priori* knowledge only of appearances not of reality, just as from the premiss that I wear blue spectacles I could infer not that all the physical objects I see really will be blue, but that they will look blue to me.

Besides being forms of intuition space and time are also asserted by Kant to be themselves intuitions. Kant holds that we have some sort of representation of Space and Time as a whole, and that, whenever we perceive anything, what we perceive is somehow located by us in this space and time. Now some of the passages which assert this doctrine may be interpreted as implying the apriority of space and time in a fifth sense as meaning that our apprehension of them preceded temporally our apprehension of any objects in space and time. But it would certainly be possible to hold that space and time are due to our nature as sentient beings and not to particular sensations as such without holding that we had intuitions of space and time temporally before apprehending any objects in them. All we should need to suppose is that we are so constituted that every time we perceive an object we also generate intuitions of space and time and locate the objects somewhere in this space and time, which would then be prior to particular intuitions only in a logical and not in a temporal sense. They would be innate ideas only in the sense that we are innately so constituted as to form them on suitable occasions, not in the sense that they are there from the beginning of life. This was at least Kant's usual view, but he sometimes seems to confuse the notion of this with the notion of them as temporally coming before as innate ideas in the sense which Locke had ridiculed.[1] Professor Kemp Smith holds that the passages in which he speaks as though this were so represent an earlier view of Kant and must be taken at their face-value as originally written, but, though "pre-critical," were incorporated in the Critique without a realisation of the meaning

[1] e.g. B 41, 42, 49, 60, v. Kemp Smith, Comm., p. 88 ff., contrast Paton I, p. 136 ff.

which the words naturally, and for Kant originally, bore. Or, I think more probably, the explanation is simply that Kant was somewhat careless in his use of terms and never meant to assert more than logical priority when he said "before," or perhaps just that they were before any particular experience we might choose to name.[1]

But, whether he thinks that we had intuitions of them before we had any other perceptions or not, he certainly seems to think in the *Æsthetic* that we can have intuitions of them by themselves in adult life, and he makes the latter, in the case of space, the basis of geometry. Space and time are for Kant not only forms of intuition but themselves intuitions, whether we had them before we had other intuitions or not. Even if this view is abandoned in the *Analytic*,[2] we cannot assume, without question, that therefore it is necessarily not present in the *Æsthetic*. To say we have intuitions of them is not, however, equivalent to saying that we have images of them, which would be absurd, but only that we are immediately aware of them as individual existents.

Kant's doctrine that space and time are *a priori* must not lead us to overlook the fact that for him they are also in a very important sense *given*. Though they are *a priori* in a sense this does not mean that we can prove *a priori* that there must be such things as space and time. They have a definite sensible nature which is just as much a datum as our sensations. That we should only be able to perceive phenomena in space and time is a contingent or, if you like, an empirical

[1] B 41, where he says that an *a priori* intuition means one which is found in us before (*vor*) any perception of an object is first inserted in the second edition, by which time he admittedly no longer held the view in question even if he ever did so.
[2] e.g. B 195, *v.* below, p. 63.

fact about our nature, though, unlike most empirical facts, it determines the whole character of our experience and therefore enables numerous *a priori* deductions to be made.

Further, we must not assume that, because Kant holds space and time to be due to our nature and not to external reality he therefore holds the particular shape and duration of particular phenomenal objects to be wholly determined by us. That they should have a shape and duration at all depends on us, but what the shape is presumably depends on the thing-in-itself, as in the analogous case of causal laws.[1] The spatial and temporal differences between the various objects we perceive are obviously not derived from us, since our form of sensibility is the same for them all. What their shape etc. is will depend on (a) our form of intuition, (b) some non-spatial non-temporal characteristics in the thing-in-itself, which, however, can only appear to us as spatial, just as the shade of blue we see when looking through blue spectacles will depend partly on the blueness of the spectacles and partly on the real colour of the physical object seen which cannot appear except as a shade of blue but will make its nature felt in modifying the shade.

Kant's Arguments for the view that Space is an A Priori intuition. The *Metaphysical Exposition* gives four arguments, two to prove that space is *a priori* and two to prove that it is an intuition. The first two arguments are intended to prove that space is *a priori* in the second and third senses above. He later concludes that it is therefore *a priori* in the fourth sense.

1. (B 38). This refutes the view that space is an empirical

[1] *v.* B 459. In the *Metaphysical First Principles of Natural Science* (*Berl.* IV, p. 507) he says—"For every given spatial determination there must be a ground in the object which is itself unknown."

conception derived by abstraction from the experience of
particular spatial objects by the argument that the experience
of any object as spatial cannot be explained merely as the
result of sensation but presupposes the notion of space as a
whole. It is interpreted in two different ways. (a) It is held
that the argument is to the effect that any spatial characteristics or relations logically presuppose Space as a whole (e.g.
to say that A and B are beside each other is to presuppose a
Space in which they are beside), and that therefore Space
cannot be derived from spatial characteristics or relations
without a vicious circle.[1] (b) But the argument is also
interpreted (by Professor Kemp Smith)[2] as resting on the
psychological assumption that sensations are non-spatial,
differing only qualitatively. If this assumption is made we
are forced to explain the presence of spatial characteristics in
our experience in some other way, and so Kant holds them
to be contributed by ourselves. I strongly incline to the
former interpretation not only as being an intrinsically more
reasonable argument but as seeming to me a much more
natural interpretation of Kant's language. It is also surely
significant that Kant expressly uses the argument given by
the first interpretation in the *Reflexionen*[3] and that Professor
Kemp Smith himself finds it "very strange" that Kant
(according to him) never uses it in the Critique.[4]

2. (B 38-9). This argument concludes that space is a necessary *a priori* representation on the ground "that we can
never represent to ourselves the absence of space" (literally,
"make a representation of there being no space") "though
we can quite well think it as empty of objects."

[The current objection to the argument is that for it to

[1] *v.* Caird I, p. 464, Paton I, p. 111.   [2] *Comm.*, p. 101.
[3] II, 403.   [4] *Comm.*, p. 106.

work we must be able to represent empty space in a sense in which we cannot represent the absence of space, i.e. "think" in "think space as empty of objects" must be capable of being understood in the same sense as "represent" in "represent the absence of space," but in fact we can only interpret "represent" either in a sense which allows us to represent both or in a sense which allows us to represent neither. If "represent" means "think" we can represent both; if it means "make a mental image of" we can represent neither. But Kant certainly held that we were aware of empty space otherwise than by conception (thinking) and yet may have held that we could have no image of it, and then he would avoid the dilemma, provided we really have this peculiar consciousness of space and it is not to be explained as an abstraction or generalisation. For, if this is so, there is a sense in which we can be said to be always aware of space even when all particular spatial objects are taken away, while we are not aware in this sense of anything which is not temporal or spatial. It does not seem obviously untrue to say that some vague consciousness of space as indefinitely extending around us is always present in our experience and that, though there would be no self-contradiction in supposing that there might be a world which was non-spatial, there is still a sense in which space cannot be thought away, while no object conditions our thought *in the sense* in which space does, though in fact we may be always aware of our body and causally conditioned by it. It must be admitted, however, that the argument is badly stated.]

We shall now turn to the arguments by which Kant seeks to prove that space is an intuition, at least as his main point, deferring the third argument in the first edition in support of the view that space is *a priori*, as it is the same in principle

as the argument of the "transcendental exposition."[1] In
discussing the question whether space is an intuition Kant
only recognizes two alternatives. He assumes that it must
be either a universal concept or an intuition, presumably
because there is no third operation besides thinking and
sensing, all knowledge being for him covered by these two.
In asserting that it is an intuition he is asserting that Space
is neither an *a priori* concept derived from formal logic nor
an empirical concept derived by abstraction or construction
from a number of particular experiences, but a sensuous
individual entity. Kant indeed refers to space and time
several times as "concepts" (*Begriffe*). It has been suggested that he is here using the word in a wide sense to cover
all representations or at least all of which we are clearly
conscious, but it seems to me quite possible that what was
an intuition as originally given may be said without contradiction to become a concept as an object of reflective
thought. Its basis is intuition and not, as with the categories, thought, and from the intuition its whole content and
nature is derived, yet when subsequently abstracted in reflection it is not unintelligible that it should be described as a
concept. It can be, and emphatically is in the *Æsthetic*, the
object of conceptual thought, but its origin is alleged to lie in
intuition.

In the first argument of the two given to show that space
is an intuition (3 in B, 4 in A) Kant makes use of the fact
that different particular spaces can only be regarded as parts
of Space as a whole. This shows at least that space is in a
radically different position from any other universal concept
(if we exclude time). To think of a number of different
things as spatial is to think of them as all in Space, to think

---

[1] *v.* below, p. 39 ff.

of them as e.g. red is not to think of them as all in one big "Red." But why should it show that space is not a universal concept at all but an intuition? Two reasons may be given. (a) Space is a single individual, for there is only one space. But it is intuition which gives the individual, not conception. What we perceive are individual things, what we conceive universals.[1] (b) Kant thinks of any concept which is not itself simple as made by the mind putting together its constituent parts, but in the case of space the constituent parts presuppose Space as a whole and not vice versa, so that space cannot be constituted in this way and is therefore not a concept at all (in origin).

The second argument for the view that space is an intuition (4)[2] is still more puzzling. It is to the effect that space is infinite. The chief difficulty here is how we can possibly be said to intuit sensibly an infinite space. A hint as to a possible answer is provided by the remark in the first edition argument that the notion of the infinity of space arises from the "limitlessness in the progression of intuition." This would seem to mean that our belief in the infinity of space is founded on the fact that, however far we go, we can always intuit or image further space beyond. In that case it is not that we intuit infinite space, but that our belief in the infinity of space is derived from the characteristics of space as sensibly intuited and imaged. This, I think, is true at least psychologically. We tend to think space infinite because an absolute end to space is something that can neither be perceived nor imagined, since to image space as finite we must image it as having boundaries and a boundary implies another space outside it. (The finite

[1] v. 4th argument about time (B 47).
[2] This argument is the fifth in the first edition.

but unbounded space of modern physics, whether conceivable or not, and whether a physical fact or not, is certainly unimaginable.) Kant's argument might then be restated thus: Space is known to be infinite because an end of space cannot be pictured. We see that this proves space to be infinite. But it could only prove space to be infinite if space is on principle picturable and so is the sort of thing that is known by intuition primarily and not by concepts. If, on the other hand, we take the view of Professor Kemp Smith that at the time of writing all or most of the *Æsthetic* Kant thought of us as having a ready-made idea of Euclidean space from the beginning, we should have to suppose that it was already infinite as an innate idea and no such explanation as that suggested by me could, I think, be given of its infinity. Another solution is provided by Caird, who connects Kant's argument with the general view that, since the object of perception is always individual, it must always be regarded as infinite, though only in a potential sense, because it can never be reduced without remainder to a limited number of characteristics as a concept can.[1] Further, if we apply to space Kant's assertion about time that to call it infinite means only that " every determinate magnitude of time is possible only through limitations of one single time that underlies it "[2] the argument becomes hardly distinguishable from the preceding one (3).[3] This passage is therefore one of which it is impossible to give any confident interpretation.

The actual argument used, however, differs in the two editions, though in both it is based on the infinity of space. In the first[4] it takes the form that we can never deduce the

[1] I, pp. 267-72.
[2] B 47-8.
[3] *v.* Paton I, p. 118 ff.
[4] A 25 (5).

quantity of anything from a universal concept of its qualitative nature, but the quantity of space is known *a priori*, i.e. it is known that it is infinite, therefore space is not a concept. The argument used in the second edition,[1] on the other hand, is that a concept cannot, like space, have an infinite number of parts, though it may have an infinite number of possible instances. A concept according to Kant must either be simple or be derived by putting together a limited number of characters, and therefore space cannot be a concept.[2]

The Argument from Geometry. (The student should read in conjunction with this the section of the *Methodology* entitled *The Discipline of Pure Reason in its Dogmatic Employment* (B 740 ff.).) In the second edition the argument is given in the exposition which Kant calls transcendental because it is an argument from the fact of knowledge to the realisation of certain conditions which Kant thinks a necessary presupposition of that knowledge. In the first edition the argument is given as the third among the arguments in the previous section in so far as geometry is held to presuppose the *a priority* of space. That it establishes its intuitional character also is not mentioned in the first edition.

Kant regards this as the most important of the arguments for the view that space is an *a priori* intuition. It may be stated very simply as follows :

[1] B 39-40 (4).
[2] " It may also be maintained that the connexion with sensibility is shown by the fact that space and time are conditions of objects being given to sense, and not conditions of their being thought. We simply *see* red as extended, and so as spatial, while we *think* that it is a quality of a substance. Similarly we are immediately aware of sensa as before and after, while we *think* that events are connected as cause and effect." (Paton I, p. 165.)

Geometry, the science of space, is synthetic. Therefore space is an intuition.

Geometry is *a priori*. Therefore space is *a priori*.

The argument assumes as premiss the validity and truth of
geometry. This Kant never questions. His position is that,
since geometry is undoubtedly valid and true, it proves the
truth of any epistemological principles without which it
would not be so. This argument backwards from knowledge which we are admitted to possess to its presuppositions is sometimes called "the analytic method" and contrasted with "the synthetic method" which proceeds in the
reverse direction. It is important to distinguish this use of
the terms, analytic and synthetic, from their use as applied
to propositions. The analytic method starts with certain
synthetic *a priori* propositions the truth and necessity of
which were generally admitted (in this case the propositions
of geometry), and argues back to the existence of certain
conditions without which they could not have the truth and
necessity which in fact they have. The synthetic method
on the other hand does not assume the validity of the *a priori*
propositions, but proves it by showing that they are involved
in the necessary conditions of ordinary experience. It is
the method which is most usually employed by Kant, being
the method of e.g. the arguments about space in the metaphysical exposition, the transcendental deduction and the
proofs of the separate categories. In the *Prolegomena* Kant
suggests the substitution of the terms "regressive" for
"analytic" and "progressive" for "synthetic" (as applied
to the general method, not of course to propositions,
and this terminology seems to me to constitute an
improvement).

[Kant must not be blamed because he assumes the truth of Euclidean geometry. A philosopher has a right to accept and use as data the established conclusions of a science. If the geometers of the day were wrong in holding the physical world to be Euclidean it was a defect in their geometry or physics, and we must not blame the philosophers for it. But it may be thought that, even if Kant has taken the most rational view possible in the light of the science of his day, the change in the science which he took as his premiss vitiates his whole argument. We shall now ask whether this is necessarily so. It may be contended that, since it is now generally admitted to be impossible to know *a priori* that space is Euclidean, Kant's problem how we can know this *a priori* just does not arise. In this connection we ought, however, to distinguish (1) the question of the axioms, (2) the question of the proofs of the theorems. It may well be the case, and in fact would, I suppose, be generally held now that, while the axioms are mere assumptions which cannot be proved, most at least of Euclid's theorems follow in strict logic from the axioms. Therefore, even if the modern account of the axioms is accepted, pure Euclidean geometry remains an *a priori* science, because it is concerned solely with seeing what follows logically from certain assumptions, i.e. it consists of hypothetical *a priori* propositions to the effect that if certain axioms are true certain theorems will follow. What we cannot say *a priori* is that either the theorems or the axioms are true of physical space; but the surprising extent to which we can carry *a priori* reasoning in this science in striking contrast to most others still calls for explanation.]

But let us first consider Kant's account of the axioms. Here I am unable to be clear which of two views Kant held. But, whichever interpretation we adopt, the main principle of his theory of axioms is not, I think, necessarily refuted by the modern development of non-Euclidean geometries. (1) Kant's account suggests that the axioms are simply propositions about the *de facto* nature of our intuition of space.[1] If this is his view he agrees with modern geometry in denying the logical necessity of the axioms, but asserts that they are perceptually necessary, i.e. that we cannot perceive what is not subject to them. There would be no contradiction in a space which was non-Euclidean, but we could not perceive such a space, and therefore, since space is only our form of intuition, there can be no such space in our world at least. What is really necessary *a priori* on this view is not that the axioms should be true of our form of intuition—but that, since they are in fact true, the phenomenal world should conform to them, otherwise it could not exist, since being phenomenal it only exists for us. The position then seems to be this. We observe empirically that in our pure intuition, e.g., the shortest distance between two points is always a straight line (pure geometry). We know (it is not very clear how) that everything that we can perceive (other than ourselves as appearance) must be located by us in this pure intuition of space. Therefore all external phenomena must conform to this principle (applied geometry). This account is obviously not incompatible with the logical possibility of non-Euclidean geometries, but it is incompatible with their application to perceptual space, and Kant identifies perceptual and physical space.

[1] *v*. Kemp-Smith, pp. 565-6.

[This solution is open to the objection that if the axioms are merely known by observing our pure intuitions we have no guarantee whatever that they will always be true, for we cannot know that our pure intuition might not change a little. If it changed very radically—ceased to be spatial for instance—Kant would reply that we should lose our identity and that therefore there would no longer be any phenomena for us; but suppose the change were slight, e.g., such that the sum of the angles of a triangle became 175 instead of 180 degrees, this retort could hardly be made. Such a change would not make as great a difference to our experience as many normal changes which are admittedly compatible with self-identity. Yet the mere possibility of such a change defeats Kant's main purpose here, which was to establish the universality and necessity of the principles of geometry, for it precludes us from being able to predict that they always will hold or even from ruling out the possibility that they have often changed without our noticing it in the past, and they could no longer be said to be necessary, as Kant insisted they were.]

(2) But Kant does not make it clear that we merely arrive at the axioms by this *de facto* observation, and he would certainly never apply the term empirical to them (though it must be admitted that this may be merely because he uses *a priori* to mean not only or chiefly " logically necessary " but "universal condition of experience "). It is thus possible to interpret him as meaning that the Euclidean axioms are necessarily involved in any kind of space. This is in accord with his view that, while there might be non-human beings who had forms of intuition other than Euclidean space, no such form could be spatial. The axioms would be logically necessary propositions about what

follows if there is a space, i.e. if human beings intuit objects in space, though it would not be a logically necessary proposition, but only a contingent proposition in fact true, that there is a space, i.e. that there are human beings who intuit objects in space. The axioms would still be based on our intuitive nature in that they would be propositions about what we must intuit, but Kant's view would now escape the objection that our intuitive nature might change, because it would now be a logically necessary proposition that as long as we perceived things in space at all they would be subject to the Euclidean axioms, and we need not be concerned with the possibility that we might cease altogether to perceive things in space, for the strongest defender of Euclid would not maintain that his axioms would be valid of what was not in space at all. By this is not meant that Euclid's axioms are included in the definition of space, which would make the *a priori* propositions of Euclid analytic, but that nothing could have any of the characteristics we describe as spatial without also conforming to all Euclid's axioms. Since the possession of any spatial characteristics would on this view synthetically imply the possession of all the characteristics of Euclidean space, we could know *a priori* that "non-Euclidean spaces" were not possible objects of intuition for any being whatever, not only for men. This view of the axioms would not be incompatible with non-Euclidean geometries as hypothetical sciences, but it would imply that the latter were not really about any sort of space but only about conceptual constructions which have some analogy to space.

[Kant seems to me right in holding that the reason for our strong tendency to think of space as Euclidean is rooted in our perceptual faculties. While it is too much to say that perceptual space is Euclidean, for it is not infinite and therefore the question in the strict sense cannot reasonably be asked, at any rate Euclid's axioms seem to be based on our total inability to see or imagine any except certain kinds of spatial constructions. Thus we still find in the modern Logic that for long was regarded as a kind of standard text-book for Cambridge the statement that "the axioms of Euclid represent the manner in which we actually intuit our space."[1] We may perhaps conceive but we cannot imagine a "curved space," or a space in which a straight line is not the shortest distance between two points, or a space in which two different straight lines through the same point can both be parallel to a third straight line, in the sense in which we can imagine Euclidean space. It may be indeed objected that we cannot perceive or imagine straight lines at all since they have only one dimension, but we can at least imagine and perceive lines in the sense of boundaries. Again it may be objected that no boundary we perceive or imagine is ever absolutely but only approximately straight, but this objection rests on a confusion, for even if no physical object we encounter· ever has a boundary which is absolutely straight, we certainly can perceive and imagine lines, in the sense of boundaries, which appear absolutely straight, and there is no *perceptual* difference between this and perceiving or imagining them as absolutely straight. But for these and similar reasons I should prefer to substitute the term "are based on" for the term "represent" in the passage from Johnson's *Logic* just quoted by me. It seems also at least plausible to hold that our inability to perceive or imagine these things is not merely a factual but a logical impossi-

[1] Johnson, *Logic* II, p. 202.

bility. (I must admit that in considering these questions I have confined myself to visual space. None of the other senses give me a sufficiently definite perception of any considerable extent of space at the same moment to enable me to answer the question in their case.)

But even if the impossibility is merely factual as in the first interpretation of Kant's argument, it would still follow that we must either hold physical space to be Euclidean or distinguish perceptual and physical space as different not only numerically but in kind. The latter distinction is quite in accord with prevailing tendencies of the present day in the philosophy of science. Kant, however, adopted the former course, because he viewed the physical world as merely appearance and therefore thought it impossible to distinguish perceptual and physical space, and because his theory explained what everybody of his time regarded as a fact, the *a priori* necessity of Euclid not only as a hypothetical science but as an account of physical space. He did not anticipate that scientific arguments worthy of serious consideration could ever be put forward to show that physical space was non-Euclidean, but, if anybody accepted a theory like Kant's on general grounds, I doubt whether he would have much difficulty in squaring it with modern science. For (a) Einstein himself admits that physical space *may* be Euclidean, and, if there are good reasons for thinking it Euclidean, we are then at liberty to replace the " may be " by an " is "; (b) scientific propositions asserting the non-Euclidean character of space could no doubt be analysed in some " Pickwickian " way. (Anybody who adopts Kant's view of the physical world will in any case have to analyse all the propositions of physical science in a " Pickwickian " way.) But I must admit that I do not possess the mathematical and physical knowledge needed for an adequate discussion of these subjects. All I want to show is that some solution like Kant's must not be dismissed at once as necessarily undeserving of any further consideration even to-day.]

But Kant's theory, besides providing an account of the axioms, also claimed to provide an account of the inferences in geometry. Besides the problem how we can have valid synthetic *a priori* axioms there is also the problem how we can draw conclusions in geometry which are not included in the premises. Kant might have held that, though the axioms were synthetic, the conclusions followed from them analytically, in which case the second problem would not arise,[1] but this is not at any rate his usual view. He certainly holds that intuition is necessary not only for the axioms but also for the inferences, and he attributes our ability to make these inferences to the sensuous character of the subject-matter of geometry. But it is not very clear exactly how he thought this helped. The mere fact that we can see the characteristics a and b together in our pure intuition of space would explain why we should think they both belonged to objects in space, but would not explain how we can see a necessary connection between one and the other. And Kant certainly did not intend to reduce geometry to mere observation, he thought that there was genuine synthetic inference, but that this inference was only rendered possible by the fact that we could draw or imagine geometrical figures. He seems to have held that the difficulty of seeing synthetic *a priori* connections disappeared where (a) the connection was one which ultimately depended on us, (b) it was one which could be made clear to

[1] This interpretation is supported by B 14.

us by constructing images, such as geometrical figures, which belonged to pure intuition and did not require for their formation any empirical data.[1] For space and time were the only things which were both individual, and therefore capable of being given in intuition, and also capable of serving as the source of universal and necessary propositions since they were conditions of all experience. This would then explain why mathematics can alone of the sciences develop a vast system of *a priori* propositions, a fact which has always seemed most puzzling to philosophers. For, whatever Kant's exact view of arithmetic and algebra, he certainly held that the reasoning in them was synthetic and that these synthetic *a priori* sciences were only possible because we could illustrate them in time and space.

[Here Kant's view does seem really to be inconsistent with the modern developments of geometry, for (a) these show that the *a priori* character of geometrical inferences is due to logical concepts and not to the actual sensible character of space as present in our experience; (b) if Kant's view of geometrical inference were true it would be impossible to have any non-Euclidean geometry even as a purely hypothetical science, at least he would either have had to deny that non-Euclidean geometry was synthetic, in which case he could not well have held that Euclidean geometry was, or he would have been forced to admit that we could have synthetic *a priori* inferences which were not dependent on our form of intuition. Further, Kant's account does not clearly distinguish the two problems, (a) how is it that pure geometry can apply to phenomena? (b) how is it that within pure geometry we can make inferences of a synthetic character? His answer to the first does not

[1] *v.* B 741 ff., 762 ff.

in any way solve the second, and his answer to the second is not worked out with sufficient fulness for it to be intelligible just how the reference to intuition is supposed to solve the difficulty. Mere intuition (observing) will not explain logical necessity. Kant's theory explains the alleged necessity that physical objects must conform to whatever theorems are proved in pure geometry by saying that they are phenomena and therefore subject to our forms of intuition, but this is not the same as explaining the necessity with which a theorem in geometry (whether pure or applied) follows from its premisses. It seems almost as though Kant had confused the two necessities and thought that he had explained the latter when he had really only explained the former at the most.]

It is a curious fact that in the first work he ever published (1747) Kant admits not only the possibility of non-Euclidean geometries but the logical possibility that they might have been true of the physical world if the laws of motion had been different.[1] He thought then that the nature of space followed *a priori* from the laws of motion, which were themselves contingent not necessary, and suggested the possibility of a metageometry which would deduce the Euclidean axioms from the existing laws of motion and other axioms from other possible laws of motion. It is a pity that he gave up the idea in later life, otherwise he might have worked out some very interesting anticipations of modern views of space and geometry.

Conclusions. (a) Kant here at once draws the conclusion that space is subjective. It must be admitted that the passage in which he does so rather supports Professor Kemp Smith's view that he is thinking of temporal priority, as

[1] *Berl.* I, 23-5.

does the corresponding passage about time.[1] "For no determinations, whether absolute[2] or relative, can be intuited prior to the existence of the things to which they belong, and none, therefore, can be intuited *a priori*."

It has been a common objection against Kant that at the best his arguments do not prove that reality is not spatial, but only that we cannot know it to be spatial. For, even if space is the form of our intuition, it is at least possible that it may also be the form of independent things. This admission would not make a great deal of difference to Kant's philosophy, because it would be at the best a bare possibility for the assertion of which there would be no ground whatever and never could be; but Kant certainly had arguments which, if valid, would disprove it conclusively even as a possibility. Only these arguments were not included in the *Æsthetic*, but in the passage on the Antinomies. There Kant claims to show that, if space and time are taken as real, we are confronted with irreconcilable contradictions, for we must hold either that the world in space and time is infinite or that it is finite, and both alternatives are equally impossible. This is regarded by him as an important confirmation of the *Æsthetic*, and if valid it would obviously lead to the conclusion not only that we cannot know space and time to belong to reality but that we can know them not to belong, because otherwise reality would be self-contradictory. Kant was probably also influenced, as with the categories, by the idea that, if space were independently real, the necessity of geometry would be lost

---

[1] B 49.

[2] By this is presumably meant *qualities* as opposed to relations. Kant is not referring here to the "absolute" view of space held by e.g. Newton.

because then spatial objects would merely happen to conform to our intuitions and not necessarily do so.[1]

Conclusion (b) expresses the central doctrine of the Æsthetic. This being so, it has already been discussed. In the first sentence of the section Kant describes space as "the form of all appearances of outer sense" (a fundamental doctrine of his), and it might be objected that this statement was of little value, since "outer" is by definition spatial. The words "*only* the form of all appearances" applied to space would be themselves sufficient to redeem the statement from the charge of tautology, but I do not think that "outer" here means "spatial" but rather "directed towards something other than oneself." What the passage asserts is that all our intuitions other than those of introspection are spatial and so only phenomenal.

In B 44 occurs for the first time the important contrast between "empirical reality" and "transcendental ideality." The general significance of this contrast will have to be discussed later.[2] Here it is sufficient to say that space and time are empirically real in the sense that phenomena are subject to them, transcendentally ideal in the sense that they do not belong to independent reality.

Immediately after introducing this distinction Kant declares that "with the sole exception of space there is no subjective representation, referring to something *outer*, which could be entitled *a priori*." This enables him to retain within phenomena the distinction between primary and secondary qualities.[3] For he recognizes different grades

---

[1] *cf.* B 167-8.   [2] *v.* below, ch. V.
[3] I am using "secondary qualities" in Berkeley's sense, not in Locke's, i.e. for the actual sensible qualities as sensed, not for the power in physical objects, though they are not conceived as themselves coloured, to produce colour-sensations etc. in us.

of subjectivity. While space and spatial characteristics are subjective relatively to things-in-themselves, they are objective in comparison with qualities such as colour, while these would again be objective, I suppose, in comparison with "illusions." But the distinction between primary and secondary qualities is no longer, as for the realist, based on the supposition that primary qualities belong to physical objects independently of us, while secondary qualities do not, but on the presence of *a priori* knowledge in regard to primary qualities and its absence in regard to secondary qualities. We can connect this way of making the distinction with Kant's doctrine in the *Analytic* that objectivity in the physical world is constituted by necessity. In the Critique[1] and in his works on science Kant takes the view that physical objects have only primary qualities. This he sees would be impossible if they were independent things, but he says that with phenomena it is quite possible.

[It seems very strange to me to speak of objects with only primary qualities as appearances. They are rather abstractions and constructions from appearances, but if this amendment were accepted it would become possible for Kant to avoid the absurdity of which any realist would be guilty who held that physical objects had only primary qualities (as opposed to the more reasonable view that, though they must have some other qualities, we do **not** know what these qualities are, and of those qualities which we perceive have only ground to ascribe to them the primary ones, not the secondary). Clearly the common element in objects of human experience abstracted by science might have these characteristics and no others, since it is not a

[1] *cf.* B 321-2, 330.

set of things existing by themselves but only an abstraction.]

The Absolute View of Space and Time. In B 49 Kant distinguishes the view that time " exists of itself " from the view that time is an objective characteristic of things, and he realises fully the existence of a corresponding distinction between two views of space, the " absolute " view held by Newton, and the view that space is reducible to the spatial relations of physical objects,[1] which is attributed by him to Leibniz, though not altogether accurately, because Leibniz did not hold that spatial relations belong to objects independently of us, but only that there are relations between independent objects (the monads) which appear to us as spatial relations but are not really spatial. Leibniz's view in fact seems very like Kant's, but differs in that he does not like Kant hold thought and sensibility to be sources of knowledge different in kind and consequently thinks that sensible appearances afford at least a partial clue to the nature of reality.

Kant himself held a view of space which reduced it to spatial relations till about 1768, when he published a pamphlet, *On the First Ground of the Distinction of Regions in Space*, in which he uses " the argument from incongruous counterparts " to establish an absolute view. He points out that the different parts of a left hand are related to each other in exactly the same way as the different parts of a right hand, yet the two hands could not coincide. The difference between them therefore cannot be explained by a difference in the relations of their parts, nor again in their relations to other bodies, for it is logically possible

---

[1] If this is called the " relative view " in opposition to the absolute, it must not be confused with modern " Relativity."

that there might be no matter in the universe at all except one single hand, in which case it would still have to be either a right or a left hand. The difference must therefore be explained as a difference in their relations to absolute space. Kant was probably also influenced by scientific reasons in adopting such a theory of space. The same "argument from incongruous counterparts" is also used by Kant for two other purposes on different occasions. In the *Dissertation of* 1770[1] and in the *Prolegomena*[2] he uses the argument in order to show that space cannot be rendered intelligible in terms of concepts, but, while he concludes from this in the *Dissertation* that space is an intuition, he concludes in the *Prolegomena* from the same argument that it is subjective. [We must remember, however, that there is not necessarily any absurdity in using the same argument to prove three different things, since it is accompanied by another suppressed premiss, which is in each case different.]

Now, though he made space and time appearances, Kant still held an absolute view of them, at least in the *Æsthetic*, in the sense that he did not believe that propositions about Space and Time were all completely reducible to propositions about spatial and temporal objects and their relations and that he held we could be immediately aware of Space and Time as wholes apart from any object in them. This doctrine he now expresses by asserting space and time to be not only forms of intuition but themselves intuitions. This seems at first sight to imply that we can have sensible images of empty infinite space and time, a view which seems obviously impossible, but probably Kant merely meant that we can be aware of them immediately in some way as in-

[1] § 15 C, *Berl.* II, 402-3.   [2] § 13.

dividual wholes. He still used the word intuition, not concept, because he believed Space and Time to be individual entities, not universal concepts which characterised a number of things. He never, I think, claims that we have an image, only a representation or an intuition, of space as such. Now, while it would be absurd to hold that we can have an image of empty infinite Space or Time, it is not obviously absurd to hold that we can be immediately aware in some way of the existence of such a thing.

He brings the following objections against the absolute view of Space and Time if conceived realistically and not as merely an account of appearances. (1) Absolute space and time are neither substances nor "anything actually inhering in substances." So what can they be?[1] (2) An empty space surrounding the world would not be anything real at all but a mere non-entity (*Unding*), and similarly with time.[2] (3) If space and time are conceived as infinite and embracing the whole of reality, there is no room for another infinite, all-embracing being, God. How can e.g. the absolute reality of space be reconciled with God's omnipresence? If space and time are conditions of all real things they must likewise condition God, but God is non-sensible.[3] Kant thinks that he has avoided these objections by making space and time appearances while retaining the doctrine that there is such a thing as space apart from objects in space, and similarly with time.

Kant's Treatment of Time. Metaphysical Exposition. The arguments about time correspond to those used about space, so I shall not discuss them at length. The comments I made on the arguments about space could for the most part be repeated here.

[1] B 70.   [2] B 49, 56, 457.   [3] B 71.

The first argument corresponds to the first argument used to prove space *a priori*,[1] and the second argument to the second. The third corresponds to the third argument in the first edition about space. It should really belong to the *Transcendental Exposition* and will be discussed briefly in connection with that.

The fourth argument corresponds to the third argument of the second edition about space. It makes it clearer that the reason why time (and so space) is to be regarded as an intuition is because it is unique and individual, but it adds an argument from the axiomatic, yet synthetic character of the proposition that different times cannot co-exist, though this really belongs to the third argument or the *Transcendental Exposition*.

The fifth argument is not, however, parallel to the fourth second edition argument about space, but rather to the third argument.[2] The reference to infinity is not fundamental and might just as well have been omitted. The argument is that different durations can only be represented as parts of Time as a whole and therefore presuppose the latter. Time, it is concluded, must therefore be an intuition, not a concept, for in the case of a concept the parts precede the whole and not as here *vice versa*.

A sixth argument is given in B 50 where Kant contends that time can be represented by a line in space, and that therefore, since " all the relations of time allow of being expressed in an intuition ", time must be an intuition itself.

Transcendental Exposition. Kant is here confronted with the difficulty that there is no *a priori* science which deals with time, as geometry does with space. He tries to fill the gap in two ways. (1) In the third argument of the

---

[1] B 38.   [2] The fourth in the first edition.

Metaphysical Exposition he adduces two axioms about time which he claims to be *a priori* and synthetic. They are (a) time has only one dimension, (b) different times are successive and not simultaneous. (2) He bases the science of motion, in so far as synthetic *a priori*, on the nature of time as he had based geometry on the nature of space.[1] But this still gives him a much less plausible case than he had in regard to space. We should remember, however, that, while it would nowadays be generally held that there is no element in the science of motion which is *a priori* except the mathematical application of laws established inductively and the fundamental presuppositions of induction itself, this was not the usual view of Kant's day. It was then commonly held that some of the laws of motion could be seen to be true *a priori*, and Kant himself tries to give an *a priori* proof of some, e.g. of the principle that action and reaction must be equal, in the *Metaphysical First Principles of Natural Science*.[2] Kant also uses the argument that change, being a combination of contradictory predicates, could not be rendered intelligible by any concepts, but only by an intuition (time). In pure conception an object cannot both have and not have a quality *a*, but it can do so if we introduce the notion of time, for then it may at one time have *a* and at another not. This is taken to prove that time is not a concept but an intuition, but further it is inferred from this that time is the basis of all synthetic *a priori* propositions in the science of motion, as time alone renders the notion of change, and so of motion, possible.

Another *a priori* science that Kant may possibly at some time have meant to base on time is arithmetic, but he seems

---

[1] Last sentence of § 5.   [2] Berl. IV, 544.

rather to have held that it was in its nature conceptual but could not be understood by us except with the help of illustrations requiring space and time.[1] Arithmetic, including algebra, is the science of quantity as such, hence its relation to intuition is different from that of geometry. Geometry can be synthetic according to Kant because it deals directly with an intuition as its subject-matter, but arithmetic and algebra[2] only because the concept of quantity can be represented in intuition by dots in space etc. or by imagining number in the form of successive moments of time. Another difference between geometry and arithmetic is that Kant denies that there are any axioms in Arithmetic in the sense of synthetic general propositions.[3] The *a priori* propositions of arithmetic are said to be either analytic, e.g. if equals be added to equals the wholes are equal, or, if they are about particular numbers, as $5 + 7 = 12$, singular though synthetic. The images display characteristics which belong to our *a priori* form of intuition and therefore apply to all objects we intuit.

§ 6. *Conclusion. Time as Form of Inner Sense.* By " inner sense " Kant does not mean to refer to sensations of our internal bodily organs but to the experience of something not spatial at all. It is the non-conceptual element in introspection. The term, *inner sense,* has been very severely criticised, e.g. by Ward,[4] but introspection certainly re-

---

[1] " The science of number, notwithstanding the succession which every construction of quantity demands, is a pure intellectual synthesis which we represent to ourselves in thought. But so far as quanta are to be numerically determined, they must be given to us in such a way that we can apprehend their intuition in successive order, and such that their apprehension can be subject to time." (*Berl.* X, p. 530, *cf.* B 299. *V.* Kemp Smith, *Comm.*, pp. 128-34.)

[2] B 745, 762.   [3] B 205.

[4] *A Study of Kant*, p. 139 ff.

sembles outer sense in the most important point for epistemology, i.e. its empirical character. It is observation and not
a priori thinking. I doubt if Kant meant more than this
when he refers it to inner sense. And even a person who
should infer on philosophical grounds that the mind is in
space does not immediately experience it as in space, as he
experiences physical objects in space, so Kant cannot possibly
be condemned for denying that space is a form of inner
sense as it is of outer.[1]

[A difficulty arises as to how on Kant's philosophy we can
distinguish inner and outer sense. If we are immediately
aware of the real self in introspection, then we know that
what we thus observe belongs to it; but if we are not aware
of it, but only of its appearances, as Kant held, then how can
we know any such thing? Kant might have replied that the
representations of inner sense and those of outer sense are
distinguished by us because they are either qualitatively
different or, if qualitatively similar, as in the case of images,
subject to different causal laws. But, even if we can distinguish the two so as to put them into separate classes, the
difficulty remains how, on Kant's view, we can know that
the one sort are appearances of oneself. This would seem to
require some sort of direct knowledge of the real self.]

The view expressed in the second paragraph that " time is
nothing but the form of inner sense " raises the difficulty
that physical objects appear as moving, or otherwise
changing, and change implies time. Kant, however,
accounts for the fact that physical objects are also in time
by arguing that, since they consist of our representations,
which can therefore be perceived by introspection, they
belong to inner as well as to outer sense, and thus acquire

[1] On inner sense, *v*. below, p. 123 ff.

the form of time.[1] That is, a physical object as perceived by
us is only an image or images, and as such is an object of
introspection, therefore it is in time, though it would not be
if it were possible for us to have outer senses without having
an inner sense also.

§ 7. One of the earliest objections that Kant encountered
was to this effect: My representations at any rate are real.
My representations change and so imply time. Therefore
time is real. Kant's answer is that I am real but that what I
observe of myself in introspection is only appearance. This
according to him gives it sufficient reality for all practical
purposes, but it remains a fact for him that if I could perceive
my states as they really are I should not perceive them as in
time at all or as being subject to change. As Kant points out
in a letter to Herz in 1772[2] this does not mean that we can
be said to be really always in the same state, for that would
itself imply that our state really was in time. We must not
attribute change to our real self, but neither must we
attribute to it unchanging duration. All we can say is that
it has some unknown mode of being which cannot be equated
with either and does not involve time.

In B56 Kant distinguishes among realist views between
(a) the Newtonian or absolute view of space as "subsistent,"
(b) the Leibnizian view of it as consisting of the relations of
objects confusedly represented.[3] It is noteworthy that here
it is the second view only which is declared to be incompatible with the *a priori* character of mathematics,[4] no doubt
because it derives space from particular perceptions and because it does not, like the first view, make it prior to and a
necessary condition of objects in space. But this is not

[1] B 50.   [2] *Berl.* X, pp. 128-9.
[3] *v.* above, p. 53 ff.   [4] B 57.

compatible with the course of Kant's argument elsewhere in the *Æsthetic*, which assumes that *any* realist view of space is to be rejected as incompatible with the *a priori* character of geometry.

§ 8. In the third and fourth paragraphs of this section the Leibnizian view is again criticised, this time on the ground that what is given in sense does not differ from intellectual concepts merely in being less clear. Kant on the contrary always regards it as very important to maintain that sensibility and intelligence are different in kind, though he does not exclude the possibility that they may ultimately have "a common root" unknowable to us. Sense-perception, he insists against Leibniz, does not merely give us the same characteristics as we could discern by thought if we were more intelligent, only in a confused form, but new characteristics different in kind from any which could conceivably be known by thought alone and from any which could belong to reality, and consequently, however clearly we thought phenomena, this would not bring us any nearer to things-in-themselves. The way in which Kant puts the argument here might suggest that we could know things-in-themselves by pure thought, which was not Kant's critical view but was held by him when he first accepted the doctrine of the unreality of space and time, i.e. in the *Dissertation* of 1770.

In the second edition Kant adds a further argument for the ideality of space and time, i.e. that outer and inner sense alike can only give relations and that a real thing could not consist only of relations.[1] Kant is including under outer sense only the so-called "primary qualities," which are really relational properties; and the reason why he holds that inner sense gives us nothing but relations is that there is nothing

[1] B 66 ff.

given by inner sense except (a) the representations of outer sense, viewed not as physical but as part of one's own history, (b) time, and that both these are reducible to relations. He excludes pleasure or unpleasure and will on the ground that these are not knowledge. [But surely they, though not cognitions, are objects of knowledge? And, even if we are right in ascribing only primary qualities to the physical world in the sense in which this is done in science, it is not true that these are the only qualities given by " outer sense."]

The distinction between illusion and appearance mentioned in B 69-71 will be discussed later.

Inconsistencies or Alleged Inconsistencies between the Æsthetic and the Analytic. The *Æsthetic* is generally held to be relatively pre-critical, chiefly because of its correspondence with the *Dissertation* of 1770, and certain passages in it are thought to be inconsistent with the views of the Analytic in the following points :

1. In the *Æsthetic* Kant talks as if perception or intuition could occur in us without conception; in the *Analytic* he is usually held to regard them as inseparable from conception. But the difference may be simply that in the *Æsthetic* Kant does not want to assume what he will only prove later, and therefore speaks as though perception were independent of conception, not because he really thinks that it is so but because he has not yet justified the view that it does imply conception and therefore cannot treat this view as established.

2. Some passages in the *Æsthetic* seem to suggest the temporal and not only the logical priority of our pure intuitions. I am doubtful whether Kant held this view even in the *Æsthetic*,[1] but if he did hold it in the *Æsthetic* there is no trace of it in the *Analytic*.

[1] *v.* above, pp. 31-2.

3. It looks as though he drew back later from his view of space and time as not only forms of intuition but themselves intuitions and so from the "absolute" view of space and time, which, as I have pointed out, might be held without making the intuition of space and time temporally prior. In particular the proofs of all three analogies[1] explicitly presuppose that "time itself cannot be perceived." Yet it is incredible that a doctrine which is a fundamental and explicit presupposition of the proofs of all three analogies should be in open contradiction with the fundamental tenets of the *Æsthetic*. That would be a flagrant conflict between two vital parts of the Critique such as we should think could hardly have escaped Kant's notice after the most cursory inspection. We are confronted here with one of the great difficulties of Kantian interpretation, and I cannot take any very confident line. But perhaps what Kant means is merely that space and time cannot be perceived in the way in which an ordinary physical object can be. What he denies in the *Analogies* is that time can be perceived in the same sort of way as an empirical object, or that it might serve as a kind of clock to measure the duration of objects; and this is compatible with our having some sort of awareness of it over and above our awareness of objects, though it is not one empirical object among others. If there is an inconsistency, it is at any rate an inconsistency not only between the Æsthetic and the Analytic, but within the latter itself. For to the passages cited we may oppose those that speak of a manifold of pure intuition,[2] one at least of which was added in the second edition.

Still harder is it to reconcile the attitude of the *Æsthetic*

---

[1] B 225, 233, 257.
[2] A 101, B 104, 160-1, 177.

as usually interpreted with the following two passages which
I quote in full in order to supplement the point of view given
in this chapter. "Even space and time," Kant says in the
Analytic, "however free their concepts are from everything
empirical, and however certain it is that they are represented
in the mind completely *a priori*, would yet be without objective validity, senseless and meaningless, if their necessary
application to the objects of experience were not established.
Their representation is a mere schema which always stands in
relation to the reproductive imagination that calls up and
assembles the objects of experience. Apart from these objects
of experience, they would be devoid of meaning."[1] In *The
Metaphysical First Principles of Natural Science*[2] he says :
" To assume as *given per se* an absolute space, i.e. a space
which, because it has no content (*weil er nicht materiell ist*),
cannot be an object of experience is to assume as a ground of
the possibility of experience something which cannot be perceived either in itself or in its consequences. Yet it is quite
clear that experience must in any case occur without it. So
absolute space is *in itself* nothing, no object at all, but signifies only any and every relative space which I can think as lying
outside whatever space is given me at the time and which I
just extend beyond every given space to infinity, as a space
which includes this given space and in which I can regard
the first as subject to movement. Because I am only thinking
of the extended, though still material, space, and know
nothing of the matter which marks it out, I abstract from
the latter. It is therefore represented as a pure, non-
empirical, absolute space. I can compare any empirical
space with it and represent the former as subject to motion

[1] B 195.
[2] Published 1786. Chapter I, Explanation I, Note 2, *Berl.* IV, 481.

in it, and for that reason it always counts as itself immovable. To make it into an actual thing is to change *logical univer-sality* . . . into a *physical universality* of actual extent." This passage definitely disagrees with the *Æsthetic* in putting forward a theory of the origin of the representation of space as such from the idea of particular spaces.[1]

4. In the *Analytic* Kant introduces the notion that space and time, like empirical intuitions, presuppose a synthesis by which the parts are put together,[2] in the *Æsthetic* he insists that in the case of space and time the whole is prior to and presupposed by the parts. It is not clear how this contradiction is to be reconciled.

[1] Contrast B 38 *ad fin.*, B 42.   [2] B 102, 160-1, 203, A 101.

CHAPTER III

THE TRANSCENDENTAL DEDUCTION OF THE CATEGORIES

For the purposes of exposition I think it best to diverge here from the order of the text and take the Transcendental Deduction first and the Metaphysical Deduction afterwards. The latter is much less important and its significance cannot be understood apart from the former. I should advise students to follow the order I have adopted also in their private reading.

The Transcendental Deduction is not intended by itself as a proof of any particular categories, but as a proof that some categories or other are necessary. Kant gives proofs of the individual categories in the *Analytic of Principles*,[1] and he also supposes that when combined with the Metaphysical Deduction the Transcendental Deduction can serve as such a proof for reasons explained later.[2] It is with the Transcendental Deduction alone that we shall be concerned in the present chapter.

It is in connection with this very important section, or rather the first edition version of it, that the theory which divides Kant's work into successive "strata" has been carried out most thoroughly, but fortunately it is not necessary to confuse the student at the start by these investigations. Even if the strata theory turns out to be substantially true, it is better for him to try to grasp the main principles of the deduction first before considering the differences between the different strata. With one exception, which I shall mention later, the alleged differences are after all matters of compara-

[1] *v.* below, p. 148 ff.   [2] *v.* below, p. 136 ff.

tive detail, and I shall say as much about them as I think it necessary for the ordinary honours student to know before the end of the chapter. The Transcendental Deduction ought to be read in both editions, at least in Professor Kemp Smith's abridged version. It is generally agreed to be the most important and central section of the whole Critique.

There is an important difference of procedure between the *Æsthetic* and the *Analytic*. In the former Kant accepts the axioms of geometry and everything that can be deduced from them by the geometrician as true and does not think it incumbent on him to give a philosophical proof of them. On the contrary, what he does is to argue backwards from them and contend that, because we know them to be true, we must accept the epistemological theory which can alone account for this knowledge,[1] i.e. the theory that space and time are *a priori* intuitions. (At least this is one, though not the only, argument for the theory in question.) But he was not willing to adopt this course with the *a priori* principles, e.g. causality, which he thought to be presupposed in all natural science. On Kant's view synthetic self-evident propositions only occur where the characteristics connected can be found or brought together in a pure intuition.[2] Where they are not thus given in intuition we can only know the proposition if we are able to introduce some third term to connect them, which term will be in the case of the categories the notion of experience in general. Therefore the categories, or rather the principles asserting their universal applicability among phenomena, must be proved and cannot be accepted as self-evident. Nor is Kant willing to accept as adequate evidence for them the fact, or supposed fact, that they are presupposed in all natural science. It is the justification of

[1] *v.* above, p. 40.   [2] *v.* B 760-2.

natural science that is itself at stake for him. He thought they were thus presupposed but did not think this in any way a proof of them. Why his attitude to natural science in this matter should be so very different from his attitude to geometry is obscure, but I suppose the reason is that in geometry we seemed to know the axioms and theorems already, while in natural science it seemed that our inductive conclusions presupposed principles that did not appear self-evident.

Kant's main object in the transcendental deduction is to justify science philosophically, i.e., prove the *a priori* principles on which he thought it depended. The only possible such proof is, Kant thinks, transcendental, i.e., a proof by asking what are the conditions without which experience would be impossible. (*Transcendental* must be carefully distinguished from *transcendent*.[1] The transcendent could not possibly be known by us according to Kant, but the transcendental could very well be known.) Now *experience* does not for Kant mean merely feeling. It is several times defined by him as " empirical judgment " (*Urteil*) or " empirical cognition " (*Erkenntnis*),[2] consequently a proof by reference to the possibility of experience is a proof of the principle by showing that it is presupposed in all empirical judgments so that if we did not accept it we should have to adopt the position of the absolute sceptic. This kind of proof may seem circular or inconclusive, but since absolute scepticism about all empirical judgments is a position that no one can seriously hold it does follow that we must accept the truth of any principle the denial of which would logically lead to this scepticism. If there are only two alterna-

---

[1] *v.* above, p. 25.
[2] e.g. in *Sieben kleine Aufsätze*, written 1788-91. (*Berl.* XVIII, 318.)

tives and one is impossible we must accept the other. And Kant is right in thinking that, if the most general principles of thought are capable of proof at all, this is certainly the only way in which they could be proved. Since there is nothing more fundamental from which they could be deduced, they could only be proved as presuppositions of our knowledge. If we do not accept a proof of this kind we must hold them to be self-evident, and Kant was unwilling ever to appeal to self-evidence, except in mathematics, for fear of its subjective character and of the readiness of people to persuade themselves that something was self-evident when it was only a blind prejudice. Kant was the first philosopher to work out systematically this method of proof, but he did not, like the advocates of the " coherence theory," think of applying it to the laws of logic. They, being " analytic," do not seem to have troubled his philosophical conscience, but the synthetic *a priori* principles of natural science caused him some qualms. But, though the proof of these categories is the ultimate object of the deduction, they far from exhaust its importance and we have a good way to go yet before we reach its conclusion in them.

We shall proceed by first giving an outline of the general train of thought, following the logical rather than the actual order, and then show what place the different parts of the chapter respectively take in this argument. Kant divided the first edition transcendental deduction into two parts, usually distinguished as objective and subjective. " The one refers to the objects of pure understanding, and is intended to expound and render intelligible the objective validity of its *a priori* concepts. It is therefore essential to my purposes. The other seeks to investigate the pure understanding itself, its possibility and the cognitive faculties upon which it rests, and so deals with it in its subjective aspect. Although this latter exposition is of great importance for my chief purpose, it does not form an essential part of it. For the chief question is always simply this : what and how much can the understanding and reason know apart from all experience?—not : how is the faculty of thought itself possible? . . . The objective deduction with which I am here chiefly concerned retains its full force even if my subjective deduction should fail to produce that complete conviction for which I hope."[1] It is important to remember this warning of Kant's and not to think that we can refute the main argument of the transcendental deduction by pointing out inconsistencies and defects in Kant's psychology, but it is impossible rigidly to separate the two parts since important epistemological truths are often expressed in a psychological form, and the second edition, which omits the subjective side of the deduction, thereby leaves a gap in the argument which it only bridges by assuming what it does not fully state or prove. Commentators would agree that one cannot obtain an adequate idea of the transcendental deduction by reading the second edition alone, largely because it omits the subjective deduction.

According to Kant himself[2] the passage A 92-3 = B 124-6 is sufficient even by itself to prove his case, so let us consider this passage first. It occurs both in the first and second editions and is not amended in the latter even verbally. Kant is asking the question how we can have knowledge of objects. This can only be possible, he says, if one of two conditions is fulfilled. Either we must be passive so that the object determines our representations entirely, which we may then regard as a sort of copy of it, or we must be

[1] A XVI-XVII.   [2] A XVII.

active and make the object ourselves so that its nature has to conform to ours. The former alternative would not account for *a priori* knowledge, which Kant thinks to be an essential ingredient even in all our so-called empirical judgments; the latter is incompatible with the fact that we depend for our information about things other than ourselves on sensations not made by us but forced on us from without. The trouble is that we are neither wholly active nor wholly passive in knowledge. We do not create what we know, yet we do not accept the evidence concerning other things passively from our senses but tamper with it by imposing on our sensations the forms of space and time and subjecting them to a synthesis. It is this dual character of human knowledge which is for Kant at once the source of all our philosophical difficulties and the key to the critical philosophy. Kant contends that philosophers had overlooked one possibility, namely, that, while our mind does not create the objects we know, yet the character we assign to them belongs to them only as objects of human knowledge. In the *Æsthetic* he had explained on these lines how we know that all phenomena must conform to geometry. He now points out that among the conditions of human knowledge are included not only *a priori* intuitions but *a priori* concepts, for to know anything we require the concept of an *object*, and this cannot be formed without the use of the categories (at least substance and, as we shall see later, causality). *A priori* concepts are consequently necessary only because they are conditions of experience. Experience contains an empirical element, i.e. the manifold given in sensation, which is due to the action of things-in-themselves on us; but it also contains an element which is due to our own nature and is therefore *a priori*, not empirical. This element is constituted by the categories which Kant more ordinarily calls the pure or *a priori* concepts of understanding. But after reading this preliminary sketch of the argument we lose sight of the categories in the intermediate stages of the proof which are perhaps in the first edition somewhat unduly protracted.

What is the premiss of the whole argument of the transcendental deduction? It is, I think, simply that *there occurs awareness of a manifold in time*.[1] I further think that the addition of the words, *in time*, is not necessary for the main argument of the transcendental deduction, though it is necessary for the particular account of the synthesis given in the first edition and for the proofs of the individual categories. In either case the premiss is one that would hardly be disputed by any philosopher, however sceptical. (I am afraid I cannot count Behaviourists among *philosophers*, however useful they may be as physiological psychologists, but I do not suppose that any will be reading this book.) From this premiss Kant tries to prove (a) that there is, in some sense to be further explained, a unified self as opposed to a mere sequence of representations; (b) that we know physical objects; (c), by means of (a) and (b), that all our knowledge is subject to the categories. He thus seeks to refute the view of Hume that there is no possibility of giving a philosophical justification of the beliefs in our self-identity, the existence of physical objects and the validity of *a priori* categories such as causality. Someone may hereupon ask: What is the use of Kant's proving what we all of us know already, even if, like Hume, we may admit that we cannot prove it? But it is the business of philosophy not only to give us new information but

[1] A 99.

also to tell us what is the real basis of the beliefs we hold in so far as they are true, and, further, we cannot separate their philosophical justification from their analysis and their significance in an ordered whole of knowledge or theory, so that to justify them philosophically is really to enrich our knowledge much more than is conveyed by the suggestion that Kant is merely inventing a new formal proof of what is self-evident. In fact Kant's mode of proof of them carried with it implications for one's whole philosophical outlook of the most far-reaching and revolutionary kind. In particular Kant thought that, while refuting Hume, he had at the same time disproved the dogmatic metaphysics of his own predecessors by showing (a) that the categories could only be proved by reference to the possibility of experience and were therefore only valid within the realm of actual and possible experience, (b) that the unity of the self, at least in so far as we could know it, was inseparable from the unity of objects known and vice versa, so that we could no longer assert either a soul-substance retaining an identity apart from its relation to objects or physical objects existing independently of us in the sense of the realist. For the full development of these implications as well as the reservations made on ethical grounds we must wait till the *Dialectic*. The kind of philosophy thus introduced, however we may like it, represents a total change from what had gone before. If we abandon the thing-in-itself, as most of Kant's important followers eventually did, we have a thorough-going idealism of the " coherence " type; if we retain the thing-in-itself, we have a positivistic philosophy of experience which at a time such as the present when anti-metaphysical and empiricist views are rampant should particularly call for attention, and may through its superior moderation and manysidedness supply some of the correctives which the unbalanced positivism of to-day so badly needs. I do not myself accept either idealism or positivism, even in its Kantian form, but perhaps the fact that I am far from being an actual disciple of the author on whom I comment is not an unmitigated disadvantage for a commentator. I have tried at any rate to keep my own philosophy in the background and avoid grinding any private axes.

The first stage in the deduction is the proof that awareness of a manifold involves a *synthesis*.[1] The more detailed account of the synthesis constitutes what Kant calls the subjective deduction,[2] but that there is a synthesis is an assumption which is essential also to the objective deduction, and when Kant suppressed the subjective deduction in the second edition he thereby suppressed also an argument which is really needed to establish the fact of the synthesis. Its place is taken by the mere assertion that combination cannot be given by sense but must be due to an act of the mind.[3]

Let us consider therefore the argument in the first edition. The student should on a first reading omit the first one and a half paragraphs under the heading *Synthesis of Reproduction in Imagination* up to the end of A 100, since Kant here confuses the issue by introducing another argument that is best considered later. The passage in question is in fact omitted in Kemp Smith's abridged edition. The chief part in carrying out the synthesis is ascribed to the "understanding" by Kant. This is his name for our capacity to form general rules. It supplies the *a priori* conceptual element in all empirical knowledge, i.e. the categories. " Pure concept of understanding " is in fact used by Kant as a synonym for category.

[1] A 99-103, B 129-30.   [2] *v*. above, pp. 69-70.   [3] B 129-30.

We must not lay too much stress on the distinction between the synthesis of apprehension, the synthesis of reproduction and the synthesis of recognition, still less conclude that Kant is asserting three syntheses instead of one. They are not, I think, to be regarded as distinct acts but only as different elements or moments in the one synthesis. More important is the distinction between the synthesis of understanding and the synthesis of imagination, but we shall have to deal with that distinction later. Kant assumes justifiably that we are aware of a manifold in time. But, he argues, we cannot be conscious even of a manifold as a manifold unless we can combine its diverse elements in thought. To do so, a threefold synthesis is required. He first points out that in order to be conscious of *a b c* it is not sufficient to think first *a*, then *b*, then *c*, we must be conscious of *a b c* together. This he calls *the synthesis of apprehension in intuition*. But I could not do this, he contends, if by the time I reached *b* I had forgotten *a*. Therefore we need a *synthesis of reproduction in imagination*. The nature of *the synthesis of recognition in a concept* is not so clear. In the first sentence under this heading Kant seems to mean that the reproduction of *a* is not sufficient by itself because we must also recognise that the *a* reproduced is the same as the *a* apprehended earlier, but at the end of the same paragraph he seems to be saying that for us to be conscious of *a*, *b* and *c* together we must be aware of them as constituting a unity such as that belonging to a single object or to the same coherent process of thought, e.g. counting. Certainly he would think the former impossible without the latter consciousness, on the ground that recall in memory requires some other link to serve as a basis of association and that recognition, if it is to amount to more than a mere feeling of familiarity, requires a definite concept of what sort of thing it is that is recognised.

There are various complications in the above argument not yet mentioned, and it is not possible to deal with all of them now. Kant seems to me gravely and unnecessarily to weaken the argument by introducing the strange suggestion that, if we are to be aware of a manifold at all, its different elements must be given separately in succession on the ground that " each representation, *in so far as it is contained in a single moment*, can never be anything but absolute unity."[1] I find it very hard to make sense of this, but we must remember that Kant is not contending that we are ever conscious of this undifferentiated unity supposed to be contained in a single moment. For consciousness of anything presupposes a synthesis, and this undifferentiated unity would only occur if there were no synthesis. There is a good deal to be said for Professor Paton's view that Kant is just saying what would happen if *per impossibile* the synthesis did not take place.[2] But, even if Kant does commit

---

[1] A 99, *cf.* below, pp. 154-5.

[2] " Kant is clearly mistaken if he means that at every moment we are given a single undifferentiated sense-impression, and that we go on to join up undifferentiated atomic sense-impressions into an intuition containing a manifold. His view is more plausible if we take it as expressing a limit reached by analysis. Let us suppose him to mean that if we were to abstract from the time-element in our consciousness, and ignore the continuous successive synthesis by which we hold together what is given at different times and in different places, we should be left with something which has no parts, outside one another, or before and after one another. For the present we must pass over the difficulties of this doctrine. It is, however, obvious that we cannot be aware of an intuition as lasting through time—and all intuitions last through some time—without holding together before the mind what is given at different times. This need not commit us to the view that in any moment, taken apart from what comes before it, we can be aware of a sense-impression which is an undifferentiated unity. There can be no idea in an isolated point

himself to the view that we cannot have two strictly simultaneous sensations, he does not hold that we ever are aware
separately of these undifferentiated single sensations. And
he expressly says that I can become empirically conscious of
the manifold either as simultaneous or as successive.[1]

Kant argues that the synthesis in all its three aspects is
presupposed not only in the awareness of particular things
but in our pure *a priori* intuitions, i.e. in the awareness of
space and time as such, hence the importance of the reference to counting. It is just because it is presupposed in the
awareness of space and time that all phenomena are subject
to the synthesis. He even speaks sometimes of a pure
manifold of *a priori* sensibility.[2] The constituents of this
manifold are presumably small durations and extensions.

[However much we may criticise Kant's statement of the
argument we must agree that, if we take any experience
which includes the cognition of anything, we find and must
always find (a) the union of diverse elements in a single
connected object of thought, for we are never conscious of
the absolutely simple and unrelated by itself; (b) the presence of memory as supplementing present perceptions, for
even the simplest perceptual judgments involve comparison
and connection with what went before; (c) the presence of
universal concepts, for we are never aware of a particular
without classifying it or some of its characteristics in some
way if only as " strange," unless we mean " by being
aware of it " merely acting as if it were present or getting

---

of time any more than there can be a colour in an isolated point of
space. The fact that we can discuss these as abstractions does not
mean that they are given elements out of which our experience is
constructed. They are, at most, elements into which our experience
can be analysed." (Paton I, 358-9.)

[1] B 139.   [2] *v.* B 102.

sensations from it as a jelly-fish might, a situation which would not be a case of experience in Kant's sense of the term. It is a fact that the threefold synthesis is present in all human cognitive experience. Before Kant's time the influence of interpretation by the mind on all, even the most simple, perceptual experiences had never been adequately realised, but thanks ultimately to Kant it has now become a commonplace of philosophy almost universally accepted. The far-reaching effects of Kant's emphasis on the activity of the mind may be traced in the Coherence Theory, in Pragmatism, in Italian Neo-Idealism, in all non-behaviour-istic modern psychologies of perception. But the interpretation of Kant's account of the synthesis raises a number of very difficult problems which we will have to leave for the present.]

From the synthesis Kant passes to the systematic unity of objects on the one hand[1] and to the transcendental unity of apperception on the other.[2] If all knowledge requires a synthesis, on the one hand the objects known must constitute or be made into a system, and on the other hand there is a unity of consciousness presupposed in all cognition, the transcendental unity of apperception. It may be objected that the term, *system*, is vague. I use it in this context to mean a set of particular facts relevantly connected so that inferences, if not *a priori*, at least inductive and probable, may be legitimately made from any one to some others and so that it cannot be split up into a number of independent sets each quite irrelevant to the others. I think this is roughly the sort of thing Kant had chiefly in mind. He certainly did not think that we could see the connection between particulars *a priori*, though the general principle

[1] A 104-6, B 130-1.   [2] A 107, 116, 117 n., B 132.

that connections of a certain type were present was for him *a priori*. The application of causality, community and substance, in so far as it can be interpreted in terms of causality, follows naturally from such a conception of system, but it is not so easy to see that the transcendental deduction should lead to the proofs of quantity, degree, and substance as an absolute permanent.

The argument for the systematic unity of objects Kant supports in the first edition by an analysis of the concept of object (*Gegenstand*). The passage in which this occurs has been widely condemned as pre-critical, but I am doubtful whether this is correct,[1] and at any rate something of the kind is needed at this stage in the argument. Kant asks what is meant by referring our representations to an object which is not itself a representation and to which they are yet supposed to correspond. If we abstract the notion of an object from our representations and regard it as something apart from experience, it is nothing more than a mere *x*. What use can it then be? Kant answers by pointing out that to ascribe different representations to the same object involves asserting a certain unity between the representations and a certain necessity governing them, e.g. if I ascribe my representations to a chair I am saying that they follow certain rules from which I can predict further representations of the same or somewhat different kinds. And since, as we have seen, there is nothing left of the concept of an object when we abstract it from our representations and their unity it follows that, when we are talking about objects, we are only talking about this unity of representations and the laws governing it. (The frequent use of the expression *a priori* in this passage is not intended to imply that we can see the

[1] *v.* below, p. 99 ff.

truth of these rules *a priori*. I think it means either that it is
a necessary *a priori* condition of our having experience in
Kant's sense that there should be rules, though not that the
particular rules which do hold actually should hold, or else
that the rules are relatively *a priori* in the sense in which we
speak of a person as arguing *a priori* when his conclusions
are based on general principles rather than directly on particular observations although the general principles are themselves ultimately based on observation.) In the second
edition deduction an object is defined as " that in the concept
of which the manifold of a given intuition is united."[1]

An object thus reduces itself to a system of representations,
and "it is only when we have thus produced synthetic unity
in the manifold of intuition that we are in a position to say
that we know the object."[2] These words laid the foundation, among other things, of the coherence theory of truth,
since they asserted that knowledge either necessarily and
always involved or was actually identical with (which Kant
means is not clear) the making of a system, though no doubt
the advocates of the coherence theory asserted that the world
and the truths about it constituted a system in a fuller sense
than Kant would have ever admitted as provable. The
difference for Kant between a proposition about physical
objects and a proposition merely about my own present
image as such is that the former proposition connects the
actual and possible representations of different observers into
a system. But even the latter proposition involves systematisation, both because the image is referred to the system of
representations constituting my appearance-self and because
I can only be aware of my images as such in contrast and
therefore connection with a presupposed material world.

[1] B 137.   [2] A 105.

We pass now to the *transcendental unity of apperception*. It is not clear how pure apperception as a power is to be distinguished from understanding except that the former word carries with it a suggestion of self-consciousness. What the whole phrase, transcendental unity of apperception, means is clearer. To assert that all phenomena presuppose this is to assert that they presuppose self-identity, but self-identity interpreted neither in terms of a substance-self distinct from its experiences nor in terms of a particular unchanging representation, but in terms of a unity of experience. The transcendental unity of apperception is to be distinguished sharply from any object of ordinary empirical perception. Kant wavers between maintaining that we are always conscious of it in some way[1] and maintaining merely that we *can* become conscious of it at any time in connection with any representation.[2] In either case we are conscious of it in a very different way from that in which we are conscious of empirical objects, for we are conscious of it as a presupposition and not as an object of knowledge. To be conscious of it as an object we should require another transcendental act of apperception to make the former its object. Hence it is irrelevant to retort that our representations are in a ceaseless flux and none of them remain identical : scepticism about the transcendental unity of apperception arises from looking for it where it could not possibly be found even if it exists. Yet in Kant's view it is equally erroneous to hypostatise it into a pure Ego theory of the self according to which we are aware of an " I " over and above all our experiences and the complex unity they form.

Kant accepted the argument for an identical self that, if there is to be knowledge of *a b c*, the same self which knows

[1] A 104, 116. [2] B 132, A 117 n.

a must also know *b* and *c*, but his originality does not consist in this. The argument was well enough known long before his time. Kant's contribution was to add that, if this is the proof of self-identity, the latter is proved only as a presupposition of knowing objects and therefore we cannot say that we are identical unconditionally but only *quâ* knowing objects, or even admit that the self-identity thus established is anything more than the unity of experience involved in knowing objects. To quote Professor Kemp Smith: "The true or transcendental self has no content of its own through which it can gain knowledge of itself. It is mere identity, I am I. In other words, self-consciousness is a mere *form* through which contents that never themselves constitute the self are yet apprehended as being objects to the self. Thus though the self in being conscious of time or duration must be conscious of itself as *identical* throughout the succession of its experiences, that identity can never be discovered in those experiences; it can only be thought as a condition of them. The continuity of memory, for instance, is not a possible substitute for transcendental apperception. As the subjective deduction demonstrates, self-consciousness conditions memory, and cannot therefore be reduced to or be generated by it. When, however, such considerations are allowed their due weight, the necessity of postulating a transcendental unity becomes only the more evident. Though it can never itself be found among appearances, it is an interpretation which we are none the less compelled to give to appearances."[1] We must add, however, that Kant's ethical thought no doubt led him to believe in the identity of the self in a fuller sense when he was considering freedom. But such identity would belong to the real self and not to

[1] *Commentary*, p. 251.

the world of experience and is not anything that can be either theoretically proved or clearly conceived, so it may be left out of account in this context.

This brings us to the next point, namely, that the unity of objects and the transcendental unity of apperception entail each other.[1] The reasons why Kant held this view are, I hope, clear from what I have already said. What we are aware of is always a diversity, but it must be a diversity in unity, otherwise we could not be aware of it even as a diversity. For that it must be thought together, but this is only possible if it constitutes or is made into a system. On the other hand self-identity can be proved in the sense that there can be no knowledge of a diversity $a\,b\,c$ unless a, b and c enter into the same unity of consciousness, but having proved it in this way we have no right to go on and say that the unity of the self is anything more than the unity of experience thus proved. The ultimate conditions of this unity are not phenomena or categories governing phenomena and therefore cannot be known by us, and there being no experience of absolute identity we can only be conscious of the identity of the self in contrast to the diversity of its representations. The self then, as far as we can tell, only has this unity in relation to objects known, and the objects we know could not exist apart from the unity of experience which constitutes the self's knowledge. (The principal arguments for the latter position are to be found not here but in the *Æsthetic* and in the *Antinomies*, where Kant argues that space and time must be appearances.) The unity of objects and the unity of the self are but different sides of the same act of synthesis which constitutes the indispensable condition of knowledge. Kant indeed sometimes seems to

[1] A 108, B 133-40.

go further still and to identify them altogether.[1] The transcendental unity of apperception, just because it is a mere form, implies content supplied from without.

Kant's argument on this point constitutes both an exposition of idealism and an attempt at a proof of the existence of physical objects. This may sound self-contradictory, but Kant would say that it is only if we are *transcendental idealists*, i.e. regard physical objects as phenomena, that we can be *empirical realists*, i.e. claim knowledge of their existence at all. In this respect he agrees with present-day phenomenalists who usually hold both that propositions about physical objects are known by us to be true and that they are only propositions about what human beings experience or would experience under given conditions.[2] Kant gives two reasons for saying that we know physical objects. (a) If physical objects were not known to exist we could not say even that our subjective representations existed, for we are only conscious of these in contrast and relation to physical objects. (b) What we know must be, in so far as we can know it, a system, and we can only systematise our representations by means of the notion of physical objects.

We must not suppose indeed that "objects," as used by Kant, covers only physical objects. The appearance self is itself one phenomenal object among others. Knowledge of it requires a synthesis, as does knowledge of physical objects,[3] and it is subject to those of the categories that are not prevented from being applicable to it by its special nature. But it is secondary and logically and chronologically posterior to

---

[1] A 105, 109, B 137.
[2] *v.* below, p. 180 ff. I think this is the clue to Kant's "Refutation of Idealism."
[3] B 153 ff.

physical objects. Introspection follows in our development consciousness of physical objects, and also logically presupposes the latter because the representations which constitute our self as it appears in introspection either consist of representations of physical objects or are related to these in some way. Some commentators have gone further and said that there was no separate manifold of inner as distinct from outer sense, but this is not consistent with Kant's recognition of emotions and desires as parts of the appearance self. The position of acts of thought and volitions is more obscure. Kant often speaks as if they belonged only to the noumenal (i.e. real) self, but they surely must have been conceived by him as having some corresponding appearances in the phenomenal self.

[We must not think that Kant was guilty of a vicious circle in deducing both unity in objects from the transcendental unity of apperception and the transcendental unity of apperception from unity in objects. It is not a vicious circle to deduce A from B and B from A, where, as here, they are both deduced from another premiss, i.e. the fact that we are conscious of a diversity. The deduction of either from the other is effected not in order to prove them but in order to show their interdependence. Their interdependence or inseparability, if a fact at all, is a most important discovery in philosophy, and the only way of proving that A and B are interdependent must be by deducing A from B and B from A.]

Finally, both the transcendental unity of apperception and the unity of objects are shown to involve the categories.[1] When Kant has occasion, in letters and other works, to express the argument for the categories as briefly as possible

[1] A 111-3, 119 ff.

he says that they are proved by the fact that they are necessary for " the unity of experience." This unity he had already shown to be a necessary condition of any knowledge, of the existence of physical objects and of self-identity. Kant has chiefly in mind the three Analogies, i.e. substance, causality, and community (mutual interaction), and it is easy to see how he might think these implied in the unity of experience. If substance did not persist and the past and present were not causally connected, he would say there would be no unity between later and earlier events in time; if different spatial objects did not interact, there would be no unity in space. Again to order our experience in any sort of system at all we must introduce the notion of things and attributes, thus using the category of substance, and we must suppose a necessary connection between different events, thus using the categories of causality and community.

But in the transcendental deduction Kant makes no attempt to give special proofs of the particular categories. He postpones that to the *Analytic of Principles*, which I shall discuss later. He does, however, think also that in the metaphysical deduction, which precedes the transcendental, he has deduced the particular categories from a consideration of the nature of thought as such, and that since he has now shown all phenomenal objects to be dependent on thought he has thereby given a proof that the categories are valid for all phenomena. In the second edition he introduces two sections which point this out,[1] but these are best discussed in connection with the *Metaphysical Deduction*, the consideration of which I have postponed to the next chapter, like that of the proofs of the particular categories. Leaving aside the question whether the particular categories that Kant men-

[1] § 19, 20. Deduct four from all numbers of sections for the Everyman translation. This translation does not include the first edition deduction.

tions are necessary for experience, the general argument that *some* categories or other are necessary may be stated thus. Kant would claim that he had proved that any objects we can know must constitute a system and that a system implies thought and therefore the *a priori* categories which belong to thought.

We have now completed our summary of the main argument of the transcendental deduction. In order to show the logical relations asserted by Kant to hold between the principal different concepts involved the following plan may be of use. I here employ an arrow to signify logical entailment, i.e. A entails B = A⟶B. The relation of logical entailment is not necessarily reversible, but it obviously may be the case both that A entails B and that B entails A, and this is so with most of the concepts here involved. Of course, if A entails B and B entails C, A entails C, but I have not thought it necessary to indicate this also.

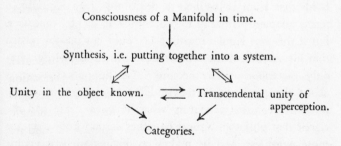

Consciousness of a Manifold in time.

Synthesis, i.e. putting together into a system.

Unity in the object known. ⟶ Transcendental unity of apperception.

Categories.

Before we proceed to comment on the text more in detail we must first discuss briefly two extremely difficult and controversial points, the nature of the synthesis and the relation between understanding and imagination. On the former there are two sharply opposed views represented by Professor Kemp Smith and Professor Paton respectively.

Professor Kemp Smith holds that the synthesis, since it creates the whole phenomenal world out of a given manifold, cannot itself be a process in time,[1] and concludes that it must be unconscious and appertain to the real non-temporal world. He adds that such a view, if carried out consistently, would make it unjustifiable to speak of the act of synthesis as the work of a self, whether phenomenal or real. He admits that Kant does not work it out consistently, but he holds that it represents a very important strain in his thought.

If this is the correct interpretation, Kant's view seems to me to be open to very serious criticism. For, if the act of synthesis is not in time and not in the phenomenal world, it should on Kant's own principles be quite unknowable, and therefore the description of it is a futile and self-contradictory undertaking when it is understood as an account of the synthesis itself and not only of its results in the phenomenal world. Professor Kemp Smith apparently holds that Kant is justified in describing it analogically in terms adapted primarily to our conscious mental processes, but if this was Kant's meaning he could not possibly claim that his account of the synthesis constituted knowledge, but only metaphor and conjecture. Yet he puts statements about the synthesis in the middle of passages which he certainly regarded as stating what he *knew*. He had declared that philosophy must be either certain knowledge or quite worthless, and he makes no distinction between his statements about the synthesis and the rest of his theoretical philosophy, for which he does claim certainty in emphatic terms. In the preface to the first edition deduction[2] he admits that the subjective deduction has some resemblance to a hypothesis (*etwas einer Hypothese ähnliches an sich*

[1] *v. Comm.*, p. 277 ff.   [2] A XVII.

hat), but he denies in the same sentence that it really partakes of this nature. And analogical statements about reality are always ruled out as illegitimate by Kant except when he is concerned with practical (ethical), not theoretical, reason. In my first book, written when I still accepted Professor Kemp Smith's interpretation, I accordingly made a sharp distinction between the doctrine of the synthesis as a description of our present knowledge, which I regarded as extremely valuable, and the doctrine of the synthesis as a theory about the origin of the phenomenal world by an act of construction on the part of the mind, which I subjected to very severe criticism.[1] But, mainly as a result of having read Professor Paton's book, I am not now by any means so sure that the theory which I criticised is really in Kant at all.

On Professor Paton's interpretation, on the other hand,[2] the syntheses " are all elements in the one temporal process which is experience." To the objection that a condition of the existence of the whole phenomenal world cannot itself be included in the phenomenal world he replies that what is a necessary condition of the existence of something need not be outside the latter but may be a necessary element in it. The description of the synthesis is not a description of how experience came to be, and the syntheses are therefore neither events in experience representing the stages which the mind passes on its way from sensation to completed knowledge nor unconscious and non-temporal noumenal[3] acts. Kant's account is an analysis of what is necessarily involved in knowing and not a sort of history

[1] *Kant's Treatment of Causality*, p. 65 ff.
[2] I, p. 572 ff.
[3] " Noumenal " is a term used by Kant of the real world.

of our coming to know. In other words, only that side of the account of the synthesis which I approved and not the side which I condemned is to be found in Kant. My personal impression now is that the general tenor of the transcendental deduction supports Professor Paton's view, though it would be harder to square with Kant's posthumous work. Kant seems to speak of the synthesis rather as an at least potentially conscious factor in experience than as a noumenal condition outside experience.

Kant distinguishes between an empirical and a transcendental synthesis, and it might be urged that Professor Paton's account was true of the empirical and Professor Kemp Smith's of the transcendental synthesis. This would be equivalent to giving the preference to the theory of the latter, because Professor Kemp Smith certainly recognises the presence of an empirical synthesis also, and it must be admitted that the distinction between the two can be explained more clearly on his theory than on Professor Paton's.[1] Yet Kant expressly says that we cannot have determinate intuition at all except " through the consciousness of the determination of the manifold by the *transcendental* act of imagination."[2] For Professor Paton the

---

[1] Other arguments for Prof. Kemp Smith's view as an interpretation of Kant are constituted by (a) the passage (B 103) which speaks of the imagination as "a blind but indispensable function of the soul of which we are scarcely ever conscious," (b) his treatment of genius as due to unconscious faculties in the *Critique of Judgment*, (c) his suggestion that sense and understanding may perhaps have a common root, (d) the needs of the doctrine of " double affection " (*v.* below), (e) the statement in the *Paralogisms* (A 363-4 n.) implying that we cannot know whether we have a unitary self at all. I do not myself think these arguments at all conclusive, but it may be that the posthumous work gives adequate justification for Professor Kemp Smith's interpretation.

[2] B 154. The italics are my own. Kant also describes the synthesis of reproduction, of which he certainly holds us to be conscious, as

transcendental and the empirical synthesis are different moments in one and the same synthesis only separable by abstraction. The synthesis quâ transcendental is the synthesis regarded as supplying the general framework, quâ empirical it is the synthesis regarded as an application of general principles to particular cases.[1]

Kant also distinguishes between the synthesis of imagination and the synthesis of understanding. The latter seems to be a necessary presupposition of all judgments, but without it we could still have images, though we presumably could not make judgments about them and say :—they are images of a particular kind. But, since they always include more than what is given in sense at the moment, images themselves presuppose a synthesis, which Kant ascribes to the imagination. As to what this synthesis does and what would be left if we took away both the synthesis of understanding and the synthesis of imagination there are conflicting views among commentators, and it is very difficult to decide.

There seem to be good grounds for the view that not only the synthesis of understanding, but also the synthesis of imagination presupposes the categories, the difference between the two syntheses being chiefly that the former applies them consciously and the latter unconsciously. The essential identity of the imagination and the understanding is asserted in B 162 n., and in B 151-2 the transcendental synthesis of imagination is expressly said to proceed according to the categories and to consist in an action of the understanding on sensibility (as also in B 154). In B 129-30, in

transcendental (A 102). Professor Kemp Smith has to dismiss this as a confusion. (*Comm.*, p. 248.)

[1] Paton I, pp. 576-7.

the most impressive place possible at the beginning of the transcendental deduction, we have the statement that all combination (*Verbindung*) comes from the understanding, which seems clearly to imply either that the imagination is just the understanding working unconsciously or that we could not have a synthesis of imagination without a synthesis of understanding, and it is common ground that a synthesis by the understanding involves the categories. It has been suggested in reply that, just as Kant started by using " reason " to cover both reason in the sense of the *Dialectic* and understanding, so he started by using " understanding " to cover both understanding, properly speaking, and imagination, and differentiated them later when the course of the argument required it. But the fact that the passage under discussion was not an early one but one only added in the second edition lessens the plausibility of this explanation. Some commentators have consequently attributed to Kant the view that we cannot even have clear, definite images, let alone be conscious of them as such, without the categories, and have concluded that apart from a synthesis employing the categories there would be left not even sense-data but only a formless unrelated manifold, nothing of which we could conceivably be conscious at all.[1]

On the other hand in the *Critique of Judgment* Kant certainly maintains as an essential part of his æsthetic doctrine that imagination can and does normally function without the categories, and in the *Prolegomena* he actually speaks of " judgments of perception " which do not require the categories (e.g. that the room is warm or sugar is sweet), but can be made into " judgments of experience " by being

[1] For a defence of this view *v*. Caird, *The Critical Philosophy of Kant* I, p. 352 ff.

brought under the categories.[1]   And in a psychological frag-
ment Kant says that "there can be clearness in intuition
even when there is absolutely no concept, e.g. when one has
no names for the manifold in a building and yet distinguishes all its details satisfactorily."[2]   Considerations like
this have led the late A. D. Lindsay to maintain that what
understanding does is only to introduce the distinction between objective and subjective and this is all for which the
categories are required.[3]   On this view we should without
the categories still be conscious of a series of images, but
we should not be able to make any distinction between the
really physical and the illusory or merely imaginary.

While I am unable to effect a reconciliation between the
Critique of Pure Reason and the *Critique of Judgment* and
Prolegomena in this matter, I am not sure that we cannot
give a consistent account which does justice to all passages
in the *Critique of Pure Reason* if we make a distinction between having images or feelings and explicitly recognising
their presence and nature so that we can say to ourselves
that we have them.   It seems to me that Kant holds that
apart from the categories we should still have consciousness
in the sense of feeling but not in the sense of cognition.   I
think Professor Kemp Smith and Professor Paton are really
agreed on this point, though the latter does not recognise it.
Professor Paton admits that "for Kant there can be no
knowledge or *experience of objects*—in the strict sense—
apart from the categories," but insists that "this is a very
different thing from saying that no *representations* can exist
for *consciousness* apart from the categories."[4]   Professor
Kemp Smith on the other hand says that because they can-

---

[1] § 18-20, *Berl*. IV, p. 298 ff.   [2] *Berl*. XV, p. 84.
[3] Lindsay, *Kant*, p. 107 ff.   [4] I, p. 330.

not apply the categories and have no capacity for self-consciousness, according to Kant " animals must also be denied
anything analogous to what we must signify by the term
consciousness,"[1] but he admits that Kant attributes to them
sensations, feelings, apprehension. They both therefore
seem to agree that without the categories we could feel or
have images but could not cognise our feelings or images.

Kant says that without a synthesis involving the categories
our experience " would not be knowledge, but a rhapsody
of perceptions that would not fit into any context according
to rules of a completely interconnected (possible) consciousness "[2] or " a mere dream,"[3] but this implies at least the
presence of images apart from the categories. On the
other hand Kant's doctrine in the *Analogies* that the categories are necessary for anything to have a determinate
position in space and time supports the view that we could
not even have images without them, but it is possible to
hold that this only means that they are necessary if we are
to be cognitively conscious of the position as determinate.

The function of the synthesis of imagination seems to
consist in fitting our present sense-data into a space and time
which include also what is not perceived at the moment
and so supplementing them by images, the function of the
synthesis of understanding in producing a consciousness of
what we perceive as belonging to physical objects in con-
tradistinction from the subjective element. What is merely
given without a synthesis is described as sensation. Some
commentators (including myself in my first book) regard
this given element as a set of terms without relations on the
ground that relation is said to be the work of mind, and
therefore they have to conclude that it is something quite

[1] *Comm.*, p. XLIX.   [2] B 195.   [3] B 247.

unthinkable and certainly incapable of existing in the phenomenal world and to blame Kant for his misuse of language in applying the term "sensation" to it. But might it not be just that element in what we call my present sense-data which is due to sensation and not memory or interpretation? We need not think of this as existing by itself in the phenomenal world before it was synthesised, but neither need we think of it as having a noumenal existence in which it is subjected to a non-temporal synthesis. It is perhaps an element in experience which never exists apart from the others in human beings and can only be separated from them by abstraction, and certainly we need not think of it as if there were always, first, sensation, then synthesis by the imagination, then synthesis by the understanding. The passage[1] which I and others regarded as conclusive for the view that all relations are imposed by the mind does not seem so to me now. It asserts that combination (*Verbindung*) is due to understanding, but *Verbindung* may simply mean synthesis, in which case the passage throws no further light on what the synthesis contributes.

Composition of Transcendental Deduction.[2] Some commentators (most notably Prof. Vaihinger[3] and Kemp Smith[4]) have divided the first edition deduction into parts which, as they think, expound inconsistent doctrines and represent different stages of Kant's development. I shall call this the "multiple theory" for short.[5] The theory was

[1] B 129-30.
[2] The reader should refer again to pp. 4-9 above. My opinion is that this passage of my book to p. 104 had better be omitted on a first reading.
[3] His separate book on *Die Transcendentale Deduktion der Kategorien*.
[4] *Comm.*, p. 201 ff.; cf. XIX ff.
[5] It is usually called the patchwork theory nowadays by critics, but in view of the suggestibility of the human mind I think that it

subjected to severe criticism by Professor Paton in 1930.[1]   I am told that it was abandoned much earlier in Germany by most scholars.

In defence of the multiple theory in general it is said (a) that Kant's opinions certainly underwent a profound and progressive alteration during the eleven years in which he was writing the Critique, that he is known to have finally composed it in a hurry in a few months, which certainly did not leave him time to write it out afresh but put him under the necessity of stringing together notes which must have been written at different periods and therefore may well express different opinions; (b) that the inconsistencies in his work are far too frequent to be explained in any other way; (c) that the whole bent of Kant's mind and method led him to tackle each problem from a number of different aspects and to sacrifice, where necessary, consistency to insight, i.e., to refuse to let one side of what he thought to be the truth go just because he could not harmonize it with the other.

I have already made some general criticisms of the theory which I shall not repeat here.[2]   (a) certainly provides a good explanation of some inconsistencies, but many think that the inconsistencies of Kant have been much exaggerated under the influence of the multiple theory.   Whether (b) is true is a matter of detailed interpretation : if we find that the inconsistencies are sufficient we must regard the tran-

---

is fairer not to start the discussion of a theory by giving it a name which has a slightly derogatory flavour.   I should be surprised to hear one of its supporters describe it as the patchwork theory by choice.

[1] In *Proceedings of Aristotelian Society*, N.S., vol. XXX, p. 143 ff.; *v*. also Lund Yates, Mind no. 155, p. 318 ff.

[2] *v*. above, pp. 4-9.

scendental deduction and perhaps the Critique as a whole as a " patchwork," but I should myself rate the number of inconsistencies very much lower. But it must be admitted that, since the first edition transcendental deduction was entirely rewritten and § 2 at least of it is said by Kant to be provisional, being intended " rather to prepare than to instruct the reader,"[1] this constitutes a part of the Critique where the application of a multiple theory is more plausible than in any other.

In support of his views as to the composition of the transcendental deduction Vaihinger has collected a considerable quantity of external evidence in the shape of Kant's own notes,[2] but unfortunately, except in two cases,[3] we have no independent evidence of the dates of these different notes. Their relative dates are ascertained mainly by the same sort of criteria as are used in dating by internal evidence the different portions of the transcendental deduction itself, and consequently, if these criteria should prove unreliable, the external evidence would do so likewise. In any case it is admitted that the main test of the theory must be whether it is necessary or helpful to the understanding of the Critique itself. This will depend on one's detailed exegesis; if it appears after examination possible to understand the transcendental deduction as a single whole, as I claim it is, the main ground for the theory will have gone. We must further remember that it is one matter to contend in general that the deduction is made up of separately composed and

[1] A 98. This last point is derived from Paton, who, however, strangely uses it in support of the opposite conclusion.

[2] This is summarised by Kemp Smith, *Comm.*, pp. 231-4.

[3] The date of one is Jan. 1780. This is taken by Vaihinger as proving that by that date Kant had not yet developed the doctrine of the threefold synthesis (the fourth stage), but it is also compatible with the supposition that he had already discarded it.

often contradictory passages, and quite another to find grounds for sorting out these correctly and determining their chronological order. Even if the multiple theory be right in general, it may still be doubted whether we have any at all reliable means of fixing which passages are early and which late in composition.

Turning to the detailed application of the theory to the transcendental deduction, we find that its holders naturally differ among themselves somewhat as to the mode of division. I shall only mention that adopted by Prof. Kemp Smith,[1] as it is most familiar to students of Kant in this country. This commentator divides the first edition transcendental deduction into four stages.

First Stage (a). II 3 (from beginning of third paragraph to end of 3) = A 104-10; (b) I § 13 (the entire section) = A 84-92 (retained in second edition as B 116-24, transitional to second stage).

Second Stage (a) I § 14 (except the last paragraph) = A 92-4 (retained in second edition as B 124-7); (b) II (the first four paragraphs) = A 95-7; (c) II 4 (the entire section) = A 110-14.

Third Stage § 14 (last paragraph) = A 94-5; whole of III = A 115-30; and (transitional to fourth stage) § 10 = A 76-9 (retained as B 102-4).

Fourth Stage II (from opening of 1 to end of second paragraph in 3) = A 98-104, and the two paragraphs immediately preceding this = A 97-8.

The stages are given in their supposed chronological order of composition. It is held that the first set of passages were written before Kant had realised the place of the categories in the synthesis, the second after he had rea-

---

[1] *Comm.*, p. 203 ff.

lised this but before he had developed the doctrine of productive imagination, and the third after he had developed the doctrine of productive imagination but before he had analysed the transcendental synthesis as threefold. Since the threefold analysis does not occur in the second edition deduction the latter constitutes a fifth stage. I am not considering the minor distinctions within each stage, and I shall only deal at length with the first stage. I select this because, if the interpretation suggested is correct, it is most radically and surprisingly different from anything else in the Critique.

Professor Kemp Smith contends that the passage A 104-10 represents a very immature stage of Kant's thought on the following grounds: (a) There is no mention of the categories, and their function seems to be fulfilled by "empirical concepts", such as that of "body", and "empirical rules."[1] (b) It is the thing-in-itself (transcendental object) which is regarded as giving phenomena unity, necessity and objectivity.[2] This seems to imply that it is treated as itself not only a cause of which they are effects, but the substance of which they are attributes.[3] Although the categories are not mentioned in the passage under consideration, the view would therefore, if carried out consistently, involve their application to the thing-in-itself, and, what is more, to the thing-in-itself alone, for there is no mention of any intermediate phenomenal object to which

[1] A 106.

[2] Point (b) is a discovery of Kemp Smith, not suggested by Vaihinger.

[3] Kant, having declared that the relation of knowledge to the transcendental object carries with it an element of necessity, gives as his reason for this statement that, in so far as our different pieces of knowledge relate to one (transcendental) object, "they must necessarily agree with one another, that is, must possess that unity which constitutes the concept of an object" (A 105 *ad fin.*), i.e. presumably a substance.

they could also be applied. According to Professor Kemp Smith, however, it had not yet occurred to Kant at the time he wrote the passage that categories were needed, and therefore the logical consequence of the view could not be drawn by Kant. If he had drawn it, it would certainly have been radically incompatible with the fundamental precepts of his critical philosophy. That the categories should be applied in some sense to things-in-themselves is not, we shall see,[1] inconsistent with Kant's mature doctrine, but that the unity and so the knowledge of phenomena should itself be constituted by the application of categories to things-in-themselves and that the categories should not be applied to phenomena at all is almost the diametrical opposite of what he considered the chief doctrine of the Critique.

(c) The absence of the phenomenal object also involves " an extreme subjectivism," i.e. in the absence of such an intermediate term between mere representations and things-in-themselves it is not open to Kant to say that our judgments about physical things are true of phenomena, and since they are not held by him to be true of things-in-themselves Kant would be in the unenviable position of the " idealists " he attacks who deny all knowledge of the physical world and make science mere illusion.

If this interpretation is correct there can be no possible doubt that the passage is pre-critical, but other commentators disagree with Professor Kemp Smith as to its interpretation. It has sometimes been taken as a passage in which Kant explains away the thing-in-itself as a mere hypostatisation of the unity of our thought, and some have, while making the " transcendental object " merely a thought of ours which gives unity to our knowledge, de-

[1] *v.* below, pp. 188-9.

nied its identity with the thing-in-itself, which exists quite independently of us.

The numerous other passages in which it is hardly possible to doubt that the transcendental object is identified with the thing-in-itself constitute an objection to the latter interpretation, and I think it requires some qualification to be made acceptable, but if as here we must choose between admitting an inconsistency in Kant's use of terminology and a fundamental and extraordinary inconsistency in views expressed, I prefer the former alternative. I think myself that Kant is starting with the common-sense conception of an object to which representations are referred and then pointing out that *for us* the reference to an object cannot mean more than that the representations constitute a system. For, he is saying, our concept of the transcendental object considered apart from this does become the empty concept of a thing-in-itself, and therefore if the concept of "object" is to help us in our thought it must take on a different meaning and be understood as an expression of the unity of our experience, i.e. he deliberately changes the meaning of "transcendental object" in order to show the reader the only sense in which the concept of an object can usefully be employed.[1] Having done this he prefers not to follow this terminology regularly himself but speaks of "objects," not "transcendental objects," when he is talking of phenomena, though no doubt it would have been more consistent with his distinction between transcendental and transcendent[2] to describe the phenomenal object as "transcendental." A thing-in-itself should be called "transcendent" not "transcendental." Kant's analysis and criticism here of the notion of an object seem

[1] *v*. Paton I, pp. 423-4.   [2] *v*. above, p. 25.

to me, apart from the ambiguities of expression which have caused such divergencies of opinion in interpreting the passage, an eminently suitable way of approaching the proof of the categories.

As regards the omission of the categories, it seems to me impossible to argue that because Kant does not mention the categories here he did not believe in their place in the synthesis when he wrote this passage. The section (2) is not by itself a proof of the categories but an introduction to their proof, and it seems to me quite fitting that they should not be mentioned till the climax of the proof was approached. The " empirical concepts " and " rules " which Professor Kemp Smith finds in Kant here seem to me to be particular applications of the categories in the sense in which particular kinds of things and particular causal laws are applications of substance and cause,[1] but Kant, quite fittingly, does not yet point this out but merely shows here that rules giving necessity are involved in the concepts of objects. Later he argues that particular objective rules presuppose the categories.[2] These rules and concepts are no doubt empirical in a sense in contrast to the categories of which I think they are particular applications, but he only once in this passage calls the concepts or rules empirical while he uses the words *a priori* or necessary in connection with them eleven times. I do not myself see any need to hold that at the time he wrote this passage Kant thought that these concepts could be formed without the help of the categories.

It is also argued that in A 107 ad hn. Kant implies that

[1] Excepting perhaps the geometrical illustration (A 105), which is still less empirical.

[2] *v.* A 126-8.

the only *a priori* concepts are space and time because he adds after "*a priori* concepts" the words "space and time" in brackets as though these were the only such concepts; but, if this is what Kant meant, the passage must have been so "pre-critical" as to have been actually "composed in the cradle."[1] It does not represent the views of any period whatever of his adult life, and if we take into account the words which immediately precede *a priori concepts*, i.e. the *purest objective unity*, we may arrive at a less surprising meaning for the passage. For, if the manifold as well as the form is given *a priori*, the resultant will be "purer" than if, as is the case with the categories, the manifold has to be given empirically, therefore it is not inappropriate to speak of space and time as constituting "the purest objective unity." The passage will then not assert space and time to be the only *a priori* concepts, but to be the ones which yield the purest objective unity.

The distinctions made between the other stages separated by Professor Kemp Smith are less important, even if justified. They all concern the subjective side of the deduction, i.e. the side which Kant regards as secondary. It would be hardly possible to maintain that Kant was completely consistent in his description of the syntheses involved in knowledge, and the inconsistencies that occur may well be due to the use of notes written at different times and not adequately revised. I think their importance should not be overrated, for we must not think of the different syntheses mentioned as sharply distinct events but rather as different aspects of the same act, and I am doubtful whether the differences that occur are not differences of language rather

[1] Paton, *Proc. of Ar. Soc.*, 1929-30, p. 171; *cf.* Paton, *Kant's Met. of Exp.* I, p. 410 n.

than of meaning. It is the case that Kant in A 98 ff. mentions three syntheses which he nowhere else distinguishes and that in A 115 he introduces another threefold distinction which it is very hard to reconcile verbally with the first one. But " there is no real contradiction if we will remember that Kant does not say that one or the other form of the synthesis is the single, complete and sufficient condition of intuition, but that each one of them is a partial condition, of which conditions apperception is the supreme and most inclusive."[1] More serious is the fact that, while in A 101-2 he admits a transcendental synthesis of reproduction, in B 152 he asserts that the synthesis of the reproductive imagination is " entirely subject to empirical laws " and "therefore contributes nothing to the explanation of the possibility of *a priori* knowledge."

However I am, after reading Professor Paton's article, sceptical as to our ability to decide which particular passages are early and which late. The main criterion employed is negative. It is argued that passages belonging to the alleged first stage do not mention the categories, passages belonging to the first and second stages do not mention the productive imagination, passages belonging to the first, second and third stages do not mention the threefold synthesis of A 98 ff., and in each case it is concluded that what Kant does not mention at the time he does not accept. But surely this is a very dangerous argument. We need not expect Kant either to mention at the beginning all the main points which are established in the course of the argument or to repeat explicitly at a later stage what had been discussed already. That passages of the second

[1] Vleeschauwer, *La déduction transcendentale dans l'œuvre de Kant*, II, p. 247.

stage do not mention the productive imagination might well be explained by supposing simply that Kant did not in these passages wish to introduce the subjective side of the deduction but only the objective. After all the *Prolegomena* and most of the second edition deduction do not mention the productive imagination, though they certainly belong to a later stage than any of the first edition.

We may now proceed to comment on particular passages, in so far as this has not already been done in the course of the discussion.

§ 13. The object of this introductory section is to show that a transcendental, as opposed to an empirical, deduction is indispensable and to point out certain difficulties in such a deduction.

Professor Paton[1] describes the difference between a transcendental deduction and an empirical deduction as being that the former deals with the origin of *a priori* concepts, the latter with the method of acquiring them. The point of this distinction is that the transcendental deduction claims to show the dependence of the categories on the mind but does not give an account of a psychological process by which we come to know and use them. This is true, but it is not the main point. The transcendental deduction of the categories does not, I think, prove their validity primarily by showing that they are dependent on the mind but by showing that "experience" would be impossible without them, and what Kant is chiefly concerned to explain is not how the categories "originated" in any sense but how it is that we can be *justified* in applying them, as is indeed clear from other passages in Professor Paton's work.

[1] I, 316.

8

With an empirical concept empirical deduction and justification do, or at least may, coincide, but it is not so with
a priori concepts. The distinguishing-marks of *a priori*
concepts were for Kant their universality and necessity,
and this made an empirical deduction impossible, meaning
by an empirical deduction a deduction from particular experiences. That even the transcendental deduction is
empirical in the sense of being a deduction by reference to
the possibility of human experience in general must not be
forgotten, but this is always sharply contrasted by Kant
with empirical deductions of the kind that can be given
of particular causal laws which are established from a
limited number of particular observations by inductive
generalisation. And Kant points out that to show how the
concepts originated empirically, as genetic psychology seeks
to do, is by no means the same as to justify their application
to objects.

In the earlier paragraphs of this section Kant includes
space and time under the *a priori* concepts. This has rather
disconcerted many commentators, since they have been declared to be intuitions, but after all he does call them concepts several times even in the *Æsthetic*, and I have mentioned earlier[1] a sense in which he was perfectly justified in
this use of the term " concept," though he ought to have
explained it more clearly. He then distinguishes the categories from the *a priori* forms of intuition and points out
that there is a difficulty about the former which does not
occur in the case of the latter, for while objects cannot even
be given in intuition without being subject to the pure
forms of space and time, they can be given in intuition,
and so appear to us, without the categories.[2] This state-

[1] p. 36.   [2] B 122.

ment as well as Kant's neglect in the present section to distinguish clearly the question of the application of the categories to phenomena from the question of their application to things-in-themselves[1] have led some commentators to regard the passage as very early. Others explain these features by saying that the section is only introductory and that Kant must not be expected to assume at the start what he is only going to prove later, but it may be replied that it is not merely a question of omission but of positive statements inconsistent with the doctrine of most of the Critique. That appearances can be given in intuition in an important sense apart from the categories is a doctrine which it may plausibly be argued was held by Kant even in his critical period,[2] but this can hardly be said of the sentence where he speaks as if the advantage of his method were that it was the *alternative* to the complete surrender of all claims to make judgments that transcend the limits of possible experience, whereas according to the general view of the Critique this surrender is in fact a *consequence* of his method itself.[3] But it is dangerous to draw conclusions from a single sentence. Occasional sentences in any philosophical book, especially when written in a hurry, are likely to be carelessly and misleadingly worded, and Kant goes on directly to talk in a way which seems to imply that it is only the question of the application of the categories to appearances which is under discussion.[4] Also, why was

---

[1] *v.* B 120.
[2] *v.* above, p. 92 ff.
[3] A 89 (= B 121).
[4] B 122-3. For the other view *v.* Kemp Smith, *Comm.*, 219-22. This writer makes the whole of § 13 transitional between his first and second stages, i.e. later than the passage on the transcendental object but earlier than any other passage in the deduction.

this passage retained in the second edition if it was as pre-critical as has been suggested?

§ 14. I have already spoken about the main argument of this section.[1] Kant's knowledge of Hume is inadequate, and his interpretation of him as a complete sceptic misleading.[2] The passage stating that there are three original sources of experience,[3] sense, imagination and apperception, is in conformity with Kant's views elsewhere if apperception be identified with or be held to involve understanding, and it does not seem impossible to connect them with the three syntheses (or, rather, the three aspects of the synthesis) mentioned in the next section. But, if so, it must be admitted that the latter section does not carry out the task of distinguishing an empirical and a transcendental employment in each case. The paragraph may have been omitted in the second edition simply because it was part of the subjective deduction, or, rather, an introductory reference to it.

First Edition Deduction. Section 2. The A Priori Grounds of the Possibility of Experience. Most of this section is provisional or preliminary and intended "rather to prepare than to instruct the reader."[4] All the same it is quite essential to the first edition deduction and fills gaps in the argument which are not adequately filled elsewhere in the first or at all in the second edition. It gives the clearest account of the reasons why Kant accepted the doctrine of the synthesis and why he regarded an object as a mere system of representations, also perhaps of his reasons for the doctrine of the transcendental unity of apperception. The section may be divided as follows: (1) Introductory

---

[1] *v.* above, pp. 70-2.　　　　[2] B 128.
[3] A 94-5, *cf.* A 155.　　　　[4] A 98.

(A 95-8), (2) the establishment of the threefold synthesis (A 98-103), (3) the analysis of the conception of an object showing that it is merely a system of representations thus synthesised (A 104-6), (4) the argument for the transcendental unity of apperception as the condition of all knowledge and of this system which constitutes objects (A 106-7), (5) the argument that not only does the unity of objects entail the transcendental unity of apperception but also *vice versa* (A 108), (6) the argument that the unity of objects and the transcendental unity of apperception involve *a priori* rules of synthetical unity, which must be the categories (A 108-14).

The arguments are, however, not kept perfectly distinct. The most important example of this is a puzzling passage extending from the beginning of the part headed *The Synthesis of Reproduction in Imagination* to the end of A 101. This logically belongs to what I have called the sixth division of the argument. Similar passages occur in A 113-4 and 121-3, so I shall discuss them together.

Kant realised that the possibility of the categories being applied or a synthesis effected depended not only on us but on the manifold given in sensation. It was logically conceivable that there might be manifolds of such intractable material that they could never be subjected to a synthesis or to the categories, and had it been the case that only such manifolds were given to us in sensation then experience would have been impossible. Further it is not enough that, e.g., everything should be caused: if the cause were too complex for us ever to discover regularities we should be as badly off as if nothing were caused, or rather we should not exist at all as human beings. It may be the case that the only true cause of anything is the whole previous state of the universe,—this indeed seems to follow if we hold with Kant that everything interacts with everything else,—but at least some parts of the universe must have less relevance to the events we are considering than others. If it is true, as Jeans has said, that every time we nod our heads we shake all the stars, at any rate astronomy presupposes that our nods are much less relevant to the motion of the stars than certain other factors and that the motions of some heavenly bodies can be calculated approximately from a few factors without taking into account all the nods that almost infinitesimally influence them. For causality to be applicable by human beings, a relatively small number of factors in the total vastly complicated cause must be of decisive importance and the influence of the others, though existent, negligibly slight, but that this should be so is not implied in the principle of causality itself. For these two reasons experience presupposes what Kant calls an " affinity " in the manifold. He brings this out in connection with the empirical principle of association of ideas. This empirical association is presupposed if we are to form any idea of a complex object or to effect any synthesis of reproduction in imagination, but if phenomena did not display some regularity in their occurrence and if there were not therefore this affinity in the manifold, association would be impossible.

Kant declines to describe the affinity as a contingent fact, and if in declaring it to be necessary *a priori* he only means that it is a principle to which all phenomena must necessarily conform because otherwise they could not be experienced by us and would not therefore be phenomena, this is perfectly in accord with his philosophy. In that case, however, the affinity will be contingent in a more ultimate sense. It might perfectly well have been the case that the only manifold given was such that it could not possibly be synthesised or subjected to the categories, only we can know *a priori* that if so there could have been no phenomena, and since, in fact, there are phenomena this is not what has happened. It may likewise be the case that besides the manifold which we can synthesise there is also produced in us another manifold which we cannot synthesise and bring under the forms of intuition and the categories, but then this second manifold can never be known by us and therefore does not constitute phenomena.

The words of Kant may, however, be interpreted as meaning that we not only impose categories on the manifold but also are responsible for this affinity of the manifold, i.e. make the manifold such that it can conform to them. If this interpretation is right it is very difficult to reconcile the passages in question with the fundamental principles of the Critique. Kant is in that case either merely putting the difficulty further back in a very naïve way or converting knowledge into pure creation and destroying the whole empirical, given element on which his epistemology lays so much stress. For we cannot bring A and B into affinity with each other unless they are such as to be capable of this affinity. But then either the capacity for affinity is independent of our mind, in which case our knowledge will still be a contingent fact, since, though the affinity which knowledge presupposes is contributed by the mind, it involves a material not contributed by the mind with an independent nature of its own; or our mind creates not only the affinity but the capacity for it, in which case we cannot stop short of saying that it creates the given manifold. If the former alternative be adopted, the supposed difficulty that our knowledge is contingent will not be removed; if the latter, this will contradict altogether the view that our knowledge depends partly on given material, which is a fundamental presupposition of the whole Critique.

But, if asked to mention the most important points in the argument about affinity, Kant would probably have said that it showed the impossibility of explaining the categories or the unity of consciousness by the principle of association of ideas, because to be ideas at all and therefore to be associated as such the ideas must be subject to the very unity they are intended to explain and to a synthesis which involves the categories, and that it was also a part of the general argument showing that phenomena constitute a system and are subject to categories.

Except for this argument about transcendental affinity with which I have just dealt I think that the section (2) up to the beginning of 4 (A 110) has been discussed sufficiently already[1] for a commentary of the present scale. *4 (A 110-4)* introduces the explicit argument for the categories. The statement in A 110 to the effect that there can only be *one* experience cannot be interpreted literally. Kant certainly did not hold, like the "Absolutists," that human perceptions are all parts of a divine, all-embracing experience. God's "experience," if it can be called experience, would not be subject to space and time and the categories, and there is no hint in Kant of the doctrine that human minds are included in God. The single experience of which Kant talks must be regarded as ideal, not actual. That is, we cannot but think of our particular experiences as experiences of physical objects, at once partially revealing these

[1] *v.* above, p. 74 ff.

objects and yet contrasted in some degree with them as they really are, and to think of physical objects as they really are is for Kant to introduce the notion of an ideal observer. Since to assert any relation between two physical things is to say something which, like everything else that we can say about them, can only be understood in reference to experience, and physical things are all interrelated, we must introduce the notion of a single experience, at least as a methodological fiction. The last three paragraphs (A 112-4) are of the nature of an appendix.

Section 3. *The Relation of the Understanding to Objects in General, and the Possibility of Knowing them A Priori.* This section is intended as a briefer and more connected account of the argument which had been already given in the preceding section. It may be summarised as follows: (a) There are three sources of human knowledge—sense, imagination and apperception. We can treat each empirically in explaining the origin of particular experiences, but we can also lay down about each of them the *a priori* principle that they are necessary conditions of all experience. We must thus contrast with empirical intuition pure intuition, which gives us the *a priori* forms of space and time, with empirical association the pure synthesis of imagination and with empirical consciousness pure apperception (first two paragraphs, A 115-6). (b) Of these the most fundamental is pure apperception. Unity of apperception is a necessary condition of all knowledge, and thus I can have no representations which are not at least capable on principle of being connected with my other representations in a single consciousness (A 116 and 117, including note). (c) But this unity of consciousness would be impossible without a synthesis by the imagination. This synthesis must be sharply distinguished from that involved in empirical memory. It is the condition of all knowledge and all phenomena (A 118). (d) "The unity of appercep- tion in relation to the synthesis of imagination is the under- standing," therefore the synthesis must involve the use of the pure concepts of understanding, i.e. the categories, and since the synthesis is a necessary condition of all know- ledge all phenomena must conform to the categories (A 119). (e) Kant then confirms his results by starting with the empirically given and working back to the tran- scendental unity of apperception. He first points out that a synthesis is necessary, on the ground that we are always conscious of a diversity in unity and sense by itself could only account for the diversity, not the unity (A 120). (f) There follows the argument concerning association and affinity which I have already discussed.[1] Its object here is to show in another way that the transcendental unity of apperception is a necessary condition of all knowledge (A 121-3). The remainder of the section enlarges on the consequences of all this. The question of the function of the imagination, on which the section turns a great deal, has already been discussed, so we may now pass on to the second edition version of the transcendental deduction.

Second Edition Deduction. This differs from the first edition in omitting any detailed account of the synthesis, and in inserting a passage which shows clearly the connec- tion between the metaphysical and the transcendental deductions,[2] and also a discussion of the phenomenal self and its relation to the transcendental unity of apperception.[3] The changes amount to a complete rewriting, but we may

---

[1] *v.* above, pp. 109-12.   [2] B 141-3.   [3] B 153-9.

agree, I think, with Kant's statement[1] that they do not involve any substantial change of view. The argument may be divided as follows. (a) § 15 proves [or states?] that all knowledge requires a synthesis. (b) § 16 proves that the synthesis requires the transcendental unity of apperception and that the latter is inseparable from the unity of our representations in a system. (c) § 17 enlarges on these points and gives a definition of "object" which makes it clear that the experience of objects and consequently their very existence presuppose the transcendental unity of apperception. (d) § 19-20 and 26 are intended to complete the proof by showing that the synthesis requires categories. § 19 and 20 attempt to fill a gap in the argument left by the first edition and show not only that some categories or other are required but that the needed categories are just those of the *Metaphysical Deduction*. § 26 connects rather with the chapter on *Schematism*. § 18 and 21-25 can be treated as notes of one kind or another rather than as contributing to the consecutive line of argument, though some commentators have classed § 22-27 as a second deduction.

§ 15. *The Possibility of Combination in General*. This section, or rather the first paragraph of it, replaces the subjective deduction in so far as it constitutes the only passage in the second edition deduction in which Kant justifies the doctrine of the synthesis.[2] And here it is rather asserted as an axiom than based on an argument, since he gives no proof of his doctrine that combination (*Verbindung*) cannot be given by the senses but must be due to the mind. (In B 201 n. *Verbindung* is identified with synthesis.) This "combination" is sharply distinguished from the pure

[1] B XLII.
[2] If we exclude B 102-3, which belongs properly to the metaphysical deduction.

forms of intuition, which are not regarded as themselves fulfilling the function of combining the manifold. One, I think the chief, reason for this is that " the sensible forms are purely receptive over against the matter to which they give form. Now this matter, being itself without any internal connection, is received by the form just as it originally is. This amounts to saying that the form of sensibility is not a synthetic function, and that the mathematicians who construct their objects in *a priori* intuition require for this end the co-operation of understanding."[1] Elsewhere he admits that the intuitions of space and time themselves presuppose a synthesis, but he distinguishes them as formal intuitions from the forms of intuition.[2] As formal intuitions they are themselves a kind, though a highly peculiar kind, of objects, and therefore they require a synthesis by the understanding. As forms they are rather the laws according to which we receive sensations passively : they are no more due to the active work of our mind than the realist thinks the physiological laws of vision to be. They are conceived as grounded in our normal nature but not in our understanding or will.

"Understanding " is used here in a very general sense to include imagination.[3] Kant points out that all analysis must according to his own doctrine presuppose synthesis. We can only analyse what has already been put together by the mind. Clearly, even if " S is P " is an analytic judgment, it must presuppose the forming of the complex conception S, of which P is a part, and therefore presupposes synthesis.

---

[1] Vleeschauwer, *La Déduction Transcendentale dans L'Œuvre de Kant*, vol. III, p. 88.

[2] B 160-1 note, *v*. above, pp. 31-2, for an explanation of this distinction.

[3] *cf*. B 137.

§ 16. *The Original Synthetic Unity of Apperception.* This is the central section of the deduction. Reverting to my division of the argument above it is clear that, while § 15 gives the first stage, the argument for a synthesis, though in such an abbreviated form that it is now a statement of doctrine rather than an argument, § 16 gives the argument for the transcendental unity of apperception and the argument that this is inseparable from the unity of our representations in a system. I need not repeat my account of these arguments given earlier.[1] Note that Kant does not maintain here that we actually are conscious of the transcendental unity of apperception, only that it must be the case that we always *can be* so conscious. " Think " in " I think " is used in the wide sense of Descartes to cover all consciousness, but " thought " in the second sentence of the section seems to be used in the narrower sense in which sensuous intuition is not thought. Note that Kant points out towards the end of the section[2] that his account only applies to an understanding which cannot produce its own manifold but is dependent on a manifold given by sense. If it could produce its own manifold the argument that self-consciousness presupposed something other than itself as the content of which to think would no longer hold.

§ 17. *The Principle of the Synthetic Unity is the Supreme Principle of all Employment of the Understanding.* This section argues that the knowledge of objects and therefore their existence as phenomena presuppose the transcendental unity of apperception. It also adds an important remark[3] to the effect that the deduction is only valid for an understanding which is dependent on a manifold given from outside

---

[1] *v.* above, pp. 81-5. [2] B 135.
[3] Last paragraph of section.

because it is only such an understanding which needs to conform the manifold to its nature by a synthesis.

Note the definition of object as "that in the concept of which the manifold of a given intuition is united."[1] That the transcendental unity of apperception is the most fundamental condition of all knowledge is emphasized very strongly. We cannot do better here than quote Professor Kemp Smith's account of the argument. "The transcendental original unity of apperception is an objective, not a merely subjective, unity. Its conditions are also the conditions in and through which we acquire consciousness of objects. An object is that in the conception of which the manifold of given intuitions is combined. Such combination requires unity of consciousness. Thus the same unity which conditions apperception likewise conditions the relation of representations to an object. The unity of pure apperception may therefore be described as an *objective* unity for two reasons : first, because it can apprehend its own analytical unity only through discovery of unity in the given, and secondly, for the reason that such synthetical unifying of the manifold is also the process whereby representations acquire reference to objects."[2]

§ 18. *The Objective Unity of Self-Consciousness*. This is an explanatory note rather than an integral part of the argument. Its purpose is to distinguish the objective unity of consciousness from the unity due to subjective associations which is purely contingent. The section is not, I think, very important and is, I know, exceedingly difficult.

§ 19. *The Logical Form of all Judgments consists in the Objective Unity of the Apperception of the Concepts which they contain*. This and the succeeding section constitute an

[1] B 137.   [2] *Commentary*, pp. 285-6.

entirely new addition intended to prove that the categories are required. The orthodox definition of judgment as "the representation of a relation between two concepts" is condemned as at once too wide and too narrow, too narrow because it does not, properly speaking, cover any except categorical judgments, too wide because it does not specify what the relation is. Kant had in mind here the point that there is also "representation of a relation between two concepts" in mere subjective association without judgment (e.g. black suggests grief), and the definition of judgment which he now gives depends on the notion of objectivity. A judgment is declared to be "nothing but the manner in which given modes of knowledge" (literally "knowledges," *Erkenntnisse*) "are brought to the objective unity of apperception." "Objective" signifies unity in an object. Kant points out that this presupposes a necessary connection, without which there could be no unity of apperception, but that does not mean that the actual judgment is itself necessary, only that it derives its objectivity from its relation to necessary principles. It is a merely contingent fact and not a necessary causal law that this or that man should be exceptionally heavy, but we could not make such judgments if we did not presuppose some causal laws or other, about e.g. weighing-machines, causality being one of the categories imposed by the transcendental unity of apperception because it is indispensably required for the systematising of experience.

§ 20. *All Sensible Intuitions are subject to the Categories as Conditions under which alone their Manifold can come together in one Consciousness.* This section brings the argument to a conclusion by claiming to show that the necessary objectivity and unity can only be secured by the application of the categories. It also makes clear for the first time the relation between the metaphysical and the transcendental deduction. For that reason it had better be reserved till the next chapter, where we speak about the metaphysical deduction.[1]

The reference to § 13 in the last sentence but one seems irrelevant. It may be a misprint for § 10 (3).

The remainder of the deduction may be described as a consideration of the application of the general principles of the deduction to *human* intuition and the situation involved in human intuition.

§ 21. *Observation*. Kant here[2] speaks as if the transcendental deduction had only just been begun, but it may be doubted whether what is left of it can be viewed as much more than an appendix. Kant seems to have been excessively preoccupied with the question of the relation of the categories to the forms of intuition when he wrote this sentence (*v.* chapter on Schematism). In the section mentioned in § 21 as though it constituted the main part of the transcendental deduction[3] he speaks as though the deduction were already completed and merely required an additional supplement.[4]

Note the contingency asserted in the last sentence. It represents a characteristic and important doctrine of Kant which it is well to remember when we accuse him of being too *a priori* in his methods. In the metaphysical deduction Kant tries to deduce the categories from the different kinds of judgment in formal logic, but that we should have these and no other forms of judgments seems to be regarded as a

---

[1] *v.* below, p. 135 ff.

[2] Third sentence of section (B 144).

[3] § 26.

[4] B 159, where he refers to the transcendental deduction in the past tense.

purely empirical matter. Whether he consistently so regarded it in the Metaphysical Deduction is another question.[1]

§ 22 and 23 assert Kant's favourite doctrine of the limitation of the categories to experience. I discuss the issues involved when I deal with the conception of things-in-themselves in Chapter V. In § 23 Kant admits that the categories "extend to objects of intuition in general, be the intuition like or unlike ours, if only it be sensible and not intellectual." The reason for this difference between the categories and the forms of intuition is that Kant thought he had by deducing the former from judgment in the metaphysical deduction shown them to be involved in the nature of all discursive thought. They were therefore essential for any being who was dependent for knowledge on a manifold that was given independently of his thinking and consequently required a synthesis before it could be made amenable to thought, though not essential for a being which was capable of non-sensuous intuition, i.e. for a being which created its own manifold by pure thought. At least in regard to such a being as that, if it exists, we could not say whether its thought would be subject to our categories or not. Further, after admitting a theoretical extension of the categories beyond our forms of intuition, Kant adds that such an extension can be of no advantage to us, because we have no forms of intuition but space and time and therefore cannot have the least idea of the kind of experience which beings with other forms of sensuous intuition would have.

The distinction between thinking and knowing at the beginning of § 22 is fundamental for the Dialectic and for Kant's doctrine of the thing-in-itself. His view as to things-

[1] *v.* below, p. 140.

in-themselves is that we can have no knowledge of them or of whether the categories apply to them, but that if we think of them at all, we must think them in terms of the categories since we have no other concepts available. This thinking, because it is purely formal and has no empirical content, cannot give knowledge, but is very important when we come on ethical grounds to accept the beliefs in God and freedom. For though we cannot know that God exists and that we have freedom in the sense in which we know scientific facts, because we can form no clear concept of God and freedom and cannot use here any of our methods of theoretical proof, yet Kant insists that the beliefs in God and freedom are rationally justified on ethical grounds, if not proved in the strictest sense, and this implies that we can think God and freedom somehow though they are not phenomena. This is the position to which Kant holds throughout his critical period. Where, as here, he is insisting on the limitations of the categories he is apt to describe their application beyond the realm of experience as meaningless, but if this statement is taken too strictly it is quite incompatible with his firm belief in God and freedom. We cannot believe in any assertion if that assertion has no meaning. What Kant signifies is rather that such metaphysical statements have not a meaning in the same sense as scientific or empirical statements, i.e. they have no clear determinate meaning but only a formal indeterminate meaning. He does not hold that they are meaningless in the sense in which the " logical positivist " of the present day so often does. They are not for him poetic expressions of emotion, still less recommendations as to the use of language, but propositions believed by him to be true of reality. We cannot conceive except in a very vague way what the reality is like of which they are true, but they do for him give some information of a metaphysical kind.

§ 24. *The Application of the Categories to Objects of the Senses in General.* The problems about the synthesis of the imagination and its relation to the understanding raised by § 24 have already been discussed.[1] More important still is the discussion of the phenomenal self in these two sections, beginning at the end of B 152.

The perception in introspection of the phenomenal self is regarded as in some respects parallel to that of physical objects. At least they both involve the same kind of synthesis. But some commentators say that, whereas outer sense has a manifold of its own produced by things-in-themselves affecting our self, inner sense is regarded as dependent on the manifold of outer sense. In that case there are not two different sets of data, one given by inner sense and the other by the outer senses. Certainly when Kant speaks of inner sense here he only speaks of it as providing a form, time, not as providing an empirical manifold. The latter consists of the sense-data of outer sense,[2] which are all also images in our mind and therefore subject to inner sense. (I can mentally picture what I have never actually perceived with my outer senses, but I can only do that by putting together what I have so perceived, e.g. I can picture centaurs though there are no centaurs, but then I have seen horses and heads of men and can therefore easily combine the two into one object in my imagination, though I have never seen such a thing.) Hence also Kant uses " affect " (*affiziren*) in a different sense in the two cases. When he speaks of things-in-themselves affecting our self he is thinking of things-in-themselves as causing (in the sense in which such things can

[1] above, pp. 91-5. [2] B 153, *cf.* B 67.

still be thought as subject to categories) our sense impressions, i.e. the empirical manifold of outer sense; but when he speaks of our self as affecting our self, he does not mean that I produce an empirical manifold in myself, but that I determine my inner sense by exercising the transcendental synthesis on it.[1] I also determine outer sense by a synthesis which combines the manifold into physical objects in space, but he does not use the term affection of this but of the production of the manifold of outer sense itself. On the other hand, while we can have external impressions, though not knowledge, of physical objects without a synthesis, we could not have even impressions of inner sense without such a synthesis, involving the transcendental unity of apperception. Thus animals, while they can have sense-impressions, are not regarded by Kant as capable of introspection, because they have not the transcendental unity of apperception, i.e. are not *selves* (as far as we can tell).

This is certainly one tendency in Kant, but it is not made really explicit and conflicts with another essential to his ethical thought. When he discusses the question of freedom he certainly regards emotions and desires as part of the phenomenal, not of the real, self. Yet they are not given by the outer senses. The most that Kant could say is that they presuppose outer sense, since they are reactions to experiences of the environment, but this is not to deny that they form a new set of data qualitatively different from those of outer sense. Nor is it easy to see how Kant could consistently have avoided including in the appearance-self volitions and thoughts, in so far as these appear in time, and they are in fact expressly included in some passages.[2]

Kant was, however, much more interested in scientific

[1] B 153.
[2] *v.* B. 67, A 357-8. I owe these references to Prof. Paton.

knowledge of physical objects, and he sometimes speaks in his letters and in the *Reflexionen* as if knowledge were limited to the latter, e.g. in a letter to Beck he says that, if the individual representation " is merely referred to the subject, its employment is æsthetic (feeling), and the representation cannot become a known fact."   But it was not his consistent opinion that introspection cannot give knowledge, which would of course be obviously false, though he does think that psychology can never become a real science on a level with e.g. chemistry, let alone physics.   The reasons he gives for this view[1] are (1) that, because time has only one dimension, the application of mathematics in psychology is limited to a single principle, the law of continuity ; (2) that we can only mentally abstract, not really separate and put together, different elements in a mental state, and thus are debarred from using the experimental method in the sense in which it is used in chemistry ;[2] (3) that we cannot observe the mental states of other people, and if we observe our own we alter them in the process, thus vitiating our observations.

Another reason which he gives elsewhere for this con-clusion is that the category of substance cannot be applied to the appearance self because it has no absolutely permanent element. One would expect indeed that, since knowledge of the phenomenal self presupposes a synthesis, it would involve all the categories, but Kant hesitates to apply to the phenomenal self either substance or community, and there are passages in which he seems to deny that it is subject to any categories. He, however, evidently thought it to be

---

[1] *Berl.* IV, 471.
[2] Kant need not be understood as excluding experimental psychology in the modern sense of the term.

subject to causality, for his whole doctrine of freedom pre-supposes the complete causal determination of everything in the phenomenal self.[1]

There is another important difference between knowledge of physical objects and knowledge of the phenomenal self. The former involves the *a priori* intuition of space as well as that of time, the latter only that of time, though Kant insists, at least in the second edition, that it is impossible to think of time or of the phenomenal self without some reference to space.

§ 25. This passage seeks to reconcile the doctrine that I can only know myself as appearance with the facts to which Descartes refers in his *cogito, ergo sum*. The apprehension of the self in the transcendental unity of apperception is merely intellectual and without sensible content. It there-fore gives me no knowledge of the self as it really is, neither can it give me knowledge of the phenomenal self apart from inner sense. In B 422 n. Kant denies that my existence can be regarded as an inference from the fact that I think, and asserts " I think " to be an empirical proposition, as expressing an " indeterminate empirical intuition," but adds that it contains a representation, the " I," which is " purely intellectual " and not at all empirical.

But the difficulty as to what it is precisely that I, on Kant's view, know in knowing that I think cannot be said to have been removed. In § 25 he says that I thus know that I am, but not what I am. This would suggest that in being aware of the transcendental unity of apperception I am conscious that there is a real (noumenal) self though I can never attain any knowledge of its nature. On the other

[1] For a detailed discussion of this whole subject *v.* my book on *Kant's Treatment of Causality*, ch. VI.

hand, all or almost all the other passages which deal with the transcendental unity of apperception imply that it is only a unity of experience and not a self independent of and, so to speak, behind all experience like the thing-in-itself. In that case we must distinguish three aspects of the self—the phenomenal self, the noumenal self and the transcendental unity of apperception. The third is not an existent but a form to which all experience is subject. Kant, however, no doubt believed, though he did not claim to *know*, that this form could only be imposed by a noumenal self and presupposed the existence of the latter.

§ 26. *Transcendental Deduction of the Universally Possible Employment in Experience of the Pure Concepts of the Understanding.* On the place of this section in the argument I shall quote Professor Vleeschauwer.[1] The problem according to him is:—" Is it evident that intuition must supply us with the manifold in such a way that it necessarily is subordinated to the unity of consciousness and the conditions of the latter? In § 13 Kant had defended the thesis that this is not evident at all, and that we consequently are under an obligation to prove it." His solution is as follows : " The manifold is given only in the forms of space and time. Now space and time are already synthetic unities determined by the categories. Therefore the manifold is only given in unities determined by the categories." The section is rendered necessary by the omission of any explicit reference to the categories in the sections 15-17, which constitute the main body of the argument. Not till § 20 are the categories mentioned and then only in connection with the metaphysical deduction, so that up to that section the de-

---

[1] *La Déduction Transcendentale dans l'Œuvre de Kant*, vol. III, pp. 234-5.

duction is not a proof of the categories at all. Now according to his own standpoint § 20 should have provided a sufficient proof of the categories for Kant, but in view of the almost universal criticism of the metaphysical deduction on which this section is based it seems highly desirable that some other proof should be given, and this is done in § 26. (I do not mean to suggest that any contemporary criticism of the metaphysical deduction constituted the reason why it was done by Kant.) It must be added, however, that to show the presence of necessity and unity as conditions of all experience, as he does in the earlier sections, might be regarded as virtually of itself a proof of the categories (though the term categories is not used), in so far as such a general proof can be given at all apart from the specific proofs of the particular categories, which are provided in at least adequate length in the *Analytic of Principles*. The section is also intended to bring the categories into connection with our particular forms of intuition as opposed to "showing their possibility as *a priori* modes of knowledge of objects of an intuition in general," which Kant claims to have done in § 20-21. In this respect the section connects with the chapter on schematism.

The proof given in this section is summarised by Professor Paton as follows.[1] "Space and time as forms of intuition are a mere multiplicity without unity.[2] It is only as pure intuitions that they possess unity. This necessary unity was treated in the *Æsthetic* as if it belonged to space and time in their own right, but space and time, as pure intuitions, possess unity only because they presuppose a synthesis which does not belong to sense at all. Unity is therefore given *along with* the pure intuitions of space and time,

[1] I, 541.   [2] *v.* B 160 n.

but it is not given *in* these intuitions. This unity of time and space is an *a priori* condition of the synthesis of apprehension. That is to say, everything that is to be represented determinately in time and space must conform to this necessary unity (or necessary combination) which is involved in the nature of time and space themselves. If we put this in less technical language, we may say that because there is only one time and one space, the manifold given must be synthesised in such a way that it can appear in one time and one space." That the categories of substance, causality and community are necessary conditions of the unity of time and space Kant claims to prove in the *Analytic of Principles*. The distinction between space and time as forms of intuitions and as intuitions seems to be the distinction between regarding them as laws which determine our representations and as single representations in which all other representations have to be somehow placed, thus securing the unity of the latter. If space were merely our form of intuition, this would ensure that all our representations of objects other than the phenomenal self should be spatial; but it would not ensure that they should be in one space, and so it would not of itself give them any unity other than what is conferred by the possession in common of a universal spatiality. But to envisage them as in one space implies a much greater unity than this. It implies that they are united in a certain definite system of relations, that they have on principle the same unity as that which belongs to a single representation, for to regard two things as in the same space is to regard them as at least potentially capable of combination in the same image, and therefore subject to the necessary conditions of unity of representation. It is not true indeed, Kant points out, that these necessary conditions are given in the intuition of space; they are to be found in the synthesis of understanding and are therefore *a priori* and not part of the sensual conditions of experience. But, though not given in them, they are given with them as their presupposition. Whatever I have said about space here equally applies to time. An adequate understanding of the application of Kant's principle to causality in B 162-3 is impossible till we have appreciated the argument of the Second Analogy which will be discussed in my next chapter. Note Kant's explicit statement at the end of the section that, though the general principle, e.g., of causality is *a priori*, we can only discover particular causal laws by the help of experience. Kant means here by experience not a transcendental argument from the possibility of experience but particular observations.

§ 27. *Outcome of this Deduction of the Concepts of the Understanding.* In this section Kant, after a brief summary of the deduction and a note explaining the sense in which the use of the categories could be extended beyond the empirical world, has recourse to biological analogies in explaining the difference between his account of the *a priori* and that provided by rival theories. That the categories should be derived from experience, as empirical generalisations, he says would be a kind of *generatio æquivoca*, the biological term for the supposed origin of the organic from the inorganic, which Kant regarded as inconceivable. He calls his own theory one of *epigenesis*, the name given to biological theories which maintained that there was a genuine development of new organs not contained in the original embryo in diminutive form. To this type of biological theory was opposed the *preformation theory*, according to which there was no development of qualitatively different parts but only an enlargement of parts already present. To this he compares the third theory of *a priori* concepts, according to which they are innate ideas implanted in us by God so as to correspond to nature, so that they are subjective and yet true of a world independent of us. Kant rejects that alternative on the ground that it is incompatible with their necessity. Even if they were subjectively necessary, and the world happened to correspond to them, it might perfectly well not have corresponded, so any objective necessity, as opposed to mere psychological inability to think otherwise, would disappear. It is not very clear why Kant applies the term epigenesis to his own philosophy. The point seems to be either that we are not given innate ideas at the start, but merely possess faculties which develop themselves under the influence of the environment and only relatively late in life attain to full consciousness, or that the categories are a new contribution to nature by our mind, not there from the beginning in something existing before we experience it.

CHAPTER IV

THE INDIVIDUAL CATEGORIES
AND THEIR PROOFS

CATEGORIES are defined in the Transcendental Deduction as "concepts of an object in general by means of which the intuition of an object is regarded as determined by one of the logical functions of judgment."[1] It is hoped that this may become clearer in the sequel.

In order to give a full list of the categories as discussed by Kant a fourfold distinction is necessary. In the *Metaphysical Deduction* Kant derives certain pure concepts of the understanding, which he sometimes describes as categories, from the logical forms of judgment, but he does not think that these can be applied to phenomena as they stand. For that application there is needed the addition of time.[2] The term *category* is used by Kant in two senses, as standing (a) for the pure concept of understanding without the addition of time, (b) for the pure concept as modified by the introduction of the time factor. In his proofs of the categories what he really claims to prove of phenomena are the categories in the second sense of the term, e.g. he claims to prove that all events have temporal causes, not that they have non-temporal grounds. I shall distinguish the two usages by calling the first *pure*, the second *schematised categories*. The *transcendental schema* is either identical with the schematised category or the time-factor in it.

Professor Paton makes a further distinction between the transcendental schema and the schematised category, and

[1] B 128. [2] Chapter on *Schematism*, B 176 ff., *v.* below, p. 145 ff.

his view is supported by the fact that Kant habitually applies different names to the two with each category. According to Professor Paton the difference is that, while the schematised category includes the schema, it also includes an element which is present in the pure category but not in the schema, the schema being not the whole category as applied to phenomena but only the additional element beyond the pure category which is necessary for its application.[1] But this distinction is only important for an ordinary student in the case of causality and community. If we identify the schema and the schematised category here, we must regard Kant as identifying phenomenal causation with regular sequence or concomitance;[2] if we do not, we may think of him as retaining the notion of ground in the schematised category. This notion of ground would be the element which logical ground, the concept expressed in hypothetical judgments, and cause have in common. Kant does not indeed regard the phenomenal cause as the logical ground of the effect, for the latter could not be inferred *a priori* from it, nor can even the pure category be easily identified with logical ground, it seems to be rather that

[1] "We must not forget that for Kant more is contained in the schematised category than is given in the transcendental schema, for the category is enriched by its connection with the form of judgment. This is true at any rate in regard to the categories of substance and cause—the two categories which we may not unreasonably conjecture to have been the starting-point of Kant's thought. Thus, in the traditional doctrine which Kant inherited, substance is regarded (1) as the ultimate subject of all predicates and (2) as the permanent substratum of change. Both of these are conceived in the schematised category. The first Kant derives from the form of judgment. The second is given in the transcendental schema and is derived from the synthesis of the manifold in time and space" (Paton II, pp. 69-70). For the statements of all the different schematised categories as distinguished from the schemata *v.id.*, p. 44ff.

[2] Note especially that Kant gives as the schema of necessity "existence of an object at all times" (B 184).

element which cause and logical ground have in common; but his frequent application of the term *necessary* to causation in cases where it can hardly mean merely that the abstract principle that every change has a cause must necessarily apply to all phenomena[1] seems quite incompatible with a mere regularity view.

Finally, the categories and schemata are not themselves principles (i.e. expressible in a universal proposition) but concepts, yet Kant's whole object is to prove certain principles concerning the universal application of these concepts, so I have completed the table by adding the principles which he actually claims to prove.

Forms of Judgment[2] (Called Logical Functions).	Pure Concepts of Understanding.[3]	Schemata.[4]	Principles Proved.
Quantity :			
Universal. Particular. Singular.	Unity. Plurality. Totality.	Number.	All intuitions are extensive magnitudes.[5]
Quality :			
Affirmative. Negative. Infinite.	Reality. Negation. Limitation.	Degree.	In all appearances the real that is an object of sensation has a degree.[6]
Relation :			
Categorical.	Inherence and Subsistence (substantia et accidens).	Permanence.	In all change of appearances substance is permanent; its quantum in nature is neither increased nor diminished.[7]

---

[1] B 124, 234, 238, 240, 244, 247.   [2] B 95.   [3] B 106.
[4] B 182-4.   [5] B 202.   [6] B 207.   [7] B 224.

Forms of Judgment (Called Logical Functions).	Pure Concepts of Understanding.[3]	Schemata.	Principles Proved.
Hypothetical.	Causality and Dependence (cause and effect).	Succession according to Rule.	All alterations take place in conformity with the law of the connection of cause and effect.[1]
Disjunctive.	Community (reciprocity between agent and patient).	Coexistence, according to a universal rule, of the determinations of different substances.	All substances, in so far as they can be perceived to co-exist in space, are in thorough-going reciprocity.[2]
Modality :			
Problematic.	Possibility— Impossibility.	Agreement with the conditions of time in general.	
Assertoric.	Existence— Non-Existence.	Existence in some determinate time.	
Apodeictic.	Necessity— Contingency.	Existence at all times.	

Relation between the Transcendental Deduction and the Metaphysical[3] Deduction. The account of this is given, though all too briefly, in § 20 of the second edition of Transcendental Deduction. In the transcendental deduction itself Kant tries to show only that some categories or other are necessary, not what these necessary categories are,

---

[1] B 232.   [2] B 256.
[3] For use of term *metaphysical v.* above, p. 25.

but he supplements his account later, in the *Analytic of Principles*, by special proofs of the individual categories. He was not, however, content with this and sought not only to prove the categories separately but to obtain an *a priori* guarantee of the completeness and correctness of his list of categories. For this he has recourse to the *Metaphysical Deduction*. Here he claims to deduce the categories from the concepts generally used in formal logic in classifying judgments. He then argues like this:—

All phenomena presuppose a synthesis by the understanding (proved in the *Transcendental Deduction*).

A synthesis by the understanding = the bringing of data under the objective unity of apperception.

But a judgment must also be defined as the bringing of data under the objective unity of apperception.[1]

∴ The synthesis must be governed by the same principles as those governing judgments.

The forms of judgments have been finally and completely classified by Aristotle.[2]

My categories are deduced from these forms in the *Metaphysical Deduction*.

∴ My categories are all valid of phenomena, and are the only categories.

We may note the summary of the argument given by Schulze, whom Kant himself recommends as his best expositor. "Thinking and judging are the same, for concepts are always predicates of possible judgments, and consequently there must be just as many pure concepts of understanding as there are different kinds of judgments."[3]

---

[1] B 141-2.

[2] This is an assumption not stated here, *v.* Pref. B VIII.

[3] *Erläuterungen über des Herrn Professor Kants Critik der reinen Vernunft*, pp. 29-30.

Kant is using *judgment* here to stand for any proposition or its mental assertion, and not, as elsewhere, for a special faculty. We must also remember that he is using *category* in a different sense from Aristotle, and that his categories are therefore not deduced from the concepts which Aristotle calls categories, but from the concepts used by Aristotle in the classification of judgments, which are different.

It may be asked why, if the above argument was valid, Kant applied to phenomena only concepts *derived* from formal logic and not exactly the same concepts as those used in formal logic, i.e. how the second column in the table I have given can be different from the first. The answer would presumably be that, while the acts of judging and of synthesis are essentially the same in kind, the conditions under which they are exercised are very different and the categories have accordingly to be modified to meet the different conditions. A judgment[1] has to give the truth about phenomena already synthesised and does not itself do the synthesising, and it is quite possible that the concepts required for the one function would have to undergo some slight modification when employed for the other.

[Kant's argument assumes (a) that the Aristotelian logic has given an exhaustive classification of the forms of judgment which can never require substantial amendment; (b) that the deduction of the categories from them follows with logical necessity in each case and is not in any way arbitrary; (c) that the synthetic thinking which makes phenomena is essentially the same as the thinking of formal logic. Most philosophers nowadays would dispute all these assumptions, and would say that the metaphysical deduc-

---

[1] In the sense in which *judgment* is employed here. The *faculty* of judgment has a share in carrying out the synthesis.

tion is now of little more than historical interest. Still it does seem to me possible to work out an argument on similar lines that is by no means despicable, though it could not at the best achieve Kant's object of proving the completeness of his list of categories. For any possible object of knowledge must surely be of such a nature as to conform to the necessary conditions of our thought, since otherwise we could not think it, and it is not unreasonable to suggest that these necessary conditions of thought can be discovered by pure logic, this being the science which considers thought as such. To pursue the argument, let us turn to the individual categories given in the second column of my table above. First, we find that classification is essential to thought; therefore, if we are to think, there must be a plurality of instances with a universal in common to give them unity, which enables them to be thought together as a whole (totality). There may be universals with only one instance or none at all, but we could hardly form any idea of such if there were not also universals with several instances in which we could recognise the common element. Secondly, since thought can make both affirmative and negative judgments about any particular, every knowable object must somehow combine in itself being and not-being, and in the objective world this combination of the negative with the positive can only be thought as a limitation. Again, " so far as thought is about reality and makes a distinction between subject and predicate, it seems to demand that the given objects should *somehow* offer us an ultimate subject as well as characteristics belonging to that subject. So far as thought is based on reasons or grounds, it seems to demand that the given objects should *somehow* offer us a combination of grounds and consequents. So far as thought separates off different classes of objects from one another within a whole, it seems to demand that the given objects should *somehow* constitute a system whose different parts mutually exclude and mutually determine one another. And so far as thought is possible, actual and necessary, it seems to demand that its objects should also be *in some way* possible, actual and necessary."[1] The argument as stated by Professor Paton and myself may be liable to some criticism, but on principle it is surely at least worth careful consideration.

Even supposing the metaphysical deduction to have totally failed in its object, the effect on Kant's philosophy would not be very disastrous. For he gives separate proofs of the individual categories in the *Analytic of Principles* and these proofs do not in the least depend on the metaphysical deduction. Anybody who rejected the metaphysical deduction but accepted the rest of Kant's philosophy would thus still be able to agree that all the categories had been shown to be valid of phenomena. All he would have to admit is that it could not, as Kant thought, be shown to be *a priori* certain that there were no other categories besides those in the list. But the fact that there might possibly be other categories would not make any breach in the structure of Kant's philosophy but only show it not to be certainly complete, a fault which no human philosophy can escape. And Kant might argue that if

[1] Paton I, pp. 295-6. The whole of this line of thought has been suggested to me by the passage mentioned, but in my account of the categories of quantity and quality here I have not followed Professor Paton's wording. I must add that I am not able to go quite as far as Professor Paton in defence of the metaphysical deduction and feel a good deal of difficulty in understanding much that he has to say on the subject.

there were any other categories occupying a position of importance at all analogous to those in his list they would have been discovered long ago. The categories of organic unity and teleology in organisms have been suggested, but he examined them in the *Critique of Judgment* and rightly concluded that, though they were not without value, we could not form a definite conception of them or strictly prove their validity. Hegel put forward some others, but it is doubtful whether anybody except Hegel has ever formed a clear idea of what they were. There is one additional category, however, which it seems to me Kant should have included under modality, namely probability.]

Kant seems to hold that it is a merely contingent fact that we should have just these forms of judgment and no more, but it may be doubted whether he could have held this if he had envisaged what it meant. He certainly did not think of the Law of Excluded Middle as a merely contingent fact, yet the classification of judgments under the heading of Quality is based on it.[1] Nor can I believe that he regarded it as a merely contingent fact that all judgments we can make are either universal or particular or singular and either problematic or assertoric or apodeictic. The classification seems based necessarily on the nature of judgment and not merely on the human mind. And the contingent view is incompatible with his doctrine that, while our forms of intuition are valid only for human beings with the human mode of sensibility, the categories are valid for all beings who have sensible perceptions of

[1] If we do choose, like Kant, to include a third class, infinite judgments, it still follows from the law of excluded middle that all judgments must either be affirmative or be negative or have a predicate of the form non-P.

whatever form (though it is impossible for us to apply them beyond the human sphere).

We shall now comment on the various sections of this part of the Critique. As it is less important than many others our comments will be brief.

Introduction to Transcendental Logic. The introduction seems to be only tacked on to the main body of the *Analytic* externally. It contains (a) a statement of the doctrine that all our knowledge requires both concepts and sense (B 74-6); (b) a classification of logic (B 76-9); (c) the definition of transcendental logic (B 79-80); (d) a discussion of the criterion of truth, in which Kant denies the possibility of any universal criterion which is more than a negative test (B 82-4); (e) the division of logic into analytic and dialectic (B 84-end). The account of the *Dialectic* here must not be accepted as giving Kant's whole view of it, i.e. he does not in fact treat it *merely* as a refutation of certain fallacies without any indication of a more positive message. The vital difference between ordinary and transcendental logic should be noted, for the latter deals with a process by which the mind not only reflects about but creates its concepts and therewith the whole phenomenal world.

Chapter I. It is asserted dogmatically that understanding is an absolute unity and that therefore its concepts must form a system derived from a single principle.[1] The point seems to be that, if anything is *a priori*, the concepts of understanding must be, and that therefore they must fit into a system *a priori*. By a system I do not think Kant means here a set of propositions mutually implying each other, but a perfect classification.

[1] B 92.

Section 1. Insists (a) that concepts and judgments do not refer to objects immediately, but only to representations immediately and to objects mediately by means of representations; (b) that concepts are inseparable from judgments, a breach with the traditional logic of the day.[1]

Section 2. *Quantity.* Kant's insistence as against the formal logic of his day on the essential distinction between the singular and the universal judgment is valid, but his assumption that the distinction can rightly be ignored even in formal logic would be questioned nowadays.

Quality. The judgment S is non-P is called infinite because the number of possible things that are lacking in any specified quality is always infinite. It can serve as the source from which the category of limitation is derived because such a judgment is essentially a limitation of the sphere of the possible. It excludes from S certain previously possible characteristics.[2]

Relation. Note that Kant regards the disjunctive judgment, S is either P or Q, as exclusive, i.e. it entails for him that S cannot be both P and Q.

Modality. This, Kant says, unlike the others, does not affect the content of judgments but only the value of the copula in relation to thought in general. I.e. to say that a judgment is e.g. problematic does not affect the "what" of the judgment but only our attitude towards it.

[Kant is criticised for omitting many distinctions on which modern logic insists. Professor Paton gives the following reply to this criticism. "It is obvious that the kinds of proposition distinguished so emphatically by

[1] For a full discussion of this section *v.* Kemp Smith, *Commentary*, p. 176 ff.

[2] For a modern criticism of this category *v.* Cook Wilson, *Statement and Inference* I, p. 249 ff.

mathematical logic—as, for example, the subject-predicate, class-membership and relational propositions—would for Kant, and indeed for any formal logician of the old school, be distinguished by their matter, and not by their form. It is important to recognise this fact, because although mathematical logic, like Kant's Formal Logic, claims to be a science of pure form, it uses the word 'form' in a different, although allied, sense. For mathematical logic the form of a proposition is what remains unchanged, although all the constituents of the proposition are altered. For Kant there can be no pure form of a proposition, unless *every possible constituent* of a proposition can be fitted into it. Thus he would not regard ' A = B ' as a form of judgment, because although many different terms may be substituted for A and B, all these terms must be quantities; that is, they must refer to a certain kind of object, while a pure form must apply to every possible kind of object."[1] In short, Kant's logic and modern mathematical logic are trying to do different things, though there is no necessary antagonism between them.]

Section 3 (§ 10). The derivation of the categories from the logical functions (forms of judgment) must be admitted to have something arbitrary about it, and it is not clear what principle governed Kant's derivation of them except the desire that its results should fit in with his preconceived views as to what the categories were. It is not by any means clear that it is logically necessary that the functions should give rise to these categories and just these alone. The derivation of two of the categories of relation calls for special comment. (a) The derivation of substance from the categorical judgment implies that all categorical judgments

[1] I, p. 210.

are of the subject-predicate form, and there is the further objection that, while the category of substance signifies that which is always a subject and never a predicate, the relation of subject and predicate in a judgment is a reversible one. (b) The derivation of community from the disjunctive judgment will seem at first sight utterly inexplicable.[1] There is, however, at least some analogy between them. For, if we are to make a disjunctive judgment about anything, our knowledge of it must constitute a kind of system. It does not involve merely one-sided connection of the one proposition with the other as in the case of hypothetical judgment, but mutual inter-connection between both. The two alternatives constitute a whole within which every possibility must fall.

§ 11. Both this and the succeeding section were first added in the second edition. Kant notes that the third category in each group arises from a combination of the first and the second.[2] It is not, however, a mere repetition of the first two, but needs " a special act of the understanding," i.e. we cannot deduce that, because the first two hold, the third will do so too, but require a separate proof of the third category.

§ 12. Kant's account of the concepts *unum, verum, bonum* cannot be taken as historically true or as giving their real use.

The Analytic of Principles.

Introduction. Judgment. Judgment as a faculty is here first distinguished from the understanding, and is defined as the faculty of subsuming particular cases under general rules, while the understanding provides the rules.[3] Among the rules to be applied the most fundamental are the cate-

---

[1] Kant explains it in B 112.   [2] B 110-1.   [3] B 171.

gories, and therefore it falls to the lot of judgment to apply to the phenomenal world the logical principles deduced in the metaphysical deduction. Judgment is thus necessary for the carrying out of the fundamental synthesis and not only for particular applications of empirical rules in ordinary life.

It is, however, misleading to describe the *Analytic of Principles* as "a canon solely for judgment," as Kant does here. The *Analytic of Principles* provides the only proofs that are given of the individual categories and is therefore essential for the categories as general principles, and it is far more concerned with this than with their application to particulars. The relation of judgment and imagination in the synthesis and the distinction between them are never made clear. It is imagination which produces the schema, not judgment as might perhaps have been expected.

Chap. I. The Schematism. Kant argues that the categories, being purely formal, cannot be applied, as they stand, to sensible intuitions, because they are too different from them. Consequently there is wanted some third factor to mediate between the categories and the intuitions. This need is met by the schemata, which are in each case derived by interpreting a pure category in terms of time. Since time is both sensible and *a priori*, it has something in common both with the sensible manifold and with the pure category, and therefore enables this mediation to be effected. (Note that it is not time itself but the schema which is the mediator.)

Kant has been rightly criticised on the ground that for a universal concept to be applied to particulars it is not necessary, or indeed possible, that it should be like the particulars.[1] If it were, another universal concept giving the

---

[1] *v.* Joseph, *Essays in Ancient and Modern Philosophy*, p. 270 ff.

point of likeness would be required. But I think this is more an objection to Kant's statement of the position than to the position itself. Perhaps the difficulty would be better stated as being that for anything to be directly subsumable under any of these concepts as they stand it would have to possess characteristics which are not compatible with its being a sensible particular.[1] If we take the category of ground, for instance, Kant was apparently thinking that it cannot be applied to sensible events as it stands, since we can see no logical connection such that one event explains another, but must be first transformed into the concept of phenomenal causation, which differs from it in being temporal and logically unintelligible but resembles it in being necessary and in justifying inferences. It is an essential doctrine of Kant that the sensible content present in the phenomenal world always prevents it from satisfying the requirements, or at least the ideal, of logic, as we shall see in the *Amphibolies*. The pure categories are too indeterminate to be scientifically useful, and in fact when Kant comes to prove the individual categories he only tries to prove them as schematised.

It might be asked why Kant schematised the categories in terms of time only and not of space, since space was also both sensible and *a priori*. The answer is perhaps simply that the second method would not work so well, for time seems essential for the formation of any tolerably clear idea of substance or causality in a way in which space is not. But in a note written for his private use he proposes to schematise the categories in terms of space as well as time. However, the nearest he ever came to this was to add the words " in space " to the definition of community in the second edition.

Kant uses the term schema also to stand for any universal

[1] *v.* Joseph, *Essays in Ancient and Modern Philosophy*, p. 273 ff.

concept, whether empirical or *a priori,* and describes a universal concept as a rule for making images, as opposed to a single image, thus giving in outline his answer to the problem how we can think of universals at all, though all images are particular.[1]

Strange to say, Kant does not give a separate schema for each category in the case of the first two groups, quantity and quality. The schemata given really correspond only to the third category in either group. The introduction of number as the schema for quantity on the ground that I "generate time" in counting raises difficulties.[2] It can hardly mean merely that counting takes time, for the same would apply to all mental operations. More probably it is meant that the units counted have to be represented as if they were successive moments of time.[3] The list of schemata will be better understood when we have considered the proofs of the separate schematised categories to which we now pass.

The question is often raised whether Kant meant all the categories to apply to everything phenomenal. I do not know of any reason for denying that Kant held this as regards everything in space. Every physical event occupies space and time (the category of quantity as interpreted later), involves the presence of a quality possessing some degree, occurs in a substance, is determined causally by previous events and is causally connected directly or indirectly with co-existing objects throughout the universe. It is also at once

---

[1] B 179-81. He distinguishes the schemata directly connected with the categories from schemata in the wider sense by calling the former transcendental schemata.

[2] B 182.

[3] *v.* above, p. 58, for Kant's doctrine of arithmetic, which seems to depend on this.

possible, actual and necessary. But Kant does not think that substance and community apply to the phenomenal self.[1] This is connected with the fact that it is not in space but only in time.

System of All Principles of Pure Understanding

The Distinction between the Mathematical and the Dynamical Principles.[2] The principal difference which Kant has in mind in distinguishing the two is that we can use the former to deduce *a priori* from empirically given particulars exact information about other particulars, while we cannot use the latter in this way. Thus if we are told that A is equal to or twice B in quantity or degree we can deduce *a priori* what B is in these respects, but if we are told that A is caused by B we cannot from that deduce *a priori* anything about B. Kant therefore calls the former principles constitutive and the latter regulative, but this must not be confused with his use of the terms constitutive and regulative in the *Dialectic*, where " regulative " implies " unproved." Neither set of principles are regulative in that sense.

Principle of the Axioms of Intuition. All intuitions are extensive quantities. " Extensive " is meant to cover duration in time as well as extension in space, so the phenomenal self, which is in time but not in space, should be subject to this category. Since the schema of the category under consideration is number, Kant may have meant his proof mainly to show that all phenomena were measurable, otherwise it seems superfluous after the *Æsthetic*. Kant holds both this and the next principle to have immediate certainty,[3] so presumably he must be understood to be not so much proving as expounding and clarifying them.

[1] *v.* below, p. 175.   [2] B 199-202, 220-3.   [3] B 199-201.

Principle of the Anticipations of Perception. In all appearances, the real that is an object of sensation has intensive magnitude, that is, a degree.

By " the real " is meant the element in phenomena of content, which is given in sensation and opposed to form. This principle is, Kant held, the only thing that we can know *a priori* about that content. Intensive magnitude is distinguished from extensive magnitude in that, in order to be conscious of a given intensive magnitude, we do not need, as in the case of extensive magnitude, to carry out a successive synthesis of the lesser magnitudes of which it is composed, but Kant was unwilling to renounce the view that even here we need some synthesis, though not a successive but an instantaneous one.

The discussion of this principle has reference to the science of the day. It was generally held that differences of weight between bodies of the same size were due solely to there being more or less empty space in them. Kant points out another possible alternative, namely, that there is no empty space at all but the differences in weight depend on a quality being present in the same extent of space in a greater or lesser degree.[1] But he leaves it an open question whether that alternative can in fact be established. He points out also that empty space and time are not possible objects of experience and cannot be legitimately inferred from experience, because any fact for which they could account could equally well be explained by assuming that matter extends everywhere but differs in intensive quantity, of which there are infinite gradations.[2]

Analogies of Experience. The introductory summary[3] of the general principle of the proofs cannot be understood

[1] B 215-6. [2] B 214. [3] B 218-220.

apart from the proofs summarised, which occur later. Kant suggests two different reasons for calling these principles analogies. One is that we can only know by means of them, e.g., that every fresh event we encounter must stand in the same *relation* to some other event as every known effect bears to its cause, without being able to deduce anything else about its cause.[1] He compares and contrasts them with mathematical analogies. From *B is* 4 and *A is to B as* 12 *is to* 6 we can infer that *A is* 8, but from *B is a death* and *there is something A which caused B*, i.e. which stands in the same relation to B as that in which some known cause stands to its effect, we cannot infer what A is. (In the Prolegomena he describes " analogy " as " a complete likeness of two relations between quite unlike things."[2]) The other reason is that the category of substance is applied to phenomena on the analogy of logical subject, the category of cause on the analogy of ground and consequent etc.[3]

The First Analogy. We had better discuss what Kant means by substance before considering his proof. In all cases what Kant tries to establish is the schematised, not the pure category, so his argument for substance is an argument that there must be a permanent element in all change. Kant expresses this by making a distinction between the two German words, *wechseln* and *verändern*, and saying that only the state of a thing can " *wechseln*," not the thing itself.[4] Professor Kemp Smith translates *wechseln* as " change " and *verändern* as " alter." The point of the distinction is that a mere state of a substance passes totally away and is replaced by another, but the thing exists permanently though its successive states all cease to exist in turn.

Now Kant could find no permanent element in the

[1] B 222.   [2] § 58 beginning.   [3] B 224.   [4] B 230.

phenomenal self, and consequently he applies substance only to physical objects. So he does not really hold that every change is a change of the attributes of a substance, but only that it presupposes the existence of some substance, though this contradicts his actual words.[1] For there is no evidence for the view that he believed our phenomenal self to be the attribute of our body. There is change in the phenomenal self, and this according to Kant presupposes permanent physical objects in contrast to which it could alone be apprehended as change, but it is not itself a change in the attributes of these permanent objects. It has frequently been suggested that Kant could have taken the transcendental unity of apperception as the permanent element in the self, but this unity is regarded by him as the source of all the categories and therefore could not be brought under a single one.

I do not, however, think it correct to say that Kant identified the first analogy with the scientific principle of conservation of matter. His position seems to be that we can tell *a priori* that there is something permanent but can only find out by empirical means what that something is. That the quantity of substances in the world must remain the same he did hold to be known *a priori,* since otherwise some substances would be created or destroyed, but he did not hold that we can know *a priori* what empirical or scientific tests can be taken as criteria to measure the quantity of substances. We must remember in this connection that Kant held every part of matter to be itself a substance.[2] Unlike modern scientists Kant thought the conception of substance essential for science.

Another difficulty is raised by the apparent incompatibility between Kant's "idealism" and his doctrine that there are

[1] B 232 (beginning of 2nd Analogy).   [2] *v. Berl.* IV, 503.

permanent substances in the phenomenal world. The substances of which he talks are certainly not things-in-themselves but phenomena. It is not, however, clear that propositions asserting the absolute permanence of physical objects
could not be analysed idealistically, for example as asserting
that we should under certain conditions always have an
experience which was the same in certain definable respects,
e.g. in those we indicate by talking about "the same weight."
Kant talks here like a realist, and he does not give the
analysis, but he may well have supposed that there was one.
For, as we have seen,[1] he does not believe that common-sense
and scientific propositions about physical objects are false,
but only that they have to be analysed in terms of what
human percipients observe.

[But this answer does not remove the difficulty altogether.
For Kant certainly did not intend to reduce substance to
causality, yet if you analyse physical substances in terms of
our representations, what is there left permanent except
causal laws?]

Kant's account suggests Locke's doctrine of an unknowable substratum. But that Kant thought such a conception
unsatisfactory is shown by a passage in B 230, where he says
that the separation of substance and accident leads to many
misunderstandings but is "unavoidable owing to the conditions of the logical employment of our understanding."
So his opinion seems to be that it would be better not to
take a substratum view, but that we cannot in practice help
separating qualities and substance in a way which implies
or at least suggests this view. [Certainly language does so.]

But really, he says, an accident of a substance is only a
special way in which the substance exists.[2] A thing is not,

[1] *v.* above, p. 84.   [2] B 229, 230.

that is, a substance and its accidents, as though these were separate bits of it, but a substance which exists in a certain way (= has certain accidents). The substance and the accidents are not different elements in the thing, but the same thing looked at from different points of view.

The second edition proof of substance[1] may be paraphrased as follows:

1. All coexistence and sequence take place in time as a substratum, time being the form of our inner intuition.

2. Time does not itself change but remains permanently. Otherwise you would need another time for it to change in. There is thus something unchanging in our experience, and it is only by being conscious of this that we can be conscious of change.

3. Time cannot be perceived *per se*. (Note Kant says "cannot be perceived" (*wahrgenommen*) not "cannot be intuited." This makes it possible, I think, to reconcile this passage with the absolute view of time in the Æsthetic.[2])

4. Therefore the permanent element in our experience proved by (2), since it cannot be found in time by itself, must be found in the objects of sense-perception as a "substratum" which "represents time" and is the condition in relation to which change and coexistence can alone be discerned. So the proposition that time is permanent involves the proposition that there is a permanent element in phenomena, and the proposition that change and coexistence can only be perceived in a permanent time involves the proposition that all change and coexistence are conditioned by a permanent substratum.

5. Such a permanent substratum is what is usually meant by substance, therefore this is a proof of substance.

[1] B 224-5.   [2] *v.* above, p. 63

11

[It is true that we cannot use "change" of time in the sense in which we use it of things in time, but neither can we use "permanence" in that sense of time. But, if we cannot apply "permanence" to time in the *same sense* as that in which we apply it to phenomena, the argument from the permanence of time to the permanence of phenomena is undermined. Further, what is the element in phenomena which "represents time"? It can only be the temporal relations of phenomena, and therefore the argument could only prove at the best the permanence of some temporal characteristics or relations, which is certainly not the same as asserting that phenomena are permanent substances.]

The chief difference between the above argument and the argument of the next paragraph[1] (really three separate arguments) is that the latter introduces the doctrine that our apprehension of the manifold is always successive. This statement occurs in all three analogies, and is in each case used for the same purpose, namely to show that we cannot identify the objective with the subjective time-order since what is coexistent in the former is successive in the latter.

[The statement may mean (1) that our apprehension always includes a succession. In that case it is true but cannot prove what it is required to prove, i.e. that the subjective time-order is different from the objective. Or it may mean (2) that our apprehension is always merely successive, i.e. we never apprehend two different things at the same time. In that case it would prove what is wanted, if it were true, since two things apprehended often objectively exist at the same time, but would be obviously false. The evidence of introspection against it might indeed be challenged on the ground that the time which has elapsed may be too short to

[1] B 225-7.

be discernible by us so that what is really successive appears as coexistent; but we could not even compare A and B if we were not aware of them, either in perception or memory, at strictly the same time, nor could we be aware of any space without being aware simultaneously of smaller spaces (I do not of course say *all* the smaller spaces) of which it is composed. If our apprehension were merely successive we could never be aware of anything but the absolutely simple, and it may be doubted whether we are ever aware of that at all. Perhaps Kant confused (1) and (2): he never asserts that apprehension is always merely successive, only that it is "successive," yet he argues as if this barred the simultaneous presence to our mind of different representations. (3) Professor Paton suggests another interpretation in order to save Kant from this charge.[1] It is that Kant is here abstracting the receipt of impressions from the act of synthesis and saying that, "although we can in one moment hold together different elements before our mind," their simultaneity can only be explained by a synthesis and not by mere passive perception. Mere succession is therefore not anything we actually experience, but only what would be left if we could *per impossibile* take away the synthesis. It is important to be clear that in none of the three analogies is this, at best doubtful, argument of Kant's at all necessary for the proof. All it is used to show is that to assert the subjective succession of B on A does not necessarily involve asserting its objective succession, so that we need some other criterion beyond the mere order of our apprehensions to determine the objective time-order, and this is obvious in any case. For, though some simultaneous events are perceived simultaneously, others are undoubtedly perceived successively.]

[1] vol. II, pp. 193-4.

Granted that some criterion is needed beyond the time-order of our perceptions to determine objective time-order, it is not so clear how a permanent substance will help. If *b* succeeds *a* as a sense-datum of mine, I can only regard *a* and *b* as co-existent if I think of them as qualities of an object or objects which persist between my sensations of *a* and *b*. Otherwise I could not say that a thing was both white and smooth because I perceived it as white at 11 and smooth at 12, and the same applies where two coexisting things perceived successively are in question. But this would only establish relative, not absolute permanence. Physical objects as ordinarily perceived are, emphatically, not absolutely permanent, and in order to be conscious of them we certainly need not be aware of anything such as the principle of conservation of matter. Kant's answer would probably be that, while substance as a category is not anything sensible, we cannot, as we have seen, distinguish subjective and objective time-order without cognising certain at least relatively persistent physical objects and we cannot cognise these without thinking them as subject to the category of substance, i.e. as implying somewhere an absolutely permanent substratum, though we do not yet know in what this permanent substratum consists.[1]

[We are certainly from the beginning conscious of them as things, i.e. substances, but whether this implies an absolutely permanent " substratum " is a more doubtful question.]

It is not contended by Kant that we need the permanent to measure time or change by it, but that we need it in order to be conscious of time or change at all. There is a verbal contradiction in B 226, where it is both asserted and denied

[1] *v.* Paton II, pp. 204-7, 218-9.

that coexistence and change are modes of time. Obviously they can be said to be modes of time in one sense and not in another. They are not attributes of time itself, but they might legitimately be called temporal modes of existence of the permanent.[1]

The argument for substance is similar to the second edition refutation of idealism, and like the latter may be regarded as an assertion of the relative independence of physical objects.

A different argument for substance is given later in the section.[2] It is to the effect that the persistence of identical substances is a necessary condition of the unity of time. This is in accord with Kant's doctrine that the real proof of all the categories is that they are necessary conditions of "the unity of experience," and it seems to me independent of the other arguments for substance given.

[The difficulty would be to show conclusively that causality without substance would not be sufficient for this purpose, but I think this to be Kant's strongest argument for substance.]

The Second Analogy. The second and third analogies would both come under the heading of causality in the usual sense of the term. The chief difference between them is that the second analogy is one-sided, the third two-sided causality, substance A affecting substance B and vice versa. Clearly it might be true that every event was completely determined by previous events and yet false that everything in the universe interacted causally with everything else, therefore the two principles needed separate proofs.

The section on the second analogy contains no less than six different proofs, but five are the same in principle and

---

[1] First sentence of B 226.   [2] B 229, 231-2.

can be treated together. In a sense indeed Kant would hold them all to be the same in principle, for he states later in the Critique that "only *one* proof can be found for each transcendental proposition" and instances this by saying that the sole possible ground of proof for the proposition that everything which happens has a cause is "that the determination of an event in time, and therefore the event as belonging to experience, would be impossible save as standing under such a dynamical rule."[1] This "sole possible ground of proof" is, however, as we see from the quotation, stated in such a general way as to be quite compatible with the existence of a number of different modes of proof under this same general principle, and in fact we find in all the Analogies a variety of proofs.

The proofs of the second Analogy are as follows:

1. B 233-4 (second paragraph in second edition).

2. B 234-9 (first four paragraphs in first edition, third to sixth in second edition).

3. B 239-41 (next three paragraphs).[2]

4. B 241-4 (next three paragraphs).

5. B 244-6 (next three paragraphs).

6. B 246-7 (next paragraph).

The first, fourth and sixth proofs are omitted in Professor Kemp Smith's abridged translation. The fifth proof differs from all the others and so will be taken separately first. It may be summarised as follows:

Precedent time necessarily determines subsequent time, since I can only reach subsequent time by passing through precedent.

---

[1] B 815-6.

[2] Perhaps it would be better to treat the third paragraph as not belonging to any special proof. Professor Kemp Smith omits this paragraph in his abridgment.

"Only in appearances can we empirically apprehend this continuity in the connection of times."

∴ Precedent phenomena determine subsequent phenomena.

[The argument, as thus stated, seems to me fallacious, because the sense in which "determine" is used in the first premiss is different from the sense in which it is used in the conclusion. That 1938 is determined by 1937 in the sense that one can only reach 1938 by passing through 1937 does not prove that the events in 1938 are causally determined or that they must happen granted the events in 1937. But it may be regarded as an imperfect expression of a general argument from the continuity of time. Time cannot be experienced by itself, Kant says, therefore the continuity of time can only be experienced as continuity of change, and continuity of change according to Kant implies causation.[1] Kant thought that causality, like substance, was provable as a necessary condition of the unity of time.]

The other argument for causality, repeated in different language in each of the remaining five proofs, depends on two main assumptions, (a) that some judgments asserting objective, i.e. physical, succession are true, (b) that these are still only judgments about actual or possible objects of experience. (a) is established by the transcendental deduction which shows that the subjective presupposes the objective, so that the latter must be admitted if we admit the former at all, (b) by the Æsthetic and indeed by Kant's whole system. The assumption, again introduced by Kant,[2] that our apprehension is always successive in a sense which debars us from distinguishing the objectively coexistent and the objectively successive by mere reference to the order of our perceptions

[1] v. Paton II, p. 256.   [2] B 234, 243, 246.

is fortunately quite unnecessary for the proof, since all that is needed is to show that what is objectively not successive is sometimes perceived successively, not that it always is so.[1] That is sufficient to compel us to distinguish between subjective and objective time-order. Finally there is the assumption that we cannot determine whether a succession is objective by perceiving time or a period of time by itself as if it were a kind of object and observing its relations to other objects.[2]

The problem in general is how we can distinguish judgments about physical objects from mere imaginations. This is a problem which must be faced by any idealist unless he is prepared to give up the distinction between science and dreams. The *Second Analogy* tackles the problem in relation to temporal sequence and asks how we can distinguish objective from subjective succession. The realist can say: If I judge that B follows A in my representations I am making a judgment only about my experience, but if I judge that B follows A physically I am judging that the sequence A B exists quite independently of any experience, but such an answer is obviously not open to the idealist. He must find a distinction between objective and subjective succession *within experience*. The distinction cannot from the nature of the case lie in the actual order of our representations, but what other distinction can there be within experience? The only one we can find, Kant suggests, is that there are certain sequences of representations which are irreversible and others which we can take in whatever order we like. Now irreversibility implies necessity, and a necessary sequence is a sequence which is determined by the category of causality. Therefore this is for Kant a proof of causality.

[1] *v.* above, pp. 154-5.   [2] B 233 *ad fin.*

Kant does not indeed mean, as Schopenhauer supposed, that if B succeeds A objectively B must be caused by A, but only that the sequence must be caused by something or other.[1] Nor does he mean that our representations of the coexistent are not determined by causal laws, as we shall see when we come to the third analogy. All he means here is that at least those representations which we regard as giving us objective succession must be determined, whether those which we regard as representations of the coexistent are also determined or not. Again he does not mean that before we can recognise a sequence as objective we must discover the particular causes by which it is determined, but that our consciousness of events as objectively successive, which we have from the beginning, is to be analysed as involving a consciousness of causal necessity. The experience of perception of the objectively sequent includes experience of the time-order of our perceptions as necessitated (forced on us whether we will it or not) and therefore includes the conception of causality even though we may be quite in the dark as to what are the causes of their having this time-order. Finally, Kant holds that particular causal laws can only be known as the result of experience, not *a priori*,[2] at least in the Critique, although in the *Metaphysical First Principles of Natural Science* the most fundamental laws of motion are deduced *a priori* from the categories.[3] The reason for the attitude of the Critique is that particular causal laws are held to depend, not only on the mind, which contributes the category, but also on the given manifold, which is due to the unknown thing-in-itself.

[Kant might have put his argument in this form. To make judgments about physical objects is always to make judg-

[1] *v.* B 244.   [2] A 127, B 165.   [3] Haupst. III Lehrs. 3, 4.

ments not merely about what I perceive at the present moment but about laws governing my own and other men's perceptions. If I judge that there is a table in this room, I judge that other people as well as myself will have visual data of a certain sort and that, if I put my hand on it, I shall have certain tactual sense-data. The proof in fact could easily be restated so as to cover both objective sequence and objective coexistence, thus :

One must distinguish propositions about physical objects from propositions merely about our actual representations.

Propositions about physical objects have to be analysed in terms of our representations.

Therefore we can only distinguish the two by introducing causal laws in our analysis of propositions about physical objects.[1]

Such an argument seems to me valid if we assume that physical objects can only be analysed in terms of what Kant called our representations and what we should now call sense-data. At any rate I cannot see any conceivable way of making the distinction which did not involve causality, at least in the sense of regular sequence. If we are on such a view to distinguish statements about our own images from statements about physical objects perceived by us, we must say that the latter sort of statements gives an account of what any other normal observer would see under given conditions, and this is to assert a causal law governing human perceptions. Without asserting or implying this we could not pass beyond our own present and remembered percep-

---

[1] Put in this general form the argument avoids the criticism that, e.g., the sequence lightning-thunder is irreversible yet not objective, for we can certainly only distinguish here what is objective and what is not by reference to some causal laws.

tions, for we cannot immediately perceive the normal observer's perceptions.

A statement that certain sense-data will occur under certain conditions, e.g. whenever another human being with normal eyesight looks where I am looking in a normal light, is an assertion of uniform sequence. Now many commentators hold that Kant never intends to assert causality of phenomena in any sense except that of uniform sequence.[1] But even if this is not so, anyone would admit that we had proved something very important if we could prove that like events would always happen under like conditions, even though we had not proved causality in a fuller sense of the term which goes beyond regularity, and most people would say that we had proved all that was needed by science. This certainly Kant claims to have proved. But I think also he would have been justified in contending that to be conscious of certain sequences as irreversible is to be conscious of them as causally necessary in a sense which cannot be reduced to uniform sequence, though there is some doubt whether he meant to maintain this or not. It might indeed be said that, e.g., the proposition—a boat is going downstream—could be analysed as expressing not a strictly universal law about sense-data but only a vaguer proposition to the effect that *most* men would have representations of a certain kind. But a prediction even about most men, like all inductive inferences, presupposes causality.

Professor Prichard's objection[2] that Kant's argument only proves necessary succession in our perceptions, not in objects, presupposes the realist point of view which Kant rejected, but I do not by any means despair of restating the argument in a way which would make it valid for the

[1] but *v.* above, pp. 133-4.   [2] *Kant's Theory of Knowledge*, p. 291.

realist.[1] However Kant himself would not agree that this could be done, and makes it an argument for his form of idealism that the categories can be proved of physical objects only if the latter are appearances. I am more doubtful whether, even on his idealist premisses, Kant has succeeded in establishing the conclusion that every change is completely determined by causes, or only in proving that the analysis of all propositions about physical events requires some reference to causal laws, by which their occurrence might still conceivably be only partly and not wholly determined.]

Of the three analogies causality is the only one which, in the Critique of Pure Reason, Kant applies to the phenomenal self.[2] Passages could be quoted which sound inconsistent with this statement, but more can be quoted in its favour, and the application of causality to the phenomenal self is absolutely essential to Kant's whole account of freedom, which he regarded as one of the most important portions of his work. The proof of the second analogy, however, raises serious difficulties in connection with this question. For causality is proved to hold of the physical world by the argument that it is needed to distinguish the objective (physical) from the subjective, but if they were both subject to causality, how could the presence of causality serve to distinguish one from the other? The argument therefore forcibly suggests that the physical world consists of all those of our representations which are causally determined and

[1] *v.* Ewing, *Kant's Treatment of Causality*, pp. 91-5. I must admit, however, that I am less confident that a proof of *universal* causality can be given than when I wrote this earlier book.

[2] For a detailed discussion of this subject *v.* my book on *Kant's Treatment of Causality*, ch. 6. In the posthumous work he also applies community.

that the rest, which fall in the phenomenal self but not in the physical world, are not subject to causation at all. But there is another possible interpretation, and since Kant certainly assumes throughout his ethical works that the *Critique of Pure Reason* has proved the states of the phenomenal self to be completely determined, it is better to adopt it. The interpretation I am suggesting is that we need causality to distinguish between subjective and objective, not because the one is subject to it and the other is not, but because we can only distinguish them by sorting them out into two different causal systems. Both involve causality, but the causal laws to which they are subject are different. Thus if I had an image of rats in my bedroom, that would be determined in any case, but it would be put in the physical world if it was found to be due to causes such that other people who came into the room would see them; but, if it was found by a psycho-analyst to be due to some suppressed desire of mine or it was discovered that the rats did not obey the causal laws which ordinary rats obey, it would be regarded as an image which only constituted part of my subjective history. This interpretation is supported by Kant's statement in B 521 that "the empirical truth of appearances . . . is adequately distinguished from dreams, if both dreams and genuine appearances cohere truly and completely in one experience, in accordance with empirical laws." The *Second Analogy* on this interpretation shows that objective succession implies causality because it is irreversible for all human percipients, but leaves open the question whether there are not causal laws also governing purely subjective representations. From the point of view of the physical scientist, with whom Kant is mainly concerned in the *Analogies*, psychological events are merely subjective; from the point of view of the psychologist they are objective and therefore presumably subject to causality. In any case all causally determined succession cannot be physically objective, because illusions are also causally determined. They are in fact felt as forced on us just as much as veridical perceptions. But even if all our representations are determined their causes vary and they may be classified accordingly. The *Second Analogy* might still serve to prove causation, for if the distinction between subjective and objective is only to be effected by putting our representations into two different causal systems it does presuppose causation just as much as if it were effected by treating one set of representations as caused and the other as uncaused. It must be admitted, however, that Kant's statement of the argument is inadequate in view of the existence of " irreversible " illusions.

But there is another proof of causality not worked out in the *Second Analogy* or elsewhere, but suggested in the *Transcendental Deduction*. There Kant argued that all empirical cognition bore reference to an " object," and that an " object " must be regarded as a necessarily connected system of representations.[1] Now a necessarily connected system of successive events in time certainly involves causality. [This argument has the advantage of being obviously applicable to the phenomenal self as well as to the physical world and of not necessarily presupposing Kant's idealism.]

The Third Analogy. Community (or reciprocity, as it is sometimes translated) differs from the second analogy in that it is a two-sided relation between different coexisting substances and not a one-sided relation between such substances or between earlier and later states of the same

---

[1] *v.* above, pp. 79, 86.

substance. It apparently may be simultaneous causation, but what Kant meant it to cover mainly were cases in which the present state of each of the interacting things is causally affected by the immediately past (not the present) state of the other and in its turn causally affects the immediately future state of the other. (It may be doubted whether simultaneous causation ever occurs, but this is not Kant's view.[1]) When the category of community is applied to all physical phenomena, it is no doubt meant to cover not only direct causal action but indirect connections such as that between ourselves and the stars, which only affect us mediately by emitting waves of light that strike our eyes ; but this is still a causal connection, though an indirect one, and one that assimilates phenomena to the coherent system envisaged by many philosophers, any particular connection presupposing the causal system as a whole. In the statement of the principle to be proved, we should note the limitation to space added in the second edition.

As I have said, Kant could have stated his proof of causality in a wider form so as to cover both successive events and coexisting objects, but he did not desire to prove merely that every change had a cause, he also wished to prove that all physical objects interacted, which is quite a different proposition. Hence he needs a separate proof.

The main proof of community[2] is best understood by bearing in mind the similar but less difficult, because less condensed, proof of causality. The difference between the

---

[1] B 247-8. Kant may seem inconsistent in introducing his examples under the heading of the second analogy and not the third, but he is not really so, for the causation is conceived as one-sided.

[2] Stated most clearly in the first paragraph of the 2nd edition (B 257-8).

perception of the successive and the perception of the coexistent had been said to be that the former was irreversible
and the latter reversible. But reversibility of our perceptions is not enough by itself to justify the assertion of objective coexistence (presumably because the perceptions might
themselves still be due to mere subjective imagination).
Kant therefore falls back on the general principle that what
is needed to give objectivity is a category involving necessary
connection, but unfortunately he does not elaborate its
application here.

[No doubt, if two things interact, they must coexist, and
therefore knowledge of interaction could serve as one
criterion among others of coexistence, but surely we can
know that two things coexist without first knowing that
they interact? If the proof is to be made parallel to that of
the second analogy, we must base it on the fact that even
when we are confronted with the coexistent we cannot
arbitrarily reverse the order of our perceptions but can only
do so by following certain rules, *e.g.*, in a house the ground-
floor and roof coexist and so we can reverse the order of
our perceptions and perceive whichever we please first, but
we cannot, e.g., obtain a perception of the roof by looking
down but only by looking up, and when we look up the
perception of the roof is forced on us so that we cannot
help having it and cannot, say, perceive the roof as thatched
when it is really composed of tiles. This shows that our
perceptions of the coexistent are subject to laws just as much
as our perceptions of the successive, and if we hold an
idealist view of physical objects we shall hold that judgments about coexistent physical objects are judgments
about these laws. But, even if we hold an idealist view of
physical objects, to say that the proposition that the sun

and moon coexist must be analysed so as to include the proposition that there is a law according to which per-cipients, if they move their sense-organs in a certain way, will perceive them first in one order and then in another is not obviously the same as to say that the sun and moon themselves interact. Kant should have shown, if possible, that the first proposition involved the second. Two events might necessarily coexist and yet have no causal connection with each other, each being determined by independent causes. Since he did not show this, he failed to prove universal interaction, and only proved at the best that all cases of coexistence as well as of sequence are necessarily determined by some causes.]

Kant adds that, if we are to apprehend A and B as co-existent, it must be possible to pass from one to the other through a *continuous* series of changing perceptions.[1] He also seems to be arguing in this paragraph that, since we could not perceive any object if it did not act on us and all phenomena can be perceived, therefore they all act on us and so presumably on each other. The last point is sup-ported by the empirical illustration of light. Light passes from all the stars to us, therefore it presumably passes from each star to all parts of the universe. He also seems to hold, for some reason which I cannot understand, that if two physical objects did not interact there would be an empty space between them.[2] Empty space, he admits, may pos-sibly exist beyond the region where our perceptions can reach, but he denies it to be a possible object of experience.

From evidence outside the Critique it is clear that Kant regarded community as provable by showing that it was a necessary condition of the unity of space, just as he had

[1] B 260-1.　　　　　　　　[2] B 259.

12

argued in one of his proofs of causality that the past conditioned the future and therefore future events must be determined by past.[1] And as each particular space, according
to Kant, presupposes Space as a whole, so the connection
between any two phenomena would presuppose the whole
physical system. When we examine the wider implications
of what Kant says we may well be inclined to agree with
Professor Kemp Smith that the notion of universal interaction presupposes or at least suggests a system such as
that envisaged by the advocates of the coherence theory.
Such a notion could not be accepted by Kant as proved,
but he seems willing to admit something like it as an un-
provable but scientifically useful "idea of reason," as he
called such concepts, and it may be, as Professor Kemp
Smith suggests, that he would have done better to treat
community as "an idea of reason" than to try to prove it
as a category.[2] He declines in the *Critique of Pure Reason*
to apply the category of community to the phenomenal self
in its relation to physical objects, but he had changed his
mind by the time he wrote his posthumously published work.

The Postulates of Empirical Thought.[3] In his discussion
of these Kant does not try to prove anything, except in-
cidentally, of the objective phenomenal world. All phenomena must according to him be at once possible, actual
and necessary (the last follows from the second and third
analogies), but from our point of view we may regard
something as being possible and yet not actual, or actual
and yet not necessary. If we know of something merely
that it can be brought under our forms of intuition and

---

[1] *v.* Kemp Smith, *Commentary*, p. 385.

[2] *Commentary*, pp. 382-3, 390-1. For "ideas of reason" *v.* below,
p. 245 ff.

[3] For term "postulate" *v.* B 285-7.

categories, we regard it as possible ;if we find also that it is given in sensation or can be inferred from something so given, it becomes actual for us; if we can succeed in also explaining it by causal laws we regard it as necessary. The postulates are therefore radically different from the other categories. While these as universal principles governing the objective world require proof, the discussion of the postulates is rather an explanation of the meaning of terms.

The treatment of possibility is mainly a criticism of Leibniz's claim for metaphysics as a science of the possible. Kant rejects the Leibnizian view that mere absence of self-contradiction is a sufficient proof of possibility. This is not, I think, a merely verbal dispute. No doubt we can say that " possibility " is used in different senses and that in one sense of possibility the absence of contradiction is a sufficient test while in another it is not, but the real difference between Leibniz and Kant was that Leibniz thought, when you were determining what was self-consistent purely *a priori*, that you were doing something of great value, Kant that you were not really saying anything positive at all, though if there were already positive evidence for a supposition the removal of apparent contradictions might be an important matter. Possibility for Kant means compatibility not only with the laws of logic, though this is a necessary condition, but with the categories and forms of intuition, and he insists that in order to pronounce something possible we must know positively that it is compatible with these, not merely be unable to see any incompatibility. This positive knowledge could only be obtained in two ways. In the case of the categories themselves and of mathematical concepts it could be given by showing them to be necessary conditions of experience or bound up inseparably with such conditions; in the case of empirical objects it could only be given by encountering actual instances of the class of object in question. It is because we never encounter such phenomena and therefore have no evidence that they are even possible that Kant forbids us to introduce even as hypotheses substances which were present in space without filling it, direct pre-cognition of the future and telepathy. Kant can hardly mean that before we can pronounce an object or event to be possible we must first know it to be actual,—this would render the use of any hypothesis impossible in science since a hypothesis is not known to be actual at the time it is introduced, yet Kant certainly holds that it must at least be known to be possible,—but he seems to mean that before we can admit anything to be possible we must know by experience that other things of the same class are actual. To suppose a new planet to account for the movements of an existing one is a legitimate hypothesis because we know by experience that there are such things as planets though we have not perceived the new one postulated, but to account for the divergence from the expected movements by suggesting that it was the work of a devil would not be a legitimate hypothesis because no instances of devils are known in experience.

Actuality is defined in a misleading fashion because conformity with the formal, not only the material, conditions of experience is obviously necessary for actuality as well as for possibility. In his discussion of actuality Kant tones down the position suggested in his account of possibility by admitting that, e.g., a magnetic matter penetrating all bodies was a legitimate scientific inference though we never perceived anything of that kind.[1] The difference between it

[1] B 273.

and the instances of hypotheses rejected above on the ground that we had no evidence of their possibility seems to be that, e.g., direct pre-cognition would be different in kind from anything we experience, while the unperceived magnetic matter would be only quantitatively different, i.e. it would have properties which belong to other material objects and only differ in degree of subtlety from any matter known to us, so that we can imagine ourselves as experiencing it by merely imagining our present senses as intensified. If the difference in the matter postulated had been qualitative we should have had no means of knowing that this difference did not make the supposition incompatible with the categories and forms of intuition and therefore impossible, but a merely quantitative difference could not, Kant thinks, have this effect. The point is of interest for its bearing on the analogous question of the compatibility of the atomic theory with (a) Kant's view as to the conditions which a hypothesis must fulfil before we can pronounce it to be possible, (b) his view that propositions about physical objects are reducible to propositions about objects of human experiences. The *Refutation of Idealism* which immediately follows the account of actuality will be discussed in my next chapter.

Necessity. Kant starts by explaining that he is referring to causal, not to logical, necessity, and that it is not the existence of things but their states which are necessary. Kant here lays down four *a priori* principles about nature.[1]

1. Everything is necessarily determined (*non datur casus*).

2. This determination is always by some other definitely specifiable condition (*non datur fatum*).

3. All change is continuous (*non datur saltus*).

[1] B 280-2.

4. There is no empty space (*non datur hiatus*).

The first and second are really both contained in the second analogy, but Kant prefers to associate the second principle with the modal category of necessity. The third is supposed to be proved at the end of the second Analogy,[1] the fourth is based on the principle repeatedly laid down by Kant that empty space is not a possible object of perception.

General Note. Here Kant puts forward the striking doctrine that " in order to understand the possibility of things in conformity with the categories, and so to demonstrate (darzutun) the *objective reality* of the latter we need, not merely intuitions, but intuitions that are in all cases *outer intuitions.*"[2] The natural conclusion that one would draw from this statement is that the categories are not applicable to the appearance self, but, as I have said, this cannot be Kant's view because in his whole account of freedom he assumes without hesitation that the appearance self is subject to causality and that the *Critique of Pure Reason* itself has proved it to be thus subject. And, after all, Kant does not say even here that the categories cannot be applied to or proved valid for inner intuitions, but only that this cannot be done till we have first had examples of their application to outer intuitions. That it can be applied afterwards he expressly says here of one category, quantity, at least.[3]

The reason why outer sense is said to be required is different in the case of each of the three analogies. With substance it is that there is nothing permanent in inner sense; with causality it is that we cannot think change without images drawn from space; with community it is

[1] B 253 ff.   [2] B 291 ff.   [3] B 293.

that except under spatial conditions we cannot conceive how different substances could interact.[1] In the cases of substance and community the objections given would be regarded by Kant as disproving the application of the category to the appearance self, and not merely as showing that before we can apply it we must understand it in terms of space, but it does not follow that this is so in the case of causality where the point mentioned by Kant, if true, shows only that to understand it we must illustrate it in terms of outer sense.

[1] *cf.* the similar difficulties of Spinoza and Leibniz about interaction between different substances.

CHAPTER V

KANT'S ATTITUDE TO MATERIAL IDEALISM. THE THING-IN-ITSELF

KANT's *Refutations of Idealism*. Kant introduces into the section on Modality a somewhat irrelevant but very important passage in which he refutes what he calls " idealism " in a derogatory sense of the term. This " idealism " he distinguishes from his own type by calling it material or empirical and his own transcendental. At this point I shall, in accordance with the usual practice of commentators, take the first edition refutation of idealism, i.e. the fourth *Paralogism* (A 366-80), though this occurs later in the book, and set it against the second edition refutation in the *Postulates of Empirical Thought*, in order to bring out the puzzling contrast between the two. Both are intended as refutations not so much of the " dogmatic idealism " attributed by Kant to Berkeley, according to which physical things are mere illusions, as of the " problematic idealism " according to which, though they are held to exist independently of us, they are not immediately perceived and their existence, being a mere causal inference, is therefore at least uncertain. Kant is thus using idealism in a wider sense to cover any variety of realism which admits a representative theory of perception. Against problematic idealism he claims in both cases to prove that physical objects are immediately perceived and are consequently known with certainty to exist. I shall now summarise briefly the main argument of the first edition refutation, and set it against that of the second, which I shall quote in full, as it is already too condensed to summarise.

First Edition (*A* 370-1). I am immediately aware of my representations.

> Physical objects are only a species (*Art*) of my representations.
> ∴ I am immediately aware of physical objects.
> ∴ Physical objects are known with certainty to exist.

Second Edition (*B* 275-6). " I am conscious of my own existence as determined in time. All determination of time presupposes something *permanent* in perception. But this permanent cannot be an intuition in me. For all grounds of determination of my existence which are to be met with in me are representations; and as representations themselves require a permanent distinct from them, in relation to which their change, and so my existence in the time wherein they change, may be determined.[1] Thus perception of this permanent is possible only through a *thing* outside me and not through the mere *representation* of a thing outside me; and consequently the determination of my existence in time is possible only through the existence of actual things which I perceive outside me. Now consciousness [of my existence] in time is necessarily bound up with consciousness of the [condition of the] possibility of this time-determination; and it is therefore necessarily bound up with the existence of things outside me, as the condition of the time-determination. In other words, the consciousness of my existence is at the same time an im-

[1] I have made here the change in the text which Kant says in B XXXIX n. ought to be made.

mediate consciousness of the existence of other things outside me."

It will be seen at once that the second edition refutation verbally contradicts the first. In the first physical objects are asserted to be merely our representations; in the second it is denied that they are anything in us at all. And in this respect the second edition refutation seems at first sight at least to contradict also many other passages in the *Critique*. This has driven many commentators to adopt the view that Kant is referring here to things-in-themselves and not to phenomena; but this interpretation seems to me and would, I think, generally be held now to be quite impossible. The principal objection to it is that he speaks of the "things outside me," to which he is referring here, as "objects in *space*." We should also note that this argument is essentially the same as that of the first analogy, which admittedly only refers to phenomena. Yet Kant says that the introduction of the second edition refutation is only a change in "the method of proof,"[1] and the second edition of the *Critique* as a whole, as much as the first, is based on the doctrine that everything in space and time is only appearance, though the first edition refutation of idealism itself is not retained in the second edition.

Vaihinger[2] solves the puzzle by pointing out that the self we observe empirically is just as much an appearance as physical objects and therefore physical objects must be regarded as independent of it. Consequently physical objects, while mere representations relatively to our real self, are "things outside us" relatively to our self as determined in time, and the realism of the second edition refutation is

[1] B XXXIX n.
[2] In his separate book on *Kant's Widerlegung des Idealismus*.

actually a necessary consequence of Kant's philosophy, for the phenomenal self, being only one appearance among others, could not create the whole phenomenal world. In this connection Vaihinger draws attention to the doctrine of "double affection." Kant recognises the possibility of an empirical, psychological and physiological account of sense-perception that would explain causally why we were conscious of A rather than B, but holds that such an account could never explain the fact of consciousness itself. We thus have, on the one hand, a causal connection in the phenomenal sense between physical objects and the appearance self which they affect, and on the other some relation, which we can only think, however imperfectly, in terms of causality, by which things-in-themselves affect the real self and thus produce the manifold which is synthesised to constitute appearances.[1] This interpretation is supported by Kant's posthumous work, which, unlike any of the earlier works, explicitly and not only implicitly maintains the doctrine of double affection and develops with greater emphasis and in much more detail both the view that we make phenomena and the view of them as independent relatively to the appearance self, saying expressly that they should be treated in science as if they were things-in-themselves relatively to us as empirical beings, though certainly not relatively to us as noumenal beings.

Professor Kemp Smith, while accepting this interpretation of Vaihinger's, asserts an irreducible inconsistency between the tendency of Kant to reduce statements about physical objects to statements about what human beings experience or would experience under given conditions

---

[1] For the possibility of two kinds of causality concerned with the same event *v.* account of freedom below, p. 230 ff.

and the tendency to ascribe to them an independent existence as in the present passage and in the *First Analogy*. But I think we can reconcile the two points of view if we bear in mind a distinction which Professor G. E. Moore has made and which seems to me to express in different language and in the context of a very different philosophy the same sort of thing that Kant himself is saying when he declares that physical objects are both empirically real and transcendentally ideal. A number of philosophers who were in the thirties described as members of the "Cambridge school" insisted both that "common-sense propositions" about physical things are known to be true and that they have to be analysed in terms of "sense-data," meaning that they are only propositions about what human beings see or feel or would see and feel etc. under certain conditions,[1] but in saying this they are only putting in their own words something like what Kant means when he says that physical objects exist and are known immediately but are only appearances. Kant differed indeed from these philosophers in holding that all judgments required *a priori* categories (which he would no doubt have sharply distinguished from linguistic conventions if the question had been raised in his time), and in maintaining the doctrine of the thing-in-itself, and I do not wish to minimise the differences between his and their philosophy, but I think that on this particular point there is sufficient parallelism to throw a valuable light on Kant's meaning. I do not therefore think that Kant in the Critique ever means to assert the existence of physical objects in any sense which could

---

[1] This must not be confused with the view suggested by myself that physical objects are groups of "unsensed sensa" (*Idealism*, ch. 7, § 3).

not be reduced to propositions about what human beings experience or would experience under given conditions.

In this light we can understand Kant's assertions about the relation between empirical realism and transcendental idealism.[1] Material (or empirical) idealism is classified as (a) problematic, (b) dogmatic, problematic idealism being the doctrine which asserts the existence of physical things to be doubtful, dogmatic idealism the doctrine that they do not exist at all but are merely imaginary entities (*Einbildungen*). To both these forms of idealism is opposed empirical realism, according to which physical objects are immediately known to exist and can be made the objects of true scientific judgments. But the empirical realist may still be a transcendental idealist, i.e. he may hold that physical objects, though they certainly exist, are only appearances. For he will not then be denying the truth and validity of scientific and common-sense propositions, but merely re-interpreting them in terms of experience. An empirical realist who is also a transcendental idealist will hold that propositions about physical things are known to be true but are still only propositions about what human beings experience.

Kant then contends that, if you are a transcendental realist, you are logically bound to be an empirical idealist, so that to escape the latter objectionable position you must adopt transcendental idealism. He has several reasons for this, not all expressly stated. (1) If physical objects are viewed as things-in-themselves, you can know nothing of their nature and assert no true propositions about them. (2) If space and time are viewed as existing independently of us, they can be shown to be self-contradictory notions,

[1] A 369 ff., B 274.

and this will make everything in them mere illusion. (3) Unless physical objects are merely phenomena, it will be impossible to prove of them the categories which all science and common-sense propositions presuppose. For these reasons you cannot claim any knowledge of physical objects if these are supposed to be transcendently real, but if they are only appearances you can and indeed must do so. Kant was considerably offended by a review of the first edition which accused him of being an idealist and of out-Berkeley-ing Berkeley, and the second edition refutation is his reply. He wrongly interpreted Berkeley as denying the existence of physical objects and reducing all science to mere illusion, though in reality it would be much fairer to say that the latter was an "empirical realist," but Kant had probably never read Berkeley, except in quoted extracts, owing to his lack of knowledge of English. Whether the difference between saying that physical objects do not exist because there are no extended things independent of us and saying that they do exist but are not things independent of us in the realist sense is as great as Kant would like to believe might be questioned, but that he thought it extremely important, just as the "Cambridge school" did, is an obvious matter of fact.

Professor Kemp Smith draws a distinction between "phenomenalism" and "subjectivism" and regards them as inconsistent tendencies in Kant. In so far as he means by phenomenalism empirical realism I have tried to show that it is not inconsistent with transcendental idealism, and I think that both views constitute an essential part of Kant's thought throughout, though no doubt he emphasises sometimes one side, sometimes the other, as even the most consistent writer must do. In so far as Professor Kemp Smith means to cover by "phenomenalism" the view that the synthetic acts mentioned as transcendental conditions of our knowledge are of a noumenal and totally unconscious character and by "subjectivism" the view that they consist of cognitive processes of the individual human mind observable by introspection, I have discussed this already in my chapter on the transcendental deduction.

We have, however, so far hardly mentioned a point on which Kant laid great stress. He wished not only to justify the belief in physical objects but to do so in a way which would finally get rid of the representative theory of perception. In the first edition refutation he argues that, since physical objects are only my representations, I must perceive them immediately; in the second he argues that, though they are not representations of mine, they are presupposed by my consciousness of my own states and therefore must be, like the latter, perceived immediately. Kant thought this an important contribution chiefly because it removed any possible theoretical doubt about the existence of physical objects, whereas the doubt might always recur if it were admitted that we did not perceive them immediately. Kant assumes that if they are perceived immediately they are known immediately, and that conversely we cannot know them immediately unless we perceive them immediately.

[But even if we assume a transcendental idealist view of physical objects the first edition refutation is defective, for even then a physical object never consists only of representations of my own. That there is a chair in this room is not anything which I can perceive immediately even on the idealist view, for it is a fact not only about my representations but about the actual or possible representations of other human beings, and the same applies not only to the chair as a whole, all of which I do not in any case see, but even to that part of its surface which I should ordinarily be said to be seeing at the moment, for to say that even that part of it exists physically is not merely to say something about a representation of mine. It is also to say at least that other people would have similar representations, and their representations I can assuredly not perceive. It is indeed less difficult for the realist (transcendental) than for the idealist to say that physical objects are perceived immediately, because, whether it is *plausible* or not, it is certainly not *impossible* for a realist to maintain that we sometimes perceive the surface of a physical object immediately. The idealist cannot maintain this, for he certainly has not immediate perception or knowledge of the representations of others or of the merely possible representations which yet on his view make up an essential part of the notion of any physical object, even the notion of a mere physical surface, and which are comprised in the meaning of any possible statement about physical objects. All propositions about physical objects have therefore still to be justified inductively, and the view that they are known with certainty is still open to the objection that inductive arguments can only give probability.

Kant brought forward what might perhaps be described as the two strongest arguments for realism, (1) that the belief in physical things gives the only possible way of ordering our existence coherently, (2) that self-consciousness presupposes consciousness of independent objects. They are not indeed arguments which first led us to believe in physical objects. They could not be if the second argument is valid, for we could not in that case have the premiss, knowledge of our own experience, without already knowing the conclusion, i.e., that physical objects exist, but at the reflective stage they could still be used to justify philosophically the belief in physical objects which we have prior to reflection. As everybody knows, our common-sense belief in the existence of physical objects is not due to philosophical arguments at all. Both arguments occur in the transcendental deduction, but the second is given in a more noticeable and emphatic form in the second edition refutation of idealism. Whether empirical realism is, as Kant held, enough for these arguments or whether they do not really also establish transcendental realism is a difficult question, to which I should not be inclined to give the same answer as Kant does. Nor, while sympathetic to the general principle of the second argument, can I regard Kant's statement of it in the second edition refutation as altogether satisfactory, largely because I am unable to accept his view of substance and because I cannot see either that time-measurement as such presupposes space logically, as opposed to factually, or that it presupposes, whether logically or factually, anything *absolutely* permanent.]

In view of Kant's strong defence of realism (of a sort) the question may well be raised—Why was he an idealist at all, even in the transcendental sense? We may sum up his main reasons thus.[1] (1) He persistently asked himself the question why objects should be held to conform to our categories and our forms of intuition. This question seemed to him unanswerable unless we suppose that the objects we know are only appearances and so somehow made by us. If they are made by us they naturally must conform to the laws governing our intuition and thought, and if they are only appear-

---

[1] For a fuller answer to this question with my reply to Kant's arguments *v.* my earlier book, *Idealism* (Methuen, 1934), pp. 64-80.

ances they could not exist without so conforming since otherwise they would not appear to us. But if they were things-in-themselves this conformity would be inexplicable and the claim to know *a priori* that they did conform presumptuous. Why should reality be just what we, perhaps owing to a mere accident of our psychological constitution, must think it to be?

(2) As we have seen, Kant believed that synthetic *a priori* judgments could only be justified within the realm of actual and possible experience. They must, he held, include an empirical element which can only be supplied by sense, and the categories themselves can only be proved by showing that they are necessary conditions without which nothing could appear to us. But experience, including in this causal arguments on the basis of experience such as those we have in science, could not, he assumes, ever give us information about things as they are independently of being experienced by us.[1] Hence he is faced with the dilemma : — either science gives us no knowledge (or justified belief), or it is only concerned with things as they appear to us, not as they really are. He had no hesitation about accepting the latter horn of the dilemma rather than the former.

(3) Kant thinks that, if we suppose physical objects to exist in space and time independently of being perceived, we are involved in insoluble contradictions (the antinomies). Such a physical world would have to be either finite or infinite, yet it could not be either without absurdity. This argument does not occur till late in the *Dialectic*, but it was probably prominent in Kant's mind throughout.

[1] These words are understood here in the unvarnished realist sense, not in the sense in which they might be reduced to a complicated statement about human experience.

Another respect in which Kant differs from other idealists is in the assertion of the thing-in-itself, and we shall now turn to this doctrine.

The Thing-in-itself.[1] *Chapter III. The Ground of the Distinction of All Objects in General into Phenomena and Noumena.* This doctrine was the first part of Kant's philosophy to be abandoned by his followers, who thus arrived at what Kant would have called dogmatic idealism. The thing-in-itself has been very seriously attacked, chiefly on the following grounds.

1. We cannot say that things-in-themselves exist unless we mean something by the term thing-in-itself. But if we mean anything by the term, we are asserting something, however vague and slight, about their nature when we assert them to exist, and therefore it is inconsistent to describe them as unknowable, as Kant does. Also how could we know that there was a reality beyond appearances at all or that it was of such a nature that we could know nothing about it without already inconsistently presupposing knowledge of its nature.

2. Kant is blamed for committing the still more serious inconsistency of applying categories to things-in-themselves. This is not an adventitious slip but necessary to his philosophy. For (1) things-in-themselves must be subject at least to the category of " reality "; (2) we cannot even think of physical objects as appearances of things-in-themselves without thinking of them as determined by the latter, which involves the category of causality, and it is clear that Kant's whole conception of appearances presupposes the action on

---

[1] Adickes, *Kant und das Ding-an-sich*, gives a very good account of this subject. Caird's commentary is full of criticism of the doctrine. A spirited defence of it is given by Riehl, *Geschichte des Kritizismus.*

us of a thing-in-itself as a part-cause of our representations accounting for the empirical element in knowledge; (3) Kant later comes to the conclusion that the real self has the power of free causality and that God created the world, therefore causality is explicitly applied beyond the realm of appearances; (4) it might be doubted whether it was possible to form any conception at all of things-in-themselves without using at least the category of substance in its pure unschematised form.[1]

Kant implicitly answers both objections by his distinction between determinate knowledge and indeterminate thought.[2] We do not know anything about things-in-themselves except that they exist, but we can do what might be described as thinking them in a sort of way, and his assertion of their unknowability is not based on any positive assumptions about their nature but on the mere absence of those spatial and temporal features which are presupposed in human knowledge. Again we have no knowledge of them according to the categories, but we can and must use the categories in thinking of them, however indeterminate and formal this use must inevitably be. Vague ideas are undesirable and unphilosophical where we can have clearer and more definite ones, but in some cases indeterminate ideas may be the best we can have. For we cannot think without the categories, and beyond phenomena they cannot be applied by us as schematised, but only in their pure and therefore indeterminate form. This is for Kant a reason for abstaining from theoretical judgments that go beyond phenomena, but he held that the thought of our objects of experience

---

[1] It is said that we have to think God in terms of substance (B 703).

[2] e.g. B XXVI n., XXVIII, 166 n.

was inseparable from the thought of a reality of which they were appearances, and also that the truths of ethics constrained us to form certain theoretical beliefs about reality, so that for these two reasons he was obliged to allow the use of the categories in this indeterminate manner. Kant uses the term "categories" to mean sometimes "pure categories" and sometimes "schematised categories," and in the former sense he asserts and in the latter denies the possibility of employing them in our thought of things-in-themselves.

But is it not an essential part of the critical philosophy that the categories cannot be applied beyond the phenomenal world at all? Certainly the following three propositions are held by Kant and are essential to his philosophy: (1) the categories as schematised cannot be applied to things-in-themselves because they are schematised in terms of time; (2) the categories consequently can give no *knowledge* of things-in-themselves; (3) there is no proof possible that they apply to things-in-themselves, or at least no theoretical proof. But not one of these three propositions is incompatible with the possibility of thinking things-in-themselves in terms of them as unschematised, though the thought must necessarily be indeterminate, formal and unsatisfactory. Causality in its unschematised form is ground, which is certainly not a notion totally without meaning, and it was causality that Kant was chiefly, if not only, concerned to apply. When we think things-in-themselves in terms of causality, what we do, according to Kant, I suppose, is to think something real as related either to something else real or to a phenomenon by a relation such as that which holds between a phenomenal cause and a phenomenal effect, except that it is regarded as non-temporal. When we have subtracted time as not belonging to reality there is indeed very little left of the relation, but there is something, the notion of dependence and ground. Kant insists that we cannot understand in the least how one real thing could be inferable from another as ground, but that is not inconsistent with his still supposing that it really is inferable though human beings cannot see how this could be, and I think that in his heart of hearts Kant was a rationalist and believed, though he admittedly could not prove, that every part of the real had a sufficient reason which would, if we could only see it, explain its existence as a logically necessary consequence of other parts. In the *Prolegomena* Kant goes further than in the *Critique* in stating quite definitely that it is both legitimate and necessary to think of God in terms of the categories " substance, causality, etc."[1]

But, while the application of categories to things-in-themselves in this indeterminate way can well be reconciled with the general principles of Kant's philosophy, I am certainly not prepared to defend the verbal consistency of all his statements. In particular he repeatedly denies, especially in the chapter on *Phenomena and Noumena*, that the categories have any " meaning " at all except as applied to phenomena.[2] But if they have no meaning, things-in-themselves could hardly be even thought in terms of them. Kant in his anxiety to oppose all dogmatic metaphysics seems to have expressed himself more strongly than was compatible with his own position or with his statements about the categories when he has in view the fact that the employment in some sense of at least one of them beyond experience is absolutely

---

[1] § 58, *Berl.* IV, p. 358.
[2] A 242, B 148, 178, 300, 306, 308, 311; *v.* also B 344, which however apparently makes an exception in favour of causality.

necessary if we are to believe in, or form any sort of notion of, God or freedom.

We must also note a verbal difficulty. Since any noun must be either singular or plural it is impossible to speak about things-in-themselves without committing oneself to the view that there is either one or more than one thing-in-itself. This is, however, rather a defect of European languages than a philosophical inconsistency. Kant uses both singular and plural, but it seems to me quite groundless to suggest that his frequent use of the latter implies that he favoured some form of metaphysical pluralism.

Let us now turn to the reasons which led Kant to assert the existence of things-in-themselves.

1. The thing-in-itself is needed to account for the given element in experience. Space, time and the categories are due to our mind, but they do not constitute the whole of phenomena. Our experience is largely forced on us from outside, and it is this dependence on what is alien to us which, he thinks, explains the limitations of our *a priori* knowledge. Epistemology would be totally different and knowledge would require no empirical element if we had " created our own manifold." Since we do not know from what this empirical element is derived, we can only ascribe it to an unknown x, the thing-in-itself.

2. For Kant the *Transcendental Æsthetic* and the *Antinomies* prove that space and time and therefore the physical world cannot be real. To assume their reality is held by him to lead to the self-contradictory conclusions of the antinomies, e.g. that the series of events in time neither had a beginning nor have gone on for ever, and therefore, since Kant seems to have no doubt that the law of contradiction applies to reality, he has for his mind a completely

adequate proof that anything real must be neither spatial nor temporal in character. Now obviously there must be something real, and to assert that it consisted only of minds and their ideas would have been to dogmatise about metaphysics in just the way against which the whole of Kant's philosophy was a protest. He expressed his undogmatic position by admitting that the element in reality other than mind was a totally unknowable thing-in-itself. He did not mean in asserting things-in-themselves to rule out the possibility that reality was mental in character. It is in fact his belief that either reality is wholly mental or that at least it is ultimately dependent on a mind, God. But since he had no right to assert this in advance of his ethical proof of the existence of God, or perhaps at all for theoretical reason, he does not intrude such ideas here.

[It is clear from these considerations that it would have been wrong on Kant's principles to deny things-in-themselves, but was he justified in asserting them? In one passage he says of the thing-in-itself that " we are completely ignorant whether it is to be met with in us or outside us, whether it would be at once removed with the cessation of sensibility, or whether in the absence of sensibility it would still remain,"[1] and if this is all that is meant by the thing-in-itself no doubt its existence is proved, granting the validity of Kant's arguments against the reality of space and time. For the assertion of things-in-themselves then merely amounts to saying that there is something real which we wrongly apprehend as subject to space and time and about which we can know nothing positive. For there must be something real, and if space and time are appearances the real must be distinguished from physical objects and minds as revealed in

[1] B 344.

introspection. But usually Kant no doubt understands by the thing-in-itself something other than any human (noumenal) minds, which affects them; and the existence of this he had no theoretical right to assert, though also no right to deny. For might not reality consist entirely of human minds? Any causal argument for the existence of anything else is out of the question, since, even if we can *think* things-in-themselves in terms of the categories, we certainly cannot according to Kant *prove* anything beyond the realm of experience by means of the categories. The only arguments against the view given are arguments for God, not for things-in-themselves. It was indeed justifiable for Kant to use the thing-in-itself as a limiting, problematical concept[1] if he meant that, having no reason to suppose that human minds comprise the whole, we had better *think* of them as if they existed together with other things quite different, though it is abstractly not impossible that there might be no other things; but this is not Kant's usual view. Usually, and according to such commentators as Adickes[2] and Paton[3] even in this passage where he describes the thing-in-itself as a problematic concept, he shows no doubt of its existence.[4] Kant denies that we can know of the existence of " noumena in the positive sense of the term,"[5] but this may only mean that we can form no positive conception of what a thing-in-itself is like. To do that, he says, we should require a faculty of non-sensuous intuition, which he also

[1] B 310. [2] p. 113 ff. [3] II, p. 456 ff.
[4] but *v.* B 335. Adickes explains the passage by saying that it is not the existence of the thing-in-itself which is said to be self-contradictory but our representation of it in so far as it claims to be knowledge and yet to be independent of sensible conditions (*Kant und das Ding-an-sich*, p. 131 ff.).
[5] B 307 ff.

envisaged as an intuitive understanding that created its own manifold. He no doubt thought of such a faculty as belonging to God, but he denied any human knowledge of its very possibility.

Kant thus did not succeed in maintaining his agnostic position consistently. He was unduly dogmatic on his own premises in asserting positively the existence of things other than human selves and their representations, however total the absence of reasons for denying such things. And further he makes even in his theoretical philosophy two dogmatic assumptions about reality which everybody accepts, but which Kant on his philosophy can hardly have had any justification for accepting, (a) that the reality which appeared to him when he introspected was a self, (b) that there were other (real) selves besides his own.]

We are apt to think of the appearances as something in our mind caused by something else not in our mind, the thing-in-itself, but it has been maintained that this is quite a wrong way of regarding them and that we should think of a thing-in-itself and its appearance as the same thing in different aspects, the former being the thing as it is and the latter the thing as it appears.[1] If Kant had been asked in which way they should be viewed, I suspect he would have replied that the question was unanswerable since according to his own philosophy the relation between appearance and reality must be regarded as itself unknowable. And the thing-in-itself I cannot admit to be a very important concession to realism, seeing that it is totally different from physical objects, which are in space but only exist as phenomena.

One motive for Kant's belief in the thing-in-itself has not

[1] e.g. by Lindsay.

been mentioned. It is that we have certain intellectual ideals which are not fulfilled in the world we know but which we may at least hope to be fulfilled in some form or other in the real world behind phenomena, and the belief in which actually may be of help even in science.[1] These are the ideas of reason discussed in the *Dialectic*. Kant's next step is to point out that, if because of the presence of these ideals in our mind we think we have *a priori know-ledge* of their fulfilment, we shall commit fallacies such as those treated in the *Amphiboly*, the *Paralogisms*, the *Antinomies* and the criticism of the proofs of God, but he ends by suggesting that there is still some positive value in the ideas. Now, if there were nothing but phenomena, then the intellectual ideals in question and the ethical ideals which led Kant to belief in God could not be fulfilled, therefore the ideas of reason at least suggest a reality beyond.

The Amphiboly of Concepts of Reflection. This section should really belong to the *Dialectic*, as it is an exposure of some of the fallacies on which dogmatic metaphysics was held by Kant to be based. It ascribes the chief doctrines of Leibniz's philosophy to the assumption that phenomena can be treated as objects of pure understanding.[2] Leibniz assumes that the world is what we should expect it to be from a consideration of universal concepts, or of pure logic. Kant thinks that, if we make this assumption, the main tenets of Leibniz's philosophy follow necessarily, but he insists, that, since phenomena include a sensible element which is alogical, the assumption must not be made. Kant does not indeed mean that phenomena (or, for that matter, noumena) contradict the laws of logic. What they do contradict is an intellectual ideal which cannot be satisfied by

[1] *v.* Kemp Smith, *Comm.*, pp. 415-7.   [2] B 326.

phenomena. While it is true that whatever is contained in a universal concept must be contained in any particular which falls under that universal, it does not follow that we can reverse this and say that there can be nothing in a particular that is not contained in the universal concept under which it falls, and Kant contends that Leibniz's conclusions presuppose this false assumption. "These are particular concepts just because they include in themselves more than is thought in the universal."[1] The alleged fallacies are four in number.

1. The identity of indiscernibles. The only way of grasping the nature of anything in thought completely is to form a concept of all its inner determinations (of quality and quantity). Leibniz concludes that therefore you cannot have two different particulars with the same inner determinations. This would be a correct conclusion if it were not for the presence of space (Kant does not mention time here), which is a phenomenon, not real, and an intuition, not a concept. But two phenomena may be numerically different and yet qualitatively the same, because they differ in their position in space.[2]

2. It is logical to assume that two real things cannot contradict each other. From this would follow two important Leibnizian doctrines, (a) that evil is nothing positive, (b) that a being which has all the positive attributes there are is at least possible (involves no contradiction), for the logical contradictory of a positive can only be a negative. Kant insists in reply that in the phenomenal world there is a type of contradiction other than logical, since two things may both exist and yet contradict each other in the sense of cancelling each other's consequences.[3]

[1] B 337.   [2] B 319-20, 327-8, 337.   [3] B 320-1, 329-30, 338.

3. We assume that everything must have some internal nature independent of its relations to other things. From this follow (a) the doctrine that the real consists of simple substances (monads), for a composite substance would have an internal nature dependent on its relations to other substances (its parts), (b) the doctrine that these substances must be conceived as having properties like those we observe in introspection, since the properties science ascribes to matter are relational in character and there are no other properties left which we can assign to the monads except mental ones, (c) the doctrine that the monads cannot interact, for if they did the state of each would be dependent on its relation to other monads. These conclusions would be justified if we could assume that the objects we encounter were real things and not phenomena, but this we cannot do, and in the case of a phenomenal substance it is true that "its inner determinations are nothing but relations, and it itself is entirely made up of mere relations," i.e. Kant accepted the Cartesian view of physical objects as having only "primary qualities," but unlike the Cartesians realised that, since these so-called qualities are all merely relational properties, an object thus conceived could not be a real thing but only an abstraction from our experience.[1]

4. Matter (which here means the determinable, a sense in which it is not identical with physical matter) must be logically prior to form (the determination of the determinable), and Leibniz therefore concludes that the forms of space and time are only relations of things. But, once we realise that physical things are only phenomena, we can see that this is impossible, for space and time, as our subjective forms, must on the contrary be prior to them.[2]

[1] B 321-2, 330-1, 339-41.   [2] B 322-4, 331-2.

Phenomena thus fail to satisfy the intellectual ideals in which we are inclined to believe. Kant seems to have believed in his heart of hearts that the real world was such as to satisfy them. (It is significant that to the end of his life Kant used a standard work of the Leibnizian school, Baumgarten's *Metaphysica*, for his university lectures.) But he was convinced that there could be no proof of the validity of these ideals even for the real world.

CHAPTER VI

THE PARALOGISMS AND THE ANTINOMIES

It will be appropriate to start the consideration of the Dialectic by quoting a passage at the beginning of the Transcendental Deduction which summarises well the negative side of Kant's attitude to metaphysics. "That a concept, although itself neither contained in the concept of possible experience nor consisting of elements of a possible experience, should be produced completely *a priori* and should relate to an object, is altogether contradictory and impossible. For it would then have no content, since no intuition corresponds to it; and intuitions in general, through which objects can be given to us, constitute the field, the whole object, of possible experience. An *a priori* concept which did not relate directly to experience would be only the logical form of a concept, not the concept itself through which something is thought. Pure *a priori* concepts, if such exist, cannot indeed contain anything empirical; yet, none the less, they can serve solely as *a priori* conditions of a possible experience. Upon this ground alone can their objective reality rest."[1] Kant's negative attitude was based mainly on (1) his conviction that space and time were only appearances, (2) his inability to prove the categories except as necessary conditions of experience, (3) the lack of any concrete material for thought except what was given in experience. This did not exclude the possibility of our thinking in a sense about things-in-them-

[1] A 95.

selves, but it excluded any but merely formal and indeterminate thinking.

The sections of the *Dialectic* prior to the *Paralogisms* are
not of great importance. Kant thought that the usual meaning of " dialectic " in ancient philosophy was to signify the
sophistical use of logic in pretending to prove false or ungrounded views,[1] and so himself used the term to stand for
that branch of philosophy which refuted the sophistries and
removed the illusions to which philosophers were most
addicted.[2] It also differs from the *Analytic* in being concerned not primarily with the understanding but with the
reason. " Reason " is indeed in some passages used to cover
Understanding, but it now develops a separate meaning.
What this meaning is can only be learnt *ambulando*, but we
must bear in mind throughout that there are two aspects or
functions of reason—(1) practical, (2) theoretical. Practical
reason gives us ethical knowledge; theoretical reason provides us with certain ideal standards which are presupposed
in much of our thinking but do not necessarily represent
objective facts. The error which the *Dialectic* refutes is in
outline that of taking them as objective without justification.

In his characteristic way Kant connected the three main
cognitive faculties with the different parts of a syllogism.
Understanding, being the faculty of general rules, thinks
the major premiss; judgment, being the faculty which sub-
sumes the particular under the universal, thinks the minor;
reason draws the conclusion.[3] Since in order ultimately to
justify the conclusion we must again ask for the condition of its condition and so on, the peculiar function of
reason is to seek the unconditioned.[4] This search for the

[1] B 86.   [2] B 88.   [3] B 360-1.   [4] B 364.

unconditioned takes three directions, which Kant derives from the three recognised kinds of syllogism.[1]

1. There is the search for an ultimate subject which gives rise to the paralogisms. This is connected with the categorical syllogism because all categorical propositions are on Kant's view reducible to subject-predicate form and are thus essentially connected with the category of substance.

2. The search for series of conditions which gives rise to the antinomies is connected with the hypothetical syllogism, because it is a search for grounds and a hypothetical proposition expresses the relation between ground and consequent.

3. The idea of God is connected with the disjunctive syllogism on the ground that if we regard God as the *ens realissimum* (sum of all attributes), as the metaphysicians of the day did, we can see that this notion presupposes a vast disjunctive proposition giving all the positive alternative attributes which a finite thing may have,[2] for all these must be included in the supreme reality presupposed by all finite things.

The Paralogisms. A paralogism was the name given to a *formally* fallacious syllogism, and the arguments of rational (i.e. *a priori*) psychology are declared to be paralogisms because they commit the fallacy of ambiguous middle (*sophisma figuræ dictionis*). The nature of the fallacy is best explained in the second edition version in connection with the argument of the first of the four paralogisms, on which the other three (or at least the second and third paralogisms) depend.[3] The argument is : What can only be thought as subject is a substance. The " I " can only be thought as subject. Therefore I am a substance. The fallacy lies in using " thought "[4] and " subject "[5] in two

[1] B 379-80.   [2] B 604-5.   [3] B 411-2.   [4] B 411 n.   [5] A 349.

different senses in the two premisses. In the minor " subject " is used in a formal sense only as that which is always subject and never predicate (the category of substance as unschematised); in the major it is used to signify a permanent object (the category of substance as schematised). In the minor I think the self as subject, which I can only do in a quite peculiar sense of " think," since what is thought is here identical with what thinks; in the major I think, or, rather, try to think myself as object, as one phenomenon among others.[1] The self as thinker is always subject because by definition it is that which thinks and therefore not an attribute of anything, but this does not make it a substance. Kant indeed holds that all (phenomenal) substances are permanent (by definition), but this does not mean that we can decide that any particular thing is permanent *a priori*. On the contrary he holds that to apply the category of substance as schematised to anything we should require the evidence of particular experiences, (as we do in order to decide what caused some event), and that the experience is lacking in this case, since there is no permanent element observable in the phenomenal self,[2] while to apply it even as unschematised to the noumenal self would obviously be transgressing the limit which critical philosophy had set. In the second edition Kant also accuses all four paralogisms of the error of treating a true but analytic proposition as if it were synthetic.[3]

The importance of the second paralogism lies in the fact that the first would not by itself, even if valid, be sufficient to prove immortality. For if the self were a complex sub-

---

[1] Kant's account of the fallacy in A 402-3 applies better to the first than to the other three paralogisms.

[2] A 349-50.   [3] B 407-9.

stance it might come to an end by breaking up into parts, as e.g. a manufactured object does, without any destruction of *substance*. ("Simple" does not mean "possessing only one attribute" but "not divisible into two or more substances.") The argument of the second paralogism is to the effect that a complex thought *ab* cannot be explained by saying that one thinker thinks *a* and another *b*.[1] A thought of wolves in one thinker, a thought of eating in another, and a thought of lambs in a third cannot possibly make up the thought that wolves eat lambs. Kant would have accepted this as an argument for the transcendental unity of apperception, but he will not accept it as an argument for the view that the self is a simple substance. A passage in the antinomies, B 471, should be read in conjunction with Kant's argument.

The third paralogism is dealt with similarly to the first two. One very important remark occurs in a footnote,[2] where Kant suggests that the apparent unity of the self might be really due to the co-operation of a number of different noumenal entities, each one transmitting its state together with the states of all the preceding ones and the consciousness of them to the next, as a motion is transmitted along a row of billiard balls. This is the only passage in the *Critique* where he unequivocally questions the right to say even "I am really one self": elsewhere he denies that I can know my real self but still apparently regards it as a self.

Kant's first edition treatment of the fourth paralogism has already been discussed in its capacity as a refutation of idealism.[3] In the second edition, however, he understands the fourth paralogism as asserting, not the problematic char

[1] A 352.   [2] A 363-4 n.   [3] *v.* above, p. 177 ff.

acter of belief in the physical world, but the independence of the self in relation to physical objects, and attributes the fallacy to a confusion between the analytic proposition that I can distinguish myself from other things and the synthetic proposition that I could exist without there being any physical phenomena.[1] But he thinks that anybody who is guilty of this fallacy has logically committed himself to at least problematic idealism, because if the existence of physical objects is not necessary for the determination of time[2] we have only an ungrounded belief in them, (*v. Second Edition Refutation of Idealism*), and if it is necessary for the determination of time we could not exist apart from them (in the phenomenal world where time is a form of our intuition). *Refutation of Mendelssohn's Proof of the Permanence of the Soul.*[3] It had been suggested that, even if the soul was simple, though it could not come to an end by splitting up into parts, it might end by simply vanishing. If the assumptions of the philosophers who believed in rational psychology were true this possibility would be disproved by the mere fact that the soul was a substance, but Mendelssohn (1729-86, a personal friend of Kant's) brought an additional argument to disprove it.[4] He contended that, since the soul was not composed of parts, it could not disappear gradually but only all at once and that the latter was impossible. Kant retorts that the soul, even if simple, still must have intensive quantity (by the principle called Anticipation of Perception), though it has no extensive quantity, and this may diminish gradually.

Kant thus rejects the *a priori* proof of immortality which was the main object of rational psychology, but he was

[1] B 409.   [2] B 418.   [3] B 413-5.
[4] *Gesammelte Schriften*, 1843, II, p. 151 ff.

nevertheless a strong believer in immortality on moral grounds. "The merely speculative proof has never been able to exercise any influence upon the ordinary reason of men. It so stands upon the point of a hair, that even the schools preserve it from falling only so long as they keep it unceasingly spinning round like a top; even in their own eyes it yields no abiding foundation upon which anything could be built. The proofs which are serviceable for the world at large all preserve their entire value undiminished, and indeed, upon the surrender of these dogmatic pretensions, gain in clearness and in natural force. . . . If we judged according to *analogy with the nature* of living beings in this world, in dealing with which reason must necessarily accept the principle that no organ, no faculty, no impulse, indeed nothing whatsoever is either superfluous or disproportioned to its use, and that therefore nothing is purposeless, but everything exactly conformed to its destiny in life—if we judged by such an analogy we should have to regard man, who alone can contain in himself the final end of all this order, as the only creature that is excepted from it. Man's natural endowments—not merely his talents and the impulses to enjoy them, but above all else the moral law within him—go so far beyond the utility and advantage which he may derive from them in this present life, that he learns thereby to prize the mere consciousness of a righteous will as being, apart from all advantageous consequences, apart even from the shadowy reward of posthumous fame, supreme over all other values; and so feels an inner call to fit himself by his conduct in this world, and by the sacrifice of many of its advantages, for citizenship in a better world upon which he lays hold in idea. This powerful and incontrovertible proof is reinforced by our ever-increasing knowledge of purposiveness in all that we see around us, and by contemplation of the immensity of creation, and therefore also by the consciousness of a certain illimitableness in the possible extension of our knowledge, and of a striving commensurate therewith."[1] I have quoted this passage at length because without having such passages in view we get a very wrong impression of Kant's attitude in the *Paralogisms*, and because it is the passage in this *Critique* which goes furthest towards stating his proof of immortality on moral grounds. It is not that Kant doubted survival, and indeed immortality, but that he doubted the alleged theoretical proofs of it and the claim to comprehend its necessity. His ground for survival was the belief that the moral law set before us an ideal which is not to be attained in this life, and that the moral law being objectively valid could not command a " wild goose-chase," but it is fully developed only in the *Critique of Practical Reason*.[2]

Further even theoretically, as we shall see, Kant thought that the idea of the self as a substance was of great use as a regulative idea.[3]

As for the doctrine that mind is dependent on matter for its existence Kant claims that this has been refuted by his philosophy, for matter is only an appearance, which would be destroyed by the removal of mind.[4] This seems to disagree with his account in the second edition, where he suggested that our mind could not exist without material objects since they are necessary for the determination of time,[5] but there Kant is thinking of the phenomenal self while here he is thinking of the self as thinker.

---

[1] B 424-6.
[2] Bk. II, ch. 2, § 4.
[3] B 700, 711, *v.* below, p. 259.
[4] A 383.
[5] B 418.

Interaction between Body and Mind.[1] The stock objection that body and mind are too unlike to interact is easily overthrown by Kant, not that we need the critical philosophy to overthrow such an argument. Kant says that, if we are talking about the real self and things-in-themselves, we cannot know at all whether they are like or unlike or whether they can or cannot interact. But what about the phenomenal self and the phenomenal body? Do they interact? Kant says that " no one could dream of holding that what he has once come to recognise as mere representation is an outer cause,"[2] and Professor Kemp Smith takes this passage as denying all interaction between mind and body as phenomena on the ground that phenomena have no causal efficacy, being merely representations (*cf.* Berkeley's argument that " ideas " cannot be causes). It is possible, however, that the emphasis may be on " outer " not on " cause." In that case Kant will be saying that phenomena cannot be causes independent of the real mind, being only representations in or for the latter. Certainly it would be quite inconsistent with the rest of his philosophy to deny that phenomena could be causes. After all he had proved the category of cause of, and only of, phenomena. From his own theory one would expect him to say that phenomenal body and phenomenal mind interacted as did other phenomena, but he did not, except in his posthumous work, apply the category of community to the phenomenal self. Yet if it does interact with the body, we should expect the relation to be one of " community," for they are co-existing objects, not successive events. Perhaps the reason why Kant does not apply this category is because the phenomenal self is not a substance and community is interaction between different

[1] A 384-93, B 427-8. [2] A 390.

substances. He also expressly limits the category to interaction *in space* in the second edition.

After the end of this chapter there are, with one slight
exception,[1] no more alterations made in the second edition.
The reason Kant gives for this is both that " time was too
short to allow of further changes " and that he had not
found "among competent and impartial critics any misapprehension in regard to the remaining sections."[2] The
latter quotation should be borne in mind as suggesting both
that Kant thought the rest of the work pretty satisfactory
as it stood and that in cases of doubt a straightforward interpretation is more likely to be correct than a recondite
one.

The Antinomies. This chapter is probably on the whole
early in composition. Apart from the intrinsic interest of the
questions discussed the antinomies have an important place
in Kant's general system of philosophy for the following
reasons. (a) If valid, they prove that space and time cannot
be regarded as real without self-contradiction, thus confirm-
ing the *Æsthetic*. They indeed, if valid, not only corroborate
but extend the argument for the subjectivity of space and
time by showing not merely that we cannot justify our belief
in their independent existence, but that this independent
existence is impossible, since it would lead to self-contradic-
tions. They thus supply something of which the lack has
always been felt by critics of the *Æsthetic* and provide the
only proof that reality cannot possibly be spatial and temporal, as opposed to proofs that we cannot know reality to be
so or justify the belief that reality is so. (b) Kant's solution
claims to show that certain arguments against God and
freedom are invalid and, though also disproving the validity

[1] B 519 n.   [2] *Pref*., B XLI.

of certain arguments for them, at least opens the way for an ethical proof by the distinction between appearance and reality. (c) The chapter is at least intended to illustrate, one might almost say, prove, the impossibility of metaphysics as a science and to throw light on the possibility of metaphysics as a natural disposition.

The arguments for the theses and antitheses of the different antinomies are not regarded by Kant merely as particular fallacies of particular thinkers but as arising inevitably from the nature of the human intellect as such. He compares them to illusions of sense-perception. Just as these persist even after we have learnt not to believe in their objective reality, so he holds we have a strong tendency to accept the arguments of the antinomies as valid even after the most conclusive disproof, so that we cannot rid ourselves of them by a single demonstration but must be ever on our guard against being deceived by these fallacies.[1] The antinomies arise because we have a desire for a unity which we cannot conceive, reason giving us ideas which transcend understanding. The principle on which the thesis is founded always is that the conditioned presupposes all its conditions. Thus the argument in each thesis is in principle :

The conditioned can only arise when its conditions are complete.

If they are infinite they can never be complete.

∴ They cannot be infinite.

The antitheses, on the other hand, do not depend on a general argument about the nature of conditions but on the specific nature of space, time and causality. Neither thesis nor antithesis are proved directly but only by the refutation of the other, which at the "dogmatic" stage of philosophy

[1] B 449-50.

which the antinomies represent is believed to be the only alternative.

Note that it is not the notion of the infinite as such which gives rise to the difficulty, but the notion of a completed infinite. This is why there is no antinomy about future events or about the infinitude of effects (as opposed to causes), for in the case of the future there is no need to suppose that the series ever is completed, since it is not a condition of anything which has already happened.[1] A series might go on for ever, but it could not both go on for ever and yet be completed.

The thesis is declared to be too small for our understanding, the antithesis too large.[2] But elsewhere[3] Kant says that the antinomies arise because a unity which was adequate to reason (the thesis) would be too great for understanding, and a synthesis which was suited to understanding (the antithesis) would be too small for reason. Grounds can be given for both views. The thesis may be called too small for our understanding because understanding always demands further conditions, the antithesis too large because we cannot grasp infinity. The thesis may be called adequate to reason but too great for understanding because it is a completed unity which cannot be realised in terms of understanding; the antithesis is suited to understanding but too small for reason because, though practically valid for science, it never goes far enough to be intellectually satisfying.

First Antinomy: Introductory Comments. " The world " here stands for anything in space and time without restriction, not necessarily for the present stellar system. The truth of the antithesis would be compatible with matter having radically changed its character many times in bygone ages

---

[1] B 436-8.   [2] B 514.   [3] B 450.

provided there had always been something in space and time. It is most important to realise also that both thesis and antithesis assume space and time themselves to be infinite: the question is only whether the things in space and time also are infinite.

Argument of Thesis. The series of events prior to the present is completed (past). ∴ It cannot be infinite. ∴ The world must have a beginning in time.

We can only think the magnitude of the world by a synthesis of its parts. But, if the world were infinite in space, such a synthesis would have taken an infinite time, which we have seen by the above argument to be impossible. ∴ The world is finite in space as well as in time.

Comments. Kant is right in speaking of the series of past events as completed, though the series of events as a whole is not. From a series which has no end we can always abstract another series made by omitting all terms after a certain one, and that second, smaller series will then have an end. E.g. the series $-2, -1, 0, +1, +2$ has an end at $+2$, though the series of whole numbers has no end. So, whatever happens in the future, the series constituted by abstraction of all events prior to 11 a.m. to-day is a series with an end.

The argument about time has been severely criticised on the ground that Kant has committed the puerile fallacy of supposing that because a series of events was completed at one of its termini it must therefore be completed at both. It has been pointed out that in order to be infinite a series need not be infinite on both sides, it is sufficient that it be infinite on one.[1] But I doubt whether Kant's argument can be

---

[1] Even this is of course not necessary to make a series infinite, provided it is "continuous" or has a continuous part.

overthrown so easily. For this difficulty still remains : The events prior to, say, midday yesterday by Greenwich time are undoubtedly completed by now. They are all over, they are past. But if the world has no beginning, those events are infinite in number. Therefore an infinite number of events have been completed, and we have still a case of the completed infinite. The argument on which the thesis is based lies in the apparent self-contradictoriness of this, a difficulty which no philosopher prior to quite modern times has succeeded in solving, if indeed it has been solved now, and not in a mere careless fallacy for which Kant is specially responsible. That the infinity was due to the absence of a beginning and not to the absence of an end would be irrelevant, provided there were really an infinite number of events of any given length which were also all past, i.e. had been gone through, completed. The infinitely numerous past events have happened in succession, and this, *prima facie* at least, is as hard to reconcile with their infinity as if a mind had enumerated them in succession.[1] Only, if valid, the argument would prove not only that the series of events had a beginning but that time itself had one. We may further note that, even if events had an absolute beginning, the difficulty would still arise because time is infinitely divisible, but Kant does not mention this point.

The second part of the thesis, that which argues for the finitude of the world in space, has been criticised on the ground that, whereas the antinomies are supposed to take place at the " dogmatic " level and not to presuppose any of Kant's " critical " doctrines, it in fact assumes the critical doctrine that a physical object which could not be apprehended could not exist. For it argues that, because we cannot carry out an infinite synthesis, the infinite cannot exist.

[1] See p. 240.n.

I am not sure again whether this criticism is valid, for it seems possible to interpret Kant as meaning only that if anything has magnitude it must be at least logically possible for somebody to complete a synthesis of its parts. In that case he would only be assuming that all quantities must be enumerable, an assumption which, whether right or wrong, is certainly extremely natural to the human mind and does constitute a main reason for its objection to infinity, compatible with "dogmatic realism" and quite independent of any assumptions or fallacies peculiar to Kant. We must not expect an anticipation of modern "mathematical logic" in Kant. Unfortunately, however, the principle in question is in conflict with his own doctrine, presupposed by both sides of the antinomies, that space and time are infinite. He also expressly rejected this kind of argument against the infinite in the *Dissertation* of 1770.[1]

Kant's *Observations* on the thesis are very good. He rejects the definition of the infinite as a maximum. To say that a whole is infinite, he says, "does not represent how great it is" but only "its relation to any assignable unit in respect to which it is greater than all number."[2]

Argument of Antithesis. It is assumed that time and space are infinite, and it is contended that if the world is finite it must stand in relation to an empty space and time outside it. That it could begin after a period of empty time is denied on the ground that "no part of such a time possesses, as compared with any other, a distinguishing condition of existence rather than of non-existence." That it could be surrounded by empty space is denied on the ground that a relation to empty space would be a relation to nothing.

Comments. The argument about time might be inter-

[1] § 1 n., *Berl.* II, 388.   [2] B 459-60.

preted in two ways. (a) It might mean that the world could not begin in empty time because owing to the total absence of distinction between the different parts of empty time there would be nothing to determine causally at what point of empty time it began. (b) It might mean that there would be no sense in saying that the world arose in empty time, because this would imply that it arose at some definite point in empty time, and no point would be distinct from any other.

The argument about space assumes that the absolute theory of space is false, thus seeming to contradict the *Æsthetic*. For, if the absolute theory is true, a space outside the world is certainly not " nothing." Kant, however, used arguments of this kind against the absolute theory of space in its realist form even in the *Æsthetic*,[1] but thought that they did not apply to the form in which he held the absolute theory himself. For, he would have said, a pure intuition is something positive, though an empty space independent of mind is not.

Second Antinomy. As both thesis and antithesis in the first antinomy assumed that space and time were infinite, so here both thesis and antithesis assume that space is infinitely divisible.[2]

Argument of Thesis. The argument is that on which Leibniz based his doctrine that reality consisted of monads, except that Leibniz did not regard the monads as being in space, while, if the argument is to fulfil its purpose here in the present context and be contradictory of the antithesis, what is declared to consist of simple parts must be in space. Kant declares that, if all composition were removed in thought, there would either be simple parts left or nothing

[1] B 49, 56.   [2] B 464, 467-8.

at all, therefore there are only two alternatives—either there must be simple parts or all composition cannot be removed in thought; and he refutes the latter by appealing to the accepted notion of substance according to which composition can only be a contingent and not a necessary relation of substances. That all substances should from the nature of the case necessarily be composite would be quite irreconcilable with the at least relative independence ascribed to substance by all metaphysicians of the day.

Comment. That it is difficult to avoid holding that the composite presupposes the simple is clear, *cf.* the tendency to assume "atomic facts," and if space is real and the composite is in space it is difficult to avoid assuming that the simple things of which it is composed are also in space in the sense in which the composite is. (By "simple" is meant not "possessing only one quality" but not "divisible into two or more substances.") Kant admitted that the argument would be valid if bodies were things-in-themselves.[1] Though the self is not mentioned in the thesis, the practical interest of the antinomy for Kant lies largely in the question whether the self is to be regarded as a simple substance and therefore is immortal.[2]

In his *Observation on the Thesis* Kant expressly excludes space and time from the sphere of the argument on the ground that they are not composed of substances and it is in their case impossible to remove all composition in thought.[3] He likewise excludes alteration of the states of substances.[4] This explains why he did not also introduce an argument against the infinite divisibility of events in time. To assert all physical objects to be infinitely divisible is to assert that there are no simple substances in the physical world, to

[1] B 469 *ad fin.*   [2] B 494.   [3] B 466.   [4] B 468.

assert all events to be infinitely divisible is not to split up substances into infinite parts and therefore is not incompatible with the existence of simple substances, for to divide a process of alteration is not to divide into two or more substances the thing of which the states are being altered, at least for Kant. The thesis of the first antinomy is thus based on the metaphysical notion of substance. Had Kant used, as might have been expected, one of Zeno's arguments instead, it would also have covered space, time and change, and this is perhaps why he did not use such an argument. Space is said to differ from matter in that "its parts are possible only in the whole, not the whole through the parts."[1] That is, in the case of matter we apprehend a whole by synthesising its parts, in the case of space we apprehend its parts only as limitations of the whole and not the whole by a synthesis of its parts.

Antithesis. This argues direct from the infinite divisibility of space to the infinite divisibility of the matter which occupies space. It also adds the argument that we can have no evidence in experience for anything absolutely simple on the ground that the mere fact that we do not apprehend complexity in an object cannot prove that it is really absent.

Comments. The antithesis is not of course incompatible with an atomic (or "electronic") theory of matter, for the electron, even if in fact physically indivisible, is spatially divisible. If an electron is one ten-billionth of a centimetre in diameter there is a part of it which is one twenty-billionth, even if the parts cannot, owing to the causal laws which govern the world, be physically separated. But there is a serious gap in Kant's argument, for it is not clear that it is

[1] B 470.

necessary to assume that matter occupies space in the sense of being extended throughout it. Kant himself in 1756[1] tried to reconcile the belief that matter consisted of simple substances with the infinite divisibility of space by suggesting that the occupation of a space by a body did not involve anything more than the possession by that body of a force which excluded all other bodies from that part of space, so it is strange that he does not mention this solution. In the *Metaphysical First Principles of Natural Science* (1786) Kant declares that " the infinite divisibility of matter is very far from being proved through proof of the infinite divisibility of space," but gives a proof by adding to this premiss the additional proposition that each part of matter possesses a power of motion and therefore divisibility.[2]

In his *Observation on the Antithesis* Kant rejects the attempt to solve the problem by distinguishing physical points from mathematical points and claiming that the former can make up space though the latter could not. He retorts that mathematics (or at least the part of it in question) is itself based on the nature of space and must therefore apply to all that is in space. One might have thought that Kant would have had more sympathy with Leibniz's attempt to solve the problem by denying that the monads are really in space, but Kant says it is not to the point here since we are talking about bodies and bodies are appearances.[3] In this he is formally in the right since the thesis is asserted of " composite substances in the world," and certainly an argument of this kind was sometimes used to support the view that objects in space are divisible into simple parts.

[1] *Monadologia Physica, Berl.* I, 480 ff.
[2] *Haupst.* 2, *Lehrsatz* 4, Anm. 1, *v.* Anm. 2.
[3] B 469.

Only, while no names are given, people naturally suppose that Kant is discussing the argument of Leibniz, and that is an argument not to the effect that there are simple substances in space but that there are simple substances which appear to be but are not really in space.

Third Antinomy. This is not primarily a discussion of freedom but of the first cause argument. Its bearing on human freedom consists in the fact that, if the thesis is true, this proves the actuality of some freedom, that of God, and therefore at any rate makes it possible that we too should be free, while, if the antithesis is true, this proves all freedom impossible.[1] The arguments on the two sides are too straightforward for a summary to be required, but there are two comments to make. In the first place the same principle, causality, is used as a basis both of the thesis and of the antithesis. The explanation of this is that it has two different aspects, one of which supports or at least suggests the thesis, while the other proves the antithesis. If the cause is viewed as explaining or giving the reason of the effect, then this suggests that there must be something which is its own cause, otherwise causation gives no ultimate explanation or reason at all, just as it would be futile to give a chain of reasons for accepting a proposition if none of them could, any more than the original proposition, be seen to be true in their own right. But causality, even if it is a principle of explanation at all, is not only that, it is a principle of explanation *by preceding events*, hence the antithesis. Secondly, we should note that the thesis, as in the other antinomies, is based on the impossibility of a completed infinite, for the argument is that any event pre-

[1] For my comments on Kant's account of human freedom *v.* below, p. 227 ff.

supposes for its occurrence the fulfilment of all its causal conditions and the number of these is infinite.

Fourth Antinomy. The principal arguments on both sides are the same as in the third antinomy, but the thesis adds an argument that the unconditioned necessary being asserted must itself be in the time-series on the ground that, since it is a cause, it must precede its effect temporally, and explicitly leaves open the possibility that the necessary being may be the time-series as a whole.[1]

The antithesis replies that no member of the time-series can be absolutely necessary without violating the principle of causality, and that the series as a whole cannot be if no member is so. It also contains an argument that there can be no necessary cause of the world outside the time-series, on the ground that the causality of such a being would be in time, since it starts events, but if its causality was it itself would be so.

In the *Observation* on the Thesis Kant points out a confusion often committed concerning contingency. Empirical contingency, meaning "dependence on empirical causes," is not the same as intelligible contingency, which belongs to anything the contradictory opposite of which is possible *per se.* Now the fact that not-A follows A does not prove, Kant points out, that A is contingent in the intelligible sense, for it does not prove the existence of A at the time when it did exist not to be necessary. All it proves is that the existence of A at all times is not necessary. This digression seems to be intended to refute the argument that change shows all empirical things to be contingent and therefore to presuppose a necessary being other than themselves by replying that for anything we can prove

[1] *v.* B 484-6.

they may be themselves necessary and thus not require a necessary being beyond themselves to explain why they are what they are.

In the *Observation on the Antithesis* Kant remarks on the circumstance, characteristic also of the third antinomy, that both thesis and antithesis are founded on the very same principle. The explanation he gives of this is that the principle—the whole of past time includes the series of all conditions—is viewed from two different points of view. The thesis contends that *all* the conditions cannot be present in this series unless there is an unconditioned; the antithesis contends that because of this principle everything in time must find its conditions in the past and not in itself as a necessary being or *causa sui*. Note that both sides discuss the question of the presence of a necessary being *in* the sensible world and dismiss the postulate that there is such a being outside the world as useless for meeting the present difficulties. For the purpose of the whole discussion it is assumed that the notion of a necessary being really has sense for us, a view which Kant rejects in his treatment of the cosmological argument.

Section 3. This important section brings out what is for Kant the chief motive in his doctrine of antinomy, i.e. the practical importance of settling the questions at stake.

Section 4. Kant claims, as elsewhere, certainty for his philosophy.[1] Reason must be able to answer all its own questions since " the object is not to be met with outside its concept," though he adds that one species of answer consists in saying that the question is an improper one and can have no answer.[2] Kant, strange to say, ascribes the like certainty and ability to answer all questions to ethics,[3] for

---

[1] *v.* above, pp. 14-5.   [2] B 507 n.   [3] B 505 *ad fin*.

the same reason, though he adds the argument that if we did not *know* what we ought to do we could not be under an obligation to do it.[1] But he differentiates the cosmological questions from the others of the *Dialectic* on the ground that here alone we are dealing with phenomena and can therefore give a positive answer and not merely an answer to the effect that the question is " itself nothing."[2]

Section 5. For the contention that the antinomies arise because one side is too large and the other too small for the concept of the understanding, *v.* above p. 210.

Section 6. Professor Kemp Smith has drawn attention to the " subjectivist" character of this section, though it is combined with a protest against " empirical " or " material " idealism. B 521 and B 524 are among the few passages which explicitly assert that to talk about physical objects existing unperceived is merely to say that under certain conditions we should perceive them, but, as I have pointed out, this doctrine is not necessarily incompatible even with the *Second Edition Refutation of Idealism.*

Section 7. The first few paragraphs of this section constitute the most important part of the whole chapter, providing as they do the foundation of the solution of all the antinomies. All four antinomies Kant rightly declares to rest on the premiss :—" If the conditioned is given, the entire series of all its conditions is likewise given." This premiss, he holds, would be valid if objects in space and events in time were things-in-themselves, but as they are appearances we must substitute—" If the conditioned is given, a regress in the series of all its conditions is set us as a task (*aufgegeben*)."[3] The reason for this substitution is that phenomena are only

[1] B 504 *ad fin.*　　[2] B 507.　　[3] B 525-9.

objects of actual or possible experience. It is clear that an infinite number of objects cannot be actually experienced, therefore all but a finite number of the infinite series of conditions would in any case have only a potential existence. Consequently, while an infinite series of real things would present insuperable difficulties, an infinite series of phenomena need not, because the assertion of such a series does not imply that there ever existed or have existed an infinite number of actual entities, it does not imply a completed infinite. The existence of the infinite in a potential sense, which is all that is now involved, is innocuous since it simply means that we can go on without limit, not of course in fact, since we are prevented by particular causal laws, but as far as the spatial and temporal character of the world and the nature of causality as such are concerned, and that, however far we go, we can never experience an absolute end of phenomena in space etc.

That we can go on indefinitely does not imply that we ever actually have an infinite number of phenomena any more than the fact that we can go on counting indefinitely implies that we can ever count an infinite number. This to Kant's mind gives his position a great advantage over realism. If realism were true and physical objects and space itself therefore existed independently of being perceived, then if the physical world were infinite at all every part of the infinite whole would be literally there at once and we should have an actual and not merely a potential infinite.

Kant adds that the thesis and antithesis appear to be contradictories but are not really so, for though they cannot both be true they may both be false. There is in each case a third alternative, namely, that the world is not in space or time at all.[1] If we do not admit this possibility, Kant says, the proofs on each side of the antithesis are well-grounded and there is an insoluble contradiction. Consequently this provides a new argument for the view that the world is merely appearance.[2]

[Since phenomena are on Kant's view only infinite in a potential sense, the series of *actual* phenomena is always *finite*. Now space and time are still held by Kant to be infinite and infinitely divisible. Therefore it may seem that the arguments of the antithesis from the infinitude of space and time and the infinite divisibility of space to the infinitude of phenomena are still valid against Kant's own solution, since he in effect makes phenomena finite. He calls them infinite and then explains that they are only infinite in a potential sense and not actually infinite; but what is infinite only potentially is actually finite. Whether this objection is valid or not depends on whether Kant regarded space and time as themselves infinite and infinitely divisible in an actual or only in a potential sense. In the latter case the arguments which he uses in the first and second antitheses would no longer apply against his solution. For then, e.g., space would only be infinitely divisible in the sense that it was always theoretically possible to experience a smaller space than any yet experienced, i.e. in the same sense as that in which phenomena are infinitely divisible.

But the solution at least of the first antinomy about time would still be extremely difficult, since it seems to imply that the past only exists in the mind of a person at the present making a regress to it, a view which is still more difficult than the corresponding view about physical things.

[1] B 530-3.   [2] B 534.

To say that the past only existed in our regress to it would be to say that past events only existed as representations in the mind of somebody who looked back upon them in the present; in other words, that there was no past at all, not even past representations, for the representations in his mind would be present. But this is clearly not what Kant really believes.

This brings one to a more general objection. Kant maintained that we could have no knowledge of reality, but that we could have real knowledge of appearances, meaning by appearances what we experience under given conditions. But if so we surely know something real in time, namely, our experiences, and time must therefore be accepted as real. To say that something is an appearance is at least to say that we can really experience it. It is essential to Kant's philosophy to maintain both that we can have real knowledge of appearances and that we can have it *only* of appearances, but the two positions are incompatible. For what is from one point of view an appearance as only "our representation" is *per se* a reality equally with the physical objects of the realist, for even mere representations are real.]

Section 8. Distinction between *regressus in infinitum* and *regressus in indefinitum*. The former is said to occur where the whole is given in empirical intuition and we make a regress to its parts, i.e. in the second antinomy; the latter where a member only of the series is given from which the regress proceeds to other members, i.e. in the first, third and fourth antinomies. The distinction depends on the supposition that in the former case, as the part must be present in the whole, all the infinity is in some sense present already in our starting-point, while in the latter it need not be present in it but is only implied by it. But, since Kant did not believe that the infinite parts of a spatial object actually exist, any more than all the infinite number of unperceived spatial objects, it is difficult to see the point of the distinction.

Section 9. B 543-6 is very important as setting out the general principles of the solution, Kant's application of it to the particular antinomies somewhat less so. In applying it Kant works out the distinction of the previous section between a *regressus in indefinitum* and a *regressus in infinitum* with unnecessary elaboration. Note that the argument of the thesis of the second antinomy is now met by the reply that, while it would contradict the notion of a thing-in-itself as substance that it should be impossible " to remove in thought all composition," it does not contradict the notion of a phenomenal substance,[1] to which we have no ground for attributing the independence of relations such as composition that was always attributed by metaphysicians to real substance.

Kant then proceeds to make a distinction between the first two, which he calls mathematical, and the last two, which he calls dynamical antinomies.[2] The chief importance of this distinction lies in the fact that, while with the first two antinomies he contends that both thesis and antithesis are false, with the last two he contends that they may both be true, the antithesis of appearances and the thesis of things-in-themselves. This is possible because, while in respect of the properties with which the first and second antinomies are concerned the conditions are homogeneous, every part of space and time being quâ space and time like any other, in respect of the properties with which

[1] B 553.   [2] B 556-60.

the third and fourth antinomies are concerned they may be heterogeneous, since the cause may be different in kind from the effect. Consequently, while in the first two antinomies all the conditions must be phenomenal if the conditioned is, in the third and fourth some may be noumenal.

[It has been suggested that Kant could have equally well said that the thesis and antithesis of the mathematical antinomies might both be true, but this could only have been done in the case of the first antinomy if he had interpreted the thesis in a Pickwickian sense as being not an assertion about magnitude in space and time but an assertion that reality is a completed whole. With the second, since the thesis as stated is not an argument directly concerning space and time, it would have been easier.

Certainly each one of the antitheses might consistently with Kant's philosophy be true of appearances because an assertion of the infinity of appearances is not an assertion that there actually are an infinite number. But we cannot say that we know them to be true of appearances, for we cannot know that the nature of noumena is such as always to supply a manifold out of which we can construct appearances, however far we go in our regress. It is not clear that this last point was realised by Kant.]

Solution of Third and Fourth Antinomies. Kant reasonably takes the view that the world as appearance might include no events which are not inferable according to causal laws from earlier appearances and yet be based on a necessary being as a ground of the whole, this ground being itself not subject to phenomenal causation. (The difficulty involved in this application of the unschematised category of cause to things-in-themselves I have already discussed.)[1] Kant insists that he has not proved that there is such a necessary being or even that such a being is really possible, but only that it cannot be refuted by the argument of the antithesis.[2] In fact he criticises the notion of a necessary being very sharply in dealing with the cosmological proof, but he would still no doubt believe that the thesis contained this much of truth, (a) there was a reality related to us by some kind of non-phenomenal causation, (b) this reality could be least inadequately thought by us in the terms which theologians commonly applied to God, (at least if we except the notion of unconditional necessity which Kant was inclined to dismiss as meaningless).

Treatment of Freedom. Kant was quite convinced both that all events in time were completely determined by natural causality, and that consequently, if phenomena were things-in-themselves, there would be no room for freedom and so for moral responsibility.[3] That natural causality was universal he regarded as proved in the *Analytic*, and there is nowhere in his treatment of freedom the least hint that this proof does not apply to the phenomenal self. If the self in time were not completely determined by natural causes his whole elaborate solution would in fact be quite unnecessary. Nor does he ever in dealing with freedom distinguish between different kinds of causation in the phenomenal world. In the *Critique of Judgment* he maintains the view that besides mechanical causation there is another kind of causation even in phenomena, namely, that which accounted for the peculiar properties and behaviour of organisms, but he does not use such a distinction to help him to deal with the problem of freedom. At the time

[1] *v.* above, pp. 187-90.   [2] B 590.   [3] e.g. B 564.

when he wrote the works which discuss freedom he apparently had not yet come to this conclusion, and so does not draw any distinction within the phenomenal world between mechanical and non-mechanical causation. This remark applies to his ethical works as well as to the *Critique of Pure Reason*. He does indeed solve the problem by a distinction between different kinds of causation, but not between different kinds of causation within the world of phenomena.

Now the difficulty for Kant is not that freedom cannot be reconciled with determination by causes, but that it cannot be reconciled with determination by *previous* causes. This is most clearly expressed in *Religion within the Bounds of Mere Reason*, where Kant blames people who " by the use of the word determinism (the principle that the will is determined through internal sufficient reasons) create an illusion, as if the difficulty lay in reconciling this principle with freedom, which nobody supposes; the difficulty, on the contrary, is how *predeterminism*, according to which voluntary actions as events have their determining grounds *in the preceding time* (which with whatever it contains is no longer in our power) can be consistent with freedom, according to which the action as well as its contradictory must be at the moment it happens in the power of the subject: this it is which we want to understand and never shall."[1] What is the precise difficulty that makes freedom irreconcilable with exclusive determination by the past? To write the argument out formally, it is this: If natural causation is universal, my present acts are always determined entirely by the past, even if it be my own past. The past is not in my power now.

[1] *Berl.* VI, p. 49 n.; Abbott, *Kant's Theory of Ethics*, p. 358 n.

∴ I am not free now.[1]

The same argument can of course be applied to the acts in the past which determine my present acts, and so on *ad infinitum* or to the origin of my life. But suppose my acts were determined, but not determined by past events, this difficulty would disappear. I should be determined, but free in so far as I was determined by myself, provided it was not only by my *past* self. Hence Kant could think that the difficulty was removed if he made the causation involved timeless. For he was not, I believe, an indeterminist.[2] He held, I think, that free acts are all determined, but determined by a causality different in kind from that which determines them as phenomenal events. The nature of this causation we cannot grasp, but at any rate we know this negative point, that it is not a causation by past events. For it is a causation by the real self, and past events are only phenomena. Hence it is not open to the main objection which leads to the conflict between freedom and natural causality. Kant had one advantage over others who have sought to solve the conflict between freedom and causality by a distinction between different kinds of causality, he was exonerated from attempting to give a clear account of the distinction, since it followed necessarily from the fundamental principles of his general philosophy that, if this noumenal causality was a fact, no clear account could be given of it, at least by human beings. And he could argue that, since the conflict between freedom and causation

---

[1] *Critique of Practical Reason* (*Berl.* V, 95; Abbott, p. 188). This particular argument does not occur in the *Critique of Pure Reason*, but his whole account of the solution there shows that it was not determination but determination by past events which he holds to be inconsistent with freedom.

[2] *v.* beginning of passage from *Religion* . . . , quoted above.

arose because of the temporal character of causation as being determination by *past* events, the only logical way out was to make the causation involved in freedom non-temporal in character, even if we could not form any positive idea of what such causation was like, and that this solution was confirmed by the way in which it fitted into the rest of his philosophy.

The assertion of a noumenal freedom Kant combined with the doctrine that our actions are completely determined by natural causality quâ phenomena. That the self can be subject to this peculiar dual causality is a difficult doctrine, and from the nature of the case cannot be made clear, but Kant would say it is sufficient justification for it that it can be seen to be the only way of removing the contradiction between ethics and universal causality in nature. Two analogies—for which I have the responsibility, not Kant—may perhaps help us a little. They are not of course perfect, but no analogy could possibly be so, for all analogies must be in time and the real self is timeless according to Kant.

First, imagine a being in the situation of one of Plato's prisoners in the Cave, tied to his chair so that he cannot get up or turn his head, and imagine that he can see in front of him a looking-glass. Now suppose there are a number of men engaged in work, say, using the cave as a factory, in such a position that the prisoner cannot see them but can see their reflections in the looking-glass. We may suppose also that he is a being from another planet who has never seen men and knows nothing about their psychology or the reasons why they work in factories. Now as they work he sees their reflections moving on the glass, but thinks that those reflections are the real things. If the work was

regular manual labour he could still make generalisations
about the movements of the shapes on the glass and arrive
at a sort of science of them from which he could make predictions that usually came off, e.g. that every seventh day
they would not appear, and that when they appeared they
would perform certain further describable movements for a
period of eight hours and then disappear. Yet he would
not have the least idea of the real causes governing the
movements. This is like our position as regards phenomena,
especially if it is held that phenomenal causation according
to Kant is little more than regular sequence. It is a not
unintelligible view, and it agrees with the generally assumed
fact that we can never see why phenomena happen, only
that they happen. There is no contradiction whatever in
the appearance of B being determined by the appearance of
A in the sense that it can be inferred from the latter
according to laws capable of inductive establishment and
yet being also determined in another sense by real B itself,
as the reflections in the mirror could be inferred from previous reflections, and yet were caused in quite another
sense, not by the previous reflections, but by the beings of
which they themselves were the reflections.

My second analogy is this. I carry out some important
business which includes posting a letter. I (1) go to the
pillar-box, and (2) put the letter in. Now the second act
follows necessarily on the first in the context of my purpose,
yet this does not make it unfree, because it is not really
determined by the first but rather by my whole purpose
which determines both first and second. A purpose may
manifest itself equally in each of a whole series of temporal
steps, and, if they are each an expression of the purpose
voluntarily embraced, they may be said to be equally free.

Strictly speaking, purposes are not out of time, but even on a non-Kantian view we must admit that a purpose may determine equally each of a whole series of temporally successive events. There is no question of its being manifested more in the earlier than in the later members, it is present equally in all. The laws actually follow from the freedom. If I go to a pillar-box with a letter, my purposes determine a law according to which my act of putting the letter in follows, but this does not imply that I cannot help putting it in at the time. On the contrary it is just because I am free that I do put it in. Similarly the succession of reflection B on reflection A in the looking-glass might be ultimately determined, not at all by reflection A itself, but by the free purpose of the man who made the whole movement each part of which equally expressed his freedom; and yet it will, just because the man has a purpose, follow a regular order. Thus Kant points out that free acts, being rational, will proceed according to fixed principles, and that therefore for that very reason the appearances of them will follow laws of regular sequence. So it actually follows from our freedom as noumena that these phenomena will be determined, and does not contradict it.

Kant holds that this view is further supported by the fact that freedom in a negative sense follows even from the *Critique of Pure Reason*, and this for two reasons. (a) The real self is not in time, and therefore cannot be determined by past events. (b) Phenomenal causation only exists for the self which synthesises the phenomena according to the category of causality, and it would therefore be committing a vicious circle to suppose that the real self can itself be determined by this causality. And Kant argues in his ethical works that you can only make this negative conception of freedom in the least intelligible by adding the positive conception of determination by the moral law. In the *Critique of Pure Reason*, on the other hand, he is more inclined to insist on the opposed though complementary point of view that we cannot positively expand our *theoretical* knowledge of this freedom as a result of ethics. We have a positive conception of the moral law, i.e. of what we ought to do, and we know that we can fulfil the law, but how we do it and how such a non-phenomenal entity can influence our action is a mystery to Kant. Presumably, whether I shall lie or not on a particular occasion when I am tempted to lie could be inferred both from past phenomena and from the nature of my real self; but, while we have a knowledge of the kind of data and psychological laws that might help in the former case, we have none in the latter. Likewise Kant admits that we have none but the vaguest idea of what non-temporal causation could be like; and he adds that the very notion that purely intellectual considerations could cause emotion and action is to us utterly incomprehensible.[1]

In his ethical works Kant identifies free action and moral action. The argument for their identification (which is only intelligible to those who know something of Kant's ethics) may be put in the following form:

Free action is action undetermined by empirical conditions.

[1] I think Kant was mistaken in thinking this especially incomprehensible. Why is it more incomprehensible that a man should desire to produce what has the particular property of obligatoriness than what has the particular property of being pleasant to his son or harmful to an enemy? But, strange to say, Kant assumed a hedonistic psychology as regards all actions except those dictated by the moral law.

But if you take away all empirical conditions the only thing left to determine action is the bare form of the law.

∴ The only action undetermined by empirical conditions is action determined by the form of the law.

But action determined by the form of the law is, according to Kant's fundamental ethical principles, moral action. Therefore all free action is moral action, just as all moral action is free.[1]

Or, to put the argument in a rather more plausible way :

Free action is action by the will acording to its own laws (autonomy).

But its own laws can only be laws that it could will to be universalised (they must be laws which it could will, otherwise they would not be its own; they must be universal, otherwise they would not be laws).

But the only laws that we can will to be universalised are, according to the fundamental principles of Kant's ethics, the moral laws.

∴ Free action is action according to moral laws.[2]

It is impossible for me here to discuss the merits or demerits of Kant's conception of ethics as *a priori* on which this argument depends, but I shall just say a word to remove a common misapprehension of students on the subject. There is no need to suppose that Kant meant that empirical facts should never be considered at all in deciding what is right. According to Kant we must consider consequences, but only up to a point. We obviously must consider, e.g., the effect of our truthful words on the state of mind of the

[1] *Critique of Practical Reason*, Pt. I, Bk. I, ch. 1, § 6, Abbott, p. 117.

[2] This form of the argument is suggested by *The Fundamental Principles of the Metaphysics of Morals*, Sect. 3, 2nd paragraph, Abbott, p. 65.

person to whom we speak them so far as to determine whether they really will make the truth clear to him, but not so far as to determine whether it would give him and others more pleasure to tell a lie. What we must not do according to Kant is base the general principle forbidding us to tell lies on empirical grounds such as the bad consequences of lying or, still less, make exceptions to the law in particular cases on the ground that to tell a lie in this or that special case will produce more good than evil. With two of the categorical imperatives Kant gives—develop our talents, and help those in need—it is still more obvious that if they are to be carried out effectively much empirical knowledge is necessary. It is only the general law and not its particular applications which according to Kant can be seen to be independent of consequences and *a priori*. If we take a universal law as our major premiss it is clear that empirical knowledge is needed both to give the minor premiss, *this is an instance of the law*, and to discover the best means of carrying out the law.[1]

The conclusion that free action is always moral raises great difficulties about immoral action. Kant thought freedom to be implied by ethics largely because we should otherwise not be responsible if we did wrong, but, if all free action is moral action, how can we be responsible for immoral acts, since they are not free? Kant suggests that immoral action consists, not in the noumenal self acting, but in the noumenal self neglecting to act and thus letting phenomenal causes take their course so that the action is determined by desire, this being the only alternative to determination by the moral law. This solution is difficult to understand: it amounts to saying that morally right

[1] *v.* my article in *Philosophy*, vol. XIII, no. 49, p. 40 ff.

actions are determined by noumenal, morally wrong actions by phenomenal causes, but surely from Kant's philosophy it would follow that all actions, right or wrong, must be determined by phenomenal causes in the only sense in which in his view phenomenal causes can determine and likewise by noumenal causes in the only sense in which noumenal causes can determine. For the principle of causality (phenomenal) is certainly held to be universal among phenomena, and also all phenomena are certainly held to be appearances of noumena and therefore determined by the latter. Perhaps Kant meant that the noumenal causes of my wrong actions are to be found not in myself but in other noumena, i.e. the real counterparts of the phenomenal objects I desire. But if the noumenal self has no sensible side and no desires, why should it ever neglect to do the right thing? Is not neglect to do the right thing as much an action as doing the wrong? Kant excuses himself by saying that the occurrence of evil is in any case unintelligible, but that is no excuse for making it more unintelligible than need be.

It is not, however, absolutely necessary to the main part of Kant's account of freedom to identify free action with moral action, only he would have had to assign to the noumenal self not only reason but desires, or some noumenal counterpart of desires, which could lead to wrong actions, so that action according to the moral law would not be the only alternative to determination merely by phenomena. If there are timeless existences there are timeless factual conditions, though we cannot know what they are, and actions might be determined by these and not only by *a priori* laws. But in that case the real motive of immoral acts is always altogether unknown, which detracts from their immorality.

Other difficulties about Kant's account of freedom are as follows :

1. It is sometimes objected that, since all events in time are only appearances, they must all, including events in inanimate matter and such events in organisms as reflex acts, be equally caused by noumena and so be all free acts. To this Kant would presumably answer that, while it is not impossible, for anything we can see, that even inorganic matter may be but the appearance of selves capable of moral action, we need not assume only one kind of noumenal cause, i.e. the kind manifested in free choices. What we have to assume is (a), on theoretical grounds, that all appearances are determined by some kind of noumenal cause; (b) that, since we are conscious of obligations and the ability to fulfil them, this implies that in some cases there is noumenal causation of the voluntary kind. There may be other species of noumenal causation or at least of noumenal causes, but we have some idea only of this one.

2. It is objected that any hypothesis which involves the unreality of time, so far from saving ethics, must destroy it, for our actions can only affect the future and therefore, if the future is not real, we cannot do any good, whatever we do.[1] But Kant could answer that, since our real self is timeless, something may be dependent on its will and yet not be future, only appear so. In that case some good may exist (timelessly) that would not have existed but for our act of will, and then we shall have done good by our action.[2]

3. Kant holds that all phenomena can be inferred from

[1] Moore, *Principia Ethica*, pp. 115-6.
[2] Kant would, however, state his ethics in terms of right and duty rather than in terms of good, unlike Professor Moore.

previous phenomena, so that my whole life is predictable from what happened before my birth. Now he had explained how I might be free even though all events in my life could be predicted from earlier events in my life, but it is not at all clear how I could be free if they were predictable entirely from events not in my life. How could all phenomenal events due to my noumenal self be inferred from the appearances of other noumena if my real self was not made by these noumena? Kant would have to reply that there was a sort of harmony between noumena so that in whatever series in time noumenon A produced phenomena a, b, noumenon B would later produce phenomena y, z. It would not be a strange coincidence that all the noumena which appeared to human beings were in such harmony that we could infer phenomena of one from phenomena of others, because those which did not stand in this harmony could not produce appearances for human beings, as all our appearances must fit into a causal system if they are to be objects of experience. This need not mean that A compelled B; it may mean simply that they were of such a character that they both spontaneously acted in that way. The regular sequence would then be due not to any connection between them, but to the fixed laws, which the actions of each followed independently of the other. Or it might be *partly* explained by noumenal causal interaction of A and B, though it could not be explained wholly by this unless we assumed that A created B or vice versa, which would interfere with the freedom of the created being. My noumenal self would be in existence eternally, but, unless phenomenal pre-existence is a fact, it would not produce any phenomena which appeared in time earlier than the marriage of my parents, a circumstance that would be quite compatible with its not being brought into existence by my parents.

4. But this explanation will not save Kant's solution from an analogous difficulty about God. For he does suppose that God created us. Kant in the *Critique of Practical Reason*[1] says that the difficulty is fatal to any view except his own, but is removed by his view, though he admits that even his solution "involves great difficulty in itself, and is scarcely susceptible of a lucid exposition." The solution is that God, not being in time, created us not as appearances but as things-in-themselves. He is therefore as creator not the cause of our actions in the world of sense, which are appearances. But this solution is incomprehensible to me. For (a) it is according to Kant not our actions in the world of sense which are held to be free, but their noumenal counterparts; (b) if God creates us quâ noumena, and we quâ noumena determine our appearances, it still remains the case that these appearances are indirectly determined by God. The difficulty with which we are faced is not the difficulty of reconciling our freedom with causal determination by the past, which Kant might claim to have removed, but the difficulty of reconciling it with total determination of ourselves by another being.

5. I find it difficult to see how I could be free in doing A without knowing that I willed A, but, if I do know this, the willing of A should be a phenomenon according to the philosophy of Kant. If I know that I will it I know that I will it *now* (in time), and this knowledge seems as definite as any psychological knowledge—not just the vague analogical thinking which is all Kant admits we can have in regard to noumena. Kant might well have said that acts of

[1] *Berl.* V, pp. 101-3; Abbott, pp. 194-7.

will or choice in time are all phenomenal counterparts of real noumenal acts and therefore what I know is a phenomenal willing which corresponds to my noumenal willing; but this alternative is not adopted till the posthumous work. Elsewhere Kant seems rather to hold the view that acts of will are just noumena without corresponding phenomena, except for the images and non-moral desires that accompany these acts. Perhaps he would have said that, when I know that I will A, I know that there is a noumenal act of will connected with A, but can only define it further in phenomenal terms

---

[1] While I still feel a difficulty about supposing the world to have had no beginning, I think I was misled here by the argument that an infinite series cannot be enumerated. Certainly the enumeration could not be completed once begun, but the supposition just is that the infinite series never began. (3rd ed.) (See p. 212.)

CHAPTER VII

THEOLOGY AND THE IDEAS OF REASON

WE shall deal first with Kant's criticism of the proofs of God, and then with his general treatment of the Ideas of Reason.

Ontological Proof (§ 4).[1] This may be summarised as follows :

1. God, by definition, = the sum of all positive attributes. [This is the usual expression, but it would be more correct to say " the substance qualified by all positive attributes."] The term, positive, makes it possible to exclude evil attributes on the ground that these are only negative, if one takes this view of evil.

2. Existence is a positive attribute.

3. Therefore God exists.

The only unfortunate feature of Kant's refutation of the argument is his illustration of a hundred dollars, which is somewhat misleading. It is clear that, however a sum of a hundred dollars be defined, it would not be defined as including all the positive attributes there are, and therefore the argument given would not apply to it even if it applied to God. No supporter of the ontological proof would claim that the existence of anything else save God alone followed from its idea. In general Kant meets the argument by denying the second premiss and thus laying down a logical principle which is of great importance and is admitted by most modern logicians. It would, however, be wrong to

[1] For § 2, *v.* below, p. 254.

ascribe originality to Kant in this : he had been anticipated by several writers.

Kant also introduces into the discussion a criticism of the whole notion of a necessary being, which he had hitherto in the *Dialectic*· taken for granted as possible, though not proved. A necessary being is a being whose existence is logically necessary *per se* so that it could not be denied without self-contradiction. (No metaphysician would have called us necessary beings on the ground that God was necessary and our existence followed necessarily from God's, so the necessity must be regarded as unconditional, a necessary being was one necessary in its own right.) Kant attributes the concept to a confusion with necessary judgments. To say that a judgment is unconditionally necessary is not to say that either the subject or predicate is so. The predicate is only conditionally necessary, i.e. conditionally on the subject, for if the subject were removed the predicate could also be removed.[1] But he does not mean that we ought to deny the existence of a necessary being, only that we cannot form any conception of such a being.[2]

The Cosmological Proof (§ 5). This is sometimes called the First Cause Argument. It again involves the notion of a necessary being, but it differs from the ontological proof in starting, not from the idea of such a being, but from experience, and from the Physico-Theological proof in starting, not from the specific nature of certain experiences, but from the mere fact that there is some experience. As summarised by Kant the argument is : "If anything exists, an absolutely necessary being must also exist. Now I, at least, exist. Therefore an absolutely necessary being exists."[3]

The cosmological proof, Kant contends, covertly presup-

[1] B 622.   [2] *v.* B 820 *ad fin.*   [3] B 632.

poses the ontological proof and is therefore wrecked by the failure of the latter. For without the ontological proof, even if we could prove the existence of a necessary being, we should have no means of determining its nature. It is only if we already know by the ontological proof that a perfect being must be a necessary being and assume that no other being can be necessary that we have by the cosmological proof established the existence of God in the sense of a perfect being, but if we have already accepted the ontological proof the cosmological proof is superfluous. No doubt one might, while denying the ontological proof, hold the cosmological proof to be valid so far as to prove the existence of a necessary being. One would then be contending that there was a necessary being, but denying our ability to see how any being of which we might form an idea could be necessary. However, Kant's point is here, not that we could not hold the cosmological argument to prove the existence of a necessary being without the ontological argument, but that without the ontological argument we could not form any idea of what the necessary being was like and therefore would have no ground for describing it as God. Kant had also argued in the previous section, which probably belongs to an earlier period, that, if we admit the possibility of a necessary being at all, we cannot deny the possibility of any being whatever, however limited, being absolutely necessary, for our inability to see its necessity does not prove it not to be necessary.[1]

Kant further objects to the very conception of a necessary being, though in his treatment of the antinomies and in § 2 and 3 of the present chapter he had spoken as if he assumed it to be possible. But he admits even now that we are " con-

[1] B 616.

strained to think something necessary as a condition of existing things,"[1] and meets the difficulty by declaring it to be a regulative principle.[2] He gives a list of other fallacies committed by the cosmological argument, of which the chief is its employment of causation in an unjustified fashion beyond the realm of possible experience.[3]

The Physico-Theological Proof (§ 6), commonly called the Argument from Design. Kant's main criticism is that, if this argument is to be used to establish the kind of God the theologians want, the ontological argument is again pre-supposed.[3] For at the best the argument from design could only establish a very good, very powerful, very wise God, not a perfect and omnipotent God. Nor does it even establish the conclusion that God created the world and did not merely impose form on a pre-existing matter.[4] In order to prove more the argument from design must be supplemented by the cosmological argument, and this, as we have seen, cannot establish its conclusion without presupposing the ontological argument.[5] The existence of God is thus left to be proved, together with our immortality, by a moral argument. The moral proof of God and immortality on which Kant relies is not given in the *Critique of Pure Reason* but in the *Critique of Practical Reason*.[6]

Kant nevertheless thought very highly of the argument from design. While the two previous arguments are dismissed as of no value, this one comes for Kant practically near being sufficient to justify belief in God, though inferior to the moral argument on which that belief should primarily depend. The *Critique of Judgment* weakens the belief in one respect, strengthens it in another. It weakens it because

---

[1] B 644.   [2] *v.* below, p. 254 n.   [3] B 637-8.   [4] B 655.
[5] B 657.   [6] Bk. II, ch. 2, § 4-5; Abbott, p. 218 ff.

it shows the great difference between the purposive causation we find in animals' bodies and that involved in design by an outside agent in human art, the analogy on which the design in nature has to be conceived by us; it strengthens it because it insists that the conception of design is necessary for biology, since we must always ask for what purpose any part of an organism exists and therefore assume, at least as a regulative principle, that everything in it has a purpose, and that this cannot be separated by us from the notion of a mind having designed the whole universe, though again that is only regulative.   But I must now explain what regulative principles are and give a list of them.

The Ideas of Reason (*Regulative Principles*).   The account of these is to be found mainly in the *Appendix to the Transcendental Dialectic*.   I shall not attempt to follow the order of the text in my comments.   Kant's theory of the Ideas is extremely important and holds the balance very finely between dogmatism and scepticism.   The analogies had been distinguished earlier from the mathematical categories as being only regulative,[1] but the word is now used in a different sense in which none of the categories are regulative. In fact the difference between categories and ideas is just that the former are constitutive and the latter regulative. Regulative differ from constitutive principles in being primarily of practical (regulating) utility.   Further the categories assert the minimum of unity necessary for experience and therefore can be proved theoretically : the ideas assert more and therefore cannot.   Metaphysics as a natural disposition is explained by our mistakenly taking regulative ideas as constitutive.   But I cannot explain the distinction further without making another one and dividing regulative ideas

[1] B 222.

into two classes, which had better be treated separately as they are regulative in different senses.

The first class is constituted by the metaphysical ideas of God, freedom and immortality. These are really held by Kant to be proved, but are called regulative partly because they are not proved in a way which satisfies his standards of logical proof, though according to him quite adequately to justify the strongest belief ("knowledge" not being claimed), partly because, owing to our inability to conceive what they can be like in themselves, we can only think them in relation to ourselves as practical beings. Kant undoubtedly believed in God, freedom and immortality, and did not merely hold that we ought to act as if the beliefs were true. Neither does he, like the pragmatist, claim them to be true because they are useful, but because he thinks that they follow from our knowledge of the moral law. It is not merely that, if we did not believe in God, freedom and immortality, we should be less likely to be moral, but that if we accept moral principles at all, we cannot reasonably avoid accepting these beliefs also. Kant's position is therefore quite different from that of pragmatism, even apart from the fact that a proof by practical reason was only claimed by him for three specific beliefs, while pragmatists make utility the criterion of all truths.

Now the mere fact that a theoretical conclusion followed from "practical reason" in the sense of being deducible only from premises one of which was ethical, would not itself prevent the proof being absolutely cogent logically and giving knowledge in the strictest sense, for Kant holds that we *know* and do not merely believe in the validity of moral laws. But he still declined to claim the rank of knowledge for the metaphysical conclusions in question, chiefly because we can obtain no clear conception of the nature of what is proved. We have in fact to apply the distinction mentioned earlier[1] between knowing and thinking in a sort of a way. Kant also distinguishes between thinking God as he is in himself, which we cannot do, and thinking God as he is in relation to us, which we can do. In the *Prolegomena* Kant uses " analogy " to mean " a perfect likeness of two relations which hold between quite unlike things " and says that " by means of this analogy there is left a concept of the highest being which is adequately determined *for us*, although we have omitted everything which could determine it absolutely and *in itself*, for we still determine it relatively to the world and to ourselves, and nothing more is necessary for us."[2] Thus he says, " If I say we are constrained to regard the world as if it were the work of a supreme understanding and will, I am really saying nothing more than this: as a clock, a ship, a regiment are related to their maker, their builder, their commander, so the sensible world (or its basis) is related to the unknown. I thus know the latter not as it is in itself but as it is for me, namely in relation to the world of which I am a part."[3] And in a footnote to the first passage quoted he explains further what he means by another illustration:—" As the promotion of the happiness of their children ($=a$) stands to their parents' love ($=b$), so the welfare of the human race ($=c$) stands to the unknown element in God ($=x$) which we call love. This does not imply that it has the least resemblance to any human desire, but only that its relation to the world can be posited

---

[1] *v.* above, pp. 121-2.   [2] § 58, *Berl.* IV, 357-8.
[3] *Proleg.*, § 57, *Berl.* IV, 357.

as like a relation which things in the world have to each other." (Without admitting "religious experience," which Kant would not do, it must be difficult to give a less formal account of God's love.) The attributes ascribed by Kant to God fall into four classes in fact :—(a) analogical, as described above, (b) formal attributes, e.g. omnipotent, the conception of which is derived from the categories, but the validity of which is proved ethically as with (a), (c) negative attributes such as timeless, which distinguish God from the world of sense, (d) specifically ethical attributes. In ethics alone, Kant thinks, is it possible to have non-empirical ideas which are also clear and definite.

Kant refuses to class the beliefs in God, freedom and immortality as justified opinions or hypotheses, partly because he thinks these words too weak to express the certainty of the beliefs in question, but partly also because he thinks that such words should only be used where we have a definite concept of the nature of what we are postulating. Kant holds that, in order to assume anything as a hypothesis legitimately, " I must at least know so much of its properties that I require to assume, not its concept, but only its existence,"[1] by which he seems to mean that I must not assume as a hypothesis the existence of a new kind of thing which has never been encountered in experience, but only fresh instances of classes of which other instances have already been experienced. For I must know at least that the object is possible,[2] and of this previous experience is the only guarantee. Kant in fact limits opinion to the sphere

---

[1] *Critique of Pure Reason*, B 855. This whole section of the *Doctrine of Method* is very valuable as criticising the use of hypotheses in metaphysics and explaining the one, negative use of them which Kant allows.

[2] B 798.

of causal reasoning among phenomena, and insists that in metaphysics or critical philosophy, as in mathematics, our arguments being *a priori* either prove their conclusions with certainty or have no value at all.[1] Since propositions about God and immortality were according to him, therefore, neither cases of opinion nor cases of knowledge, he had to find a new niche for them, and did it by introducing a third class of cognitive attitude, which he called belief or practical knowledge. In the *Doctrine of Method* he distinguishes (1) opinion, which is both subjectively and objectively uncertain, (2) knowledge, which is both subjectively and objectively certain, (3) belief, which is objectively uncertain but subjectively certain,[2] and he puts the ideas of God and immortality in the third class. The position he intends to ascribe to freedom is more doubtful.

For the moral proof of God and immortality we must refer the reader to the *Critique of Practical Reason*.[3] Since Kant is not dealing with ethics in the *Critique of Pure Reason*, he does not give an account of the main positive basis of his doctrine in that work. I shall just call attention very briefly to two highly noteworthy features in his whole treatment of religion. (1) He tries to found every religious dogma which he admits on ethics and to reinterpret all the generally accepted dogmas of Christianity more or less symbolically in ethical terms. The essence of superstition is for him the supposition that we can make ourselves pleasing to God in any other way than by good moral action, a superstition of which he found abundant

---

[1] B 803 ff.; for criticism of this, *v.* above, p. 15.

[2] B 850. The same German word, *Glauben*, may be translated either " faith " or " belief."

[3] Bk. II, ch. 2, esp. § 4-5, Abbott, p. 218 ff. For a detailed account of his theological views *v.* his *Religion within the Bounds of Mere Reason*.

examples in the stressing of creeds and ceremonies as necessary to salvation. (2) He will have nothing to do with what is nowadays usually called " religious experience " either as a source of evidence for the being or nature of God or as a desirable aim for the believer in God. He recognises no such thing as communion with God. Kant took this attitude partly because he was afraid that the encouragement of attention to emotional experiences in connection with religion was dangerous as tempting people to take these as a substitute for moral goodness and also as leading to the acceptance of mere subjective fancies as communications from God, partly because the admission of such a source of knowledge or even ground for justified belief would conflict with his theory of knowledge, according to which sensation was essential for cognition, at least outside ethics. He in fact ruled out *a priori* the possibility of the experience of the non-sensible for human beings, though it is difficult to see on what grounds he could do so without unwarranted dogmatism, especially in view of the " critical " character of his own philosophy.

The question may reasonably be asked how it is that, having denied the possibility of attaining any sort of knowledge or even justified opinion about reality through theoretical reason, Kant could consistently claim to do so by means of practical reason. He would answer by pointing out the total difference (on his view) between ethical and theoretical knowledge. We could have no purely theoretical knowledge of reality because we could know no *a priori* propositions independently of experience, or at least of our forms of sensibility, in the theoretical sphere (except the " analytic " propositions of formal logic), but all pure (as opposed to applied) ethics was purely *a priori*. Ethics from the beginning can and must be independent of experience, while theoretical philosophy never can be, and so the obstacles which limit theoretical knowledge to phenomena disappear in the case of ethics. This does not mean that propositions in pure ethics give us information about reality by themselves. They cannot do this; as Kant insists, what ought to be may be very different from what is. But if, as Kant claims, though not themselves capable of giving information about what is, they have corollaries which do so, then there is no reason to limit these corollaries to experience, since they are based on propositions which are purely *a priori*, unlike those of theoretical knowledge. Ethics, Kant further thinks, must be about reality, not about appearances, just because, while it does not matter if science can only tell us what appears, not what really is, it would be futile for ethics to tell us only what appears to be our duty, not what our duty really is. If this is so, there is no reason why, if ethical propositions entail theoretical propositions at all, they should not entail theoretical propositions that do not hold merely within the realm of experience but apply to reality, although theoretical reason by itself could never reach such conclusions owing to its limitation to experience.

Kant, however, gives Ethics a kind of reference to experience by saying that it " can present its principles together with their practical consequences, one and all *in concreto,* in what are at least possible experiences," and mentions this as an advantage which it has in common with all subjects except metaphysics and which enables it to avoid " the misunderstanding due to abstraction."[1] Perhaps this explains too how it is that Kant could admit synthetic *a priori* propositions in Ethics after having asserted

[1] B 453.

the dependence of all such propositions on experience. They would be possible in Ethics, because Ethics, though intrinsically *a priori*, could at least be illustrated in empirical actual or possible actions. We may take the parallel of arithmetic, which can be synthetic because, though it is concerned with pure concepts, these concepts can be illustrated in counting or by picturing them in terms of dots on paper or successive moments of time. In that case the passage would explain a long-standing puzzle about Kant's views. Ethics would be synthetic because it could be at least applied to and illustrated by something that we experience in time. And the fact that it only requires illustration in experience, not a proof by reference to experience, might explain why it can lead to conclusions about reality. After all, arithmetic could presumably be applied to things-in-themselves, and arithmetic according to Kant's account agrees with ethics in not being proved, but only illustrated and clarified by reference to experience.

Kant holds, however, that the idea of God is important not only for ethics but also theoretically for science as a help in the systematic investigation of nature, though this is not regarded by him as constituting a proof of the existence of God. The idea is conceived as important for science in these two respects. (1) Kant thinks that the view of nature as a systematic whole in a sense of system which goes far beyond the minimum provided by the categories is very useful to science,[1] and he also contends that to look on nature as a systematic whole is the same as looking upon it *as if* it had been constructed by a rational mind with a view to making it intelligible.[2] We may compare

[1] *v.* the second class of ideas of reason discussed below, p. 255 ff.
[2] *v. Critique of Judgment Intr.*, § IV.

the view of e.g. Keynes that the assumption of causality even as universal would not be sufficient to justify induction, but that we require also to assume that the causal laws are relatively simple. Kant would put a similar point somewhat differently. He would say that in order to have any science, though not in order to make the unordered empirical generalisations and predictions of ordinary life, e.g. that fire will burn, we must think of the phenomenal world as intelligible and therefore think of it *as though* it were constructed by an intelligent mind in such a way that we could understand it, even if we do not necessarily assume the actual existence of such a mind. This is not meant to imply that he thinks we can see the connection between particular causes and their effects *a priori*, which he did not, but merely that we can "understand" phenomena in the sense in which the physical scientist claims to understand them. Even this would obviously be impossible if, though all phenomena were determined causally, the causal laws were too complicated for us ever to use or were all isolated and incapable of inter-connection in some sort of system. (2) Kant thinks that the concept of purpose is necessary for the success of biology, since biology finds it highly profitable or even essential to ask of the different parts of an organism—What is their purpose?[1]—and he further insists that to look upon organisms as purposive is to look on them *as if* they were created by a God. Both points are stressed greatly in the *Critique of Judgment*, but they also occur in the *Critique of Pure Reason*. Kant seems to think that these circumstances provide an argument,

---

[1] i.e., their purpose for the organism itself, not necessarily for man. Kant was not thinking of the teleology which says that sheep are created to provide us with wool and mutton, which would be of little use in biology.

though not a strictly conclusive argument, for the existence of God even on the theoretical side, and in one passage he goes so far as to say that opinion is far too weak a term and that "even in this theoretical relation it can be said that I firmly believe in God."[1]

Kant even thought, at least at one stage of the composition of the *Critique of Pure Reason*, that the idea of the *ens realissimum* of the ontological proof could be made serviceable as a regulative idea. This doctrine is elaborated in § 2 of the chapter. The *ens realissimum* is the idea of the sum of all ultimate, underivable predicates, therefore all our concepts can be reached by limitation of it, and Kant speaks in that section as though the idea were therefore presupposed in all our knowledge and thought, not indeed as a reality but at least as an idea, since it provides, so to speak, the store of attributes from which we must select any attributes we ascribe to anything. That the predicates attributed to the *ens realissimum* must be the highest possible in degree is not explicitly stated by Kant, but it is necessary if the *ens realissimum* is to be identified with God, and it is certainly part of the idea in the metaphysics taught by the Wolffian school which inspired this section of the Critique. All lower degrees of a quality would then be regarded as limitations of the highest degree. Negative predicates are not included by Kant, on the ground that they are derivative.[2] Even in this section Kant did not regard the utility of the notion of *ens realissimum* as proving that there was such a being.[3]

Of the three ideas under discussion freedom is given a

[1] B 854.   [2] B 602-4.
[3] Kant also gives importance as a regulative principle to the idea of a necessary being on which the cosmological argument depends (B 644), but adds that it must be supplemented by an opposite regulative principle.

special position. It is said to be " the only one of all the Ideas of Pure Reason whose object is a thing of fact (Tatsache) and to be reckoned among the *scibilia*,"[1] so that it is actually described as an object of knowledge. It is also " the only one of which we *know* the possibility *a priori* (without, however, understanding it), because it is the condition of the moral law which we know."[2] The other two ideas, God and immortality, are held to differ from freedom in that they are not conditions of our being subject to the moral law, but only conditions of its application in pursuit of the highest good. But, even if proved in a sense in which God and immortality are not, freedom resembles these ideas in being quite incomprehensible to us, and so, like them, differs from the clear definite concepts of natural science *in toto*.

We may now turn to the second class of ideas. These differ very much from the first. For (1) they consist of principles which are indeed useful but are not held to be proved (even ethically) and are not, or rather ought not to be, objects of belief. (2) Their utility is not in connection with ethical practice but in connection with science. (3) They are directly concerned with phenomena, not noumena, though, if objectively valid, some of them would have metaphysical implications, e.g. the principle of teleology. They are thus *merely* regulative in a stricter sense than the first class of ideas. For, if used rightly, they do really only regulate our scientific practice and do not give us fresh information, while it cannot be denied that the ideas of God, freedom and immortality if, as Kant thinks, they have been established by ethics, give us information about reality, at

---

[1] *Critique of Judgment*, *Berl*. V, p. 468, Bernard's transl., p. 406.
[2] *Critique of Practical Reason*, *Berl*. VI 4, Abbott, pp. 87-8.

least in relation to human beings, that we otherwise could not have attained, even if the information is not very clear and has not been proved to be true in the strictest sense, only sufficiently to justify belief.

It should be added, however, that, in so far as the idea of God is used theoretically for science, apart from its ethical proof, it belongs rather to the second than to the first class of ideas. Kant did not, at least in most moods, hold that the supposed utility of the idea of God for science justified us in believing that God existed, *only* in thinking of the world *as if* it were created by God,[1] though, since the belief was established by an ethical proof, he no doubt thought that some additional confirmation, if there was any needed, was provided by its value for scientific research.

Unfortunately Kant does not give a list of the second class of ideas, and they form a rather numerous and motley crowd. They have this point in common, that they are all concerned with the systematising of phenomena.[2] Kant says that every science must be based on an idea.[3]

[1] But *v. Critique of Pure Reason*, B 854.

[2] "If we consider in its whole range the knowledge obtained for us by the understanding, we find that what is peculiarly distinctive of reason in its attitude to this body of knowledge, is that it prescribes and seeks to achieve its *systematisation*, that is, to exhibit the connection of its parts in conformity with a single principle. This unity of reason always presupposes an idea, namely, that of the form of a whole of knowledge—a whole which is prior to the determinate knowledge of the parts and which contains the conditions that determine *a priori* for every part its position and relation to the other parts. This idea accordingly postulates a complete unity in the knowledge obtained by the understanding, by which this knowledge is to be not a mere contingent aggregate, but a system connected according to necessary laws" (B 673).

[3] "No one attempts to establish a science unless he has an idea upon which to base it. But in the working out of the science the schema, nay even the definition which, at the start, he first gave of the science, is very seldom adequate to his idea. For this idea lies hidden in reason, like a germ in which the parts are still undeveloped and barely

1. There is the principle of homogeneity of species:—that all different species can be brought under a few genera and these ultimately under one single supreme genus.[1] What is meant by this principle is not very clear to me. It obviously must mean that most or even all things are to be regarded as having something in common, but it seems also to mean something more, which we might express by saying that there is a limited number of ultimate determinable characteristics such that all things can be arranged in classes, each of which is defined by one of these, and that in these classes the defining properties of the different species will be derivable from the determinable characteristic of the genus to which they belong either through being generated by them in the sense in which a determinable can generate its more determinate varieties,[2] or, if not themselves varieties of the determinable, in the sense of being connected by causal laws with varieties or degrees of the determinable. An example would be found in the classification of the chemical elements according to their atomic weights.

2. But this is supplemented by its opposite, the principle of specification, according to which no species is to be regarded as the lowest.[3] Kant does not say that no species

---

recognisable even under microscopic observation. Consequently since sciences are devised from the point of view of a certain universal interest, we must not explain and determine them according to the description which their founder gives of them, but in conformity with the idea which, out of the natural unity of the parts that we have assembled, we find to be grounded in reason itself. For we shall then find that its founder, and often even his latest successors, are groping for an idea which they have never succeeded in making clear to themselves, and that consequently they have not been in a position to determine the proper content, the articulation (systematic unity) and limits of the science " (B 862).

[1] B 680 ff.   [2] As possibilities, not of course as actual existents.
[3] B 682 ff.

actually is the lowest, but only that we must never lose sight of the possibility of finding further diversity. We here have a regulative principle which, if taken as constitutive, would be actually self-contradictory. Kant points this out in the case of the next principle, continuity of species.

3. The principle of affinity or continuity[1] is what Hegel would have called the synthesis of the first two principles. It is the law that we should think of species as if they formed a continuous series, in which between every two there was another to be found which differed less from either of the two than they differed from each other. Kant, though he lived before the scientific establishment of the doctrine of evolution, was very interested in the notion of evolution as a possibility, and if he had been a contemporary of Darwin he would probably have pointed to evolution as a case where a regulative idea, that of continuity of species, suggested and encouraged the search for partial realisations of it even against the apparent empirical evidence, i.e. although extant species were quite distinct, and so led to the eventual finding of new empirical evidence which justified the search, e.g. that of fossils.

4. Kant also speaks of pure earth, pure air, pure water, etc. (in the chemical sense of the day) as concepts of reason.[2] They are not ordinary empirical concepts, because these have never been found empirically in their purity, and they were in Kant's time of utility in organising our knowledge in chemistry, but there is obviously an important difference between them and the more general ideas. (Kant apparently does not mean to distinguish "concepts of reason" from "ideas of reason.") Obviously there are a great number of that kind of "ideas." E.g. in physics the idea of a body ab-

[1] B 686 ff.   [2] B 673-4.

solutely unaffected by others (as in the first law of motion) is another example that Kant might have mentioned.

5. Kant speaks of the idea of a fundamental power from which all the properties of a thing could be derived.[1] He is thinking especially of the self in psychology, but also of material things.

6. Similarly he says that we ought in psychology to "connect all the appearances, all the actions and receptivity of our mind, *as if* the mind were a simple substance which persists with personal identity (in this life at least)."[2] This regulative idea, when illegitimately treated as constitutive, gives rise to the paralogisms. Rightly used it does not involve the impossible task of deriving the different properties of our soul from the notion of the soul as a thinking substance, but rather strives to derive them from each other on the ground that the different properties of the same substance must be themselves in unity with each other.[3]

7. Corresponding to the antinomies there is also a "cosmological idea" which is useful as regulative but harmful if taken as constitutive.[4] This idea, though Kant calls it an idea of "absolute totality,"[5] which may suggest the thesis, is really the principle of the antithesis that we must treat the series of conditions as if it were infinite.

8. There is the idea of teleology, which is useful in physiology and biology, where the inquirer is always asking about the purpose of different parts of an organism, thus presupposing the principle, as at least regulative, that everything in an organism has a purpose.

9. In the *Critique of Judgment* there is a new development. In the *Critique of Pure Reason* it had been assumed

---

[1] B 676 ff.   [2] B 700, *v*. 710 ff.   [3] B 701.
[4] B 537-8, 700, 712 ff.   [5] B 713.

that there was only one kind of causality among phenomena, but in the *Critique of Judgment* a distinction is drawn between the mechanistic causality prevalent in the inorganic world and the causality which accounts for the characteristic behaviour of organisms, and mechanism, instead of being identified with the category of causality in the only form in which it can be applied to phenomena and therefore held to be constitutive, is declared merely regulative. The antinomy between mechanism and teleology is thus solved by declaring both principles regulative.

10. " A constitution allowing *the greatest possible human freedom* in accordance with laws by which *the freedom of each is made to be consistent with that of all others* " is declared to be " a necessary idea, which must be taken as fundamental not only in first projecting a constitution but in all its laws."[1] This idea, though it might perhaps be conceived as bearing a relation to politics similar to what the other ideas bear to the physical sciences, differs from them in being an ethical ideal, not an idea of what is already there which we hope to find partially confirmed, but an idea of what we ought, as far as possible, to produce.

11. Kant speaks of " ideals " of reason as well as " ideas," meaning by *ideal* " an individual thing, determinable or even determined by the idea alone."[2] As an example he cites the idea of a perfect man, but the idea of God is the principal " ideal." The idea of a kingdom of ends, which is essential for Kant's ethics, would, I suppose, also be an ideal.

Why did Kant believe that the ideas were useful for science? For two reasons, I think : in the first place because they served as an inspiration and encouragement. If we think of all the different properties of a thing as de-

[1] B 373.   [2] B 596 ff.

rived from one single property or of all phenomena as mechanically caused, it will incite us to look very keenly for evidence of unity in the one case and of mechanism in the other, and as a result we are much more likely to discover what unity and mechanism there actually is. And these ideas will inspire us with a salutary discontent with explanations which readily have recourse to a number of irreducible faculties or which appeal to a *deus ex machina* or a " vital force " as soon as any difficulty arises in explaining something according to the recognised laws of nature. Secondly, we must have some policy to organise our research; if we look merely at random we are not likely to find anything of value. For the mere knowledge that an event is caused is not enough; it gives no hint where to look in order to find what causes there are. But the various more specific ideas give this hint. E.g. the " idea " that the whole physical universe was a mechanical system governed by the same laws of motion throughout suggested to astronomers ways of inquiry that led to a successful causal explanation of phenomena such as the velocities and orbits of the planets; the assumption that the different parts of the body have a purpose, applied in particular cases more specifically, suggested to biologists where to look for the causes of their movements; and even the mere general idea that the world is a unity had its utility in calling the attention of scientists to similarities that they might otherwise have overlooked, e.g. between the motion of apples falling in an orchard and the motions of the stars. We may compare Professor Broad's statement that for successful advance a science needs a " ground-plan." Kant's ideas are intended to provide this ground-plan.

Reason is said by Kant to be related to understanding as

the categories are to sensibility, i.e. just as there would be no sense-experience without the categories there would be no coherent use of understanding without reason.[1] Note that Kant does not say no "understanding" but no "coherent use of understanding." This does not destroy the analogy with the categories, for Kant only applies the term "experience" to coherent experience, i.e. he does not say that there would be no experience in the sense of sensation without the categories, but no organised sense-experience. Similarly there would no doubt be isolated judgments and empirical generalisations without the ideas according to Kant, but no science. There is, however, a certain variation of emphasis, if not inconsistency, in Kant's treatment of the ideas. The two conflicting tendencies are designated by Professor Kemp Smith respectively sceptical and idealist (in a special sense of the term which has no reference to the existence of physical objects). "On the Idealist interpretation Reason is a metaphysical faculty, revealing to us the phenomenal character of experience, and outlining possibilities such as may perhaps be established on moral grounds. From the sceptical standpoint, on the other hand, Reason gives expression to what may be only our subjective preference for unity and system in the ordering of experience. According to the one, the criteria of truth and reality are bound up with the Ideas; according to the other, sense-experience is the standard by which the validity even of the Ideas must ultimately be judged."[2] As Professor Kemp Smith[3] admits, his account of the idealist tendency goes slightly beyond the

[1] B 596 ff.

[2] *v. Commentary*, pp. 426 ff., 547 ff. B 673, 678-9, 681-2, 684, 688-9, 691, 703-4 are passages which incline more in the idealist direction, B 674-7, 693 ff., 704-6, 721, 727-9, 799 more in the sceptical.

[3] Kemp Smith, *Commentary*, p. 560.

actual words of the Critique, but expresses thoughts that were no doubt very much in Kant's mind when he wrote certain passages. It might be questioned whether, as Professor Kemp Smith holds, the ideas are necessary for the distinction between appearance and reality, since one might degrade the world of our ordinary experience to the rank of appearance, not because it fell short of the standard set by the "ideas," but because, if taken as real, it was, as the antinomies claimed to show, actually self-contradictory, but no doubt the conviction that the physical world did not conform to our ideas together with the hope that reality might in some sense do so was one of Kant's motives for making the distinction. This "idealist" tendency was the most important thing in Kant for the Hegelians.

The Transcendental Doctrine of Method. This part of the Critique should not be neglected by the student, but its clear and straightforward exposition renders the help of a commentator much less needful than is the case with the remainder of the work. It is not without significance that I have included my brief remarks on it in the chapter on Theology and the Ideas of Reason, because the questions suggested by these words constitute the main *ratio essendi* of what Kant calls (very inappropriately) the Doctrine of Method. Owing to the relative lack of difficulty in this part of the work I shall confine myself to one or two brief remarks showing its general purpose. I have already referred to three of the most important sections—*The Discipline of Pure Reason in its Dogmatic Employment, The Discipline of Pure Reason in respect of Hypotheses, and Opining, Knowing and Believing.*[1]

The *Doctrine of Method*, together with the *Appendix to*

[1] *v.* above, pp. 39, 248, 249.

the Dialectic,[1] is concerned with giving an account of the functions which reason can perform, while the *Dialectic* tries to show that it cannot perform certain functions which had been ascribed to it. The title, *Doctrine of Method*, is therefore somewhat misleading. It would also have been better to make the division at the beginning of the above-mentioned Appendix. This part of the Critique also serves to draw a general map of philosophy and sketch the connection between Kant's ethical and theoretical works. It is contrasted with the *Doctrine of Elements*, which constitutes the rest of the Critique from the introduction of the whole work to the end of the *Dialectic,* and which gives an inventory of our capacities for knowledge, while the *Doctrine of Method* investigates how they are to be used in constructing the system of knowledge, metaphorically described here as a building.[2] One would therefore expect the *Doctrine of Method* to be a much more considerable part of the book than the other, but instead of this it is more like a mere appendix. This is because Kant's investigation in the *Doctrine of Elements* had left him with the conviction that there were no materials available from which to build up a speculative philosophy, so that the function of reason became very limited. Also its constructive function is almost wholly confined to ethics, and ethics he handles in other works.

a. *The Discipline of Pure Reason.* This consists in differentiating between those spheres where we can obtain *a priori* knowledge and those where we cannot, and thus curbing the pretensions of pure reason to give us knowledge independently of all experience. The critical philosophy thus produced differs from " scepticism " in that it is founded, not merely on the empirical failures of the human mind to

[1] B 670 ff.   [2] B 735.

prove metaphysical conclusions, but on general principles which show that such a thing is impossible and at the same time prevent the extension of the distrust of reason to science and mathematics, where it is unwarranted.[1] (Reason is here sometimes used by Kant in a wider sense in which it includes " understanding " also.)

b. *The Canon of Pure Reason*. This contains the only positive contribution of pure reason, unless we call the architectonic a positive contribution. Our inextinguishable desire for knowledge through reason would be unaccountable if there were not really some positive knowledge belonging to reason, but this is not to be found in theoretical but in practical reason. The canon of pure reason, if completely given, would be a list of the supreme moral laws. Kant does not however give these here, but rather discusses the bearing of ethics on the rest of philosophy and especially on belief in God and immortality, raising his famous question—What may I hope?　He gives a condensed statement of the moral proofs of these doctrines, which proofs are given more fully in the *Critique of Practical Reason*.[2]

His statement that, if there were no God or no future life, we should have " to regard the moral laws as empty figments "[3] is not in accord with his usual view, which was that the moral law was certain whatever our metaphysical beliefs. It might indeed be contended that if, like Kant, one argues from the moral law to the existence of God and immortality, one must accept the converse proposition that, if there were no God or no immortality, there could be no binding moral law. But Kant's position would rather be that the moral law was absolutely certain, but that the inference from the moral law to God and immortality,

[1] B 788 ff.　　[2] Bk. 2, ch. 2, sect. 4-5.　　[3] B 839.

18

though adequate for all practical purposes, fell short of the highest degree of certainty. It follows that if *per impossibile* God or immortality were proved impossible, Kant should doubt, not the moral law, but the less certain proposition that the moral law implies God and immortality, and this is no doubt what he would have done. Nor is it Kant's usual view that without God and a future life the ideas of morality could not serve as springs of purpose and "continued and persistent action " (*Ausübung*), as he says in B 841.

c. *Architectonic*. This consists in a systematic classification, according to *a priori* principles, of all knowledge[1] (see page 267).

A peculiarity of this list is the admission of an empirical part of philosophy.[2] His inclusion of rational psychology under immanent metaphysics[3] disagrees with the usage of the *Dialectic*. Note that empirical psychology is denied a place of right in philosophy, but then allowed one by courtesy on the grounds that "it is not yet so rich as to be able to form a subject of study by itself, and yet is too important to be entirely excluded or forced to settle elsewhere, in a neighbourhood that might well prove much less congenial than that of metaphysics."[4]

Much more important than the architectonic is the distinction between philosophy of the schools (*Schulbegriff*), which does not aim at anything more than to make as scientific a system as possible of philosophy, and philosophy as a *conceptus cosmicus* (*Weltbegriff*).[5] The latter seeks to order all knowledge with a view to the supreme ends of humanity and would manifest itself not only theoretically, but practically in the ideally noble life of the philosopher,

---

[1] *v*. B 868 ff.   [2] B 868 *ad fin*.   [3] B 874.   [4] B 876-7.
[5] B 867-8, *cf. Logik, Berl*. IX, 23 ff.

though Kant adds that no such ideal philosopher has been found. "The idea of his legislation" is, however, to be found in the reason of every human being, and Kant strives

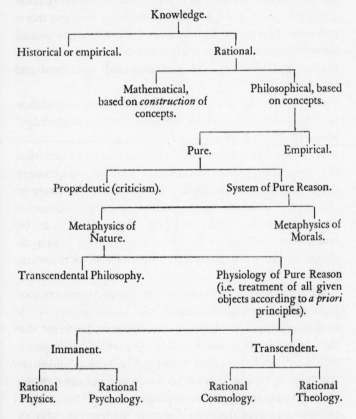

Knowledge.

Historical or empirical.   Rational.

Mathematical, based on *construction* of concepts.   Philosophical, based on concepts.

Pure.   Empirical.

Propædeutic (criticism).   System of Pure Reason.

Metaphysics of Nature.   Metaphysics of Morals.

Transcendental Philosophy.   Physiology of Pure Reason (i.e. treatment of all given objects according to *a priori* principles).

Immanent.   Transcendent.

Rational Physics.   Rational Psychology.   Rational Cosmology.   Rational Theology.

to carry it out all through his works. Philosophy thus viewed is a scheme of the ideal human life, a scheme which will fix among other things the place in it of philosophy itself. Thus Kant will only admit the pursuit of philosophy to be justified in so far as it contributes to human welfare in the highest sense. He thought that his philosophy benefited humanity by securing against the sceptic ethics, religion and science, and by delimiting their rightful position. Speculative metaphysics he thought of no value either for giving anybody a real conviction on such matters or for explaining anything scientifically, but rather regarded it as an unsettling and distracting influence and therefore did not regret its destruction.

d. *History*. Kant here uses the term "naturalist of pure reason" to stand for the members of the "common sense" school of whom Beattie was a representative, but his account hardly does them justice. The statement about Locke's view of immortality is also inaccurate. The very brief sketch given in this section seems to show that the issue in philosophy to which Kant attached most importance was that between empiricism and rationalism. This is highly appropriate, for one of the chief merits of his philosophy lies in the subtle and fruitful way in which he combined the two.[1]

Kant has been subjected to severe and persistent criticism from all sorts of different angles, and hardly anyone would wish now to defend the *ipsissima verba* of the Critique. But the extraordinary power and fertility of his thought, as evidenced by the fact that he would be almost universally admitted to be the greatest philosophical influence during the last 150 years, cannot be explained away. He combined in himself most of the main divergent tendencies of thought which have influenced philosophers throughout the ages and did so in such a way as to bring out the strength and weak-

[1] For a fuller account of his interpretation of the history of philosophy *v. Logik, Einleitung*, p. 4.

ness of each in a fashion which had never been achieved before, and provided the seed for a great number of promising developments. Almost all the varieties of nineteenth and twentieth century philosophy from positivism to absolute idealism, from pragmatism to direct realism, have their roots partly in the *Critique of Pure Reason*.

INDEX

ACTUALITY, 172-3

Adickes, 187 n., 193

Æsthetic, Transcendental, ch. II passim; aim of, 9, 11, 24; its apparent differences from rest of *Critique*, 62-5, 67, 214

Affection, Kant's use of term, 123-4; doctrine of double affection, 90 n., 179

Affinity, in the manifold, 110-2

Algebra, 48, 58

Amphiboly of Concepts of Reflection, 195-8

Analogy, meaning of term, 150, 247 ; first, 150-7 ; second, 157-66 ; third, 166-70

Analytic, Transcendental, ch. III-IV passim; aim of, 9, 11, 24

Analytic] [synthetic judgments, 18 ff., 58, 116; analytic method, 40

Animals, psychology of, 94, 124

Anticipations of Perception, Principle of, 149

Antinomies, 208-27; general principle of their solution, 221-4; their bearing on Kant's general philosophy, 208-9, 259

Appearances, argument that everything in space and time is reducible to, 30, 49-50, 61-2, 185-6, 221-4; relation to things-in-themselves, 194, 230 ff.

Apperception, use of term, 81, 113; transcendental unity of, 81 ff., 112, 113, 114, 117, 118, 124, 126-7

Apprehension, synthesis of, 75, 129

A priori, use of term, 17, 29 ff., 32-3, 80; problem of synthetic *a priori* judgments, 18 ff., 26, 30, 40 ff., 47 ff., 71-2; *a priori* element in all judgments, 71-2,

86, 130; space and time *a priori*, 29-35, 40-9, 56-7; *a priori* knowledge in mathematics, 40 ff., 47 ff.; *a priori* judgments in metaphysics, 12, 25, 199; *a priori* element in Kant's ethics, 234-5, 251-2

Aristotle, logic of, 136, 137

Arithmetic, 23-4, 48, 57-8

Association of ideas, 110-2

Atomic theory of matter, 173

Axioms, 41-6, 57, 58; *Principle of the Axioms of Intuition*, 148

Baumgarten, 198

Beattie, 3, 268

Belief,] [knowledge and opinion, 249, 254

Berkeley, 182

Body, relation to mind, 207

Caird, 1 n., 34 n., 38, 92 n., 187 n.

Cambridge school, 180

Categories, use of term, 132, 137; Kant's pre-critical view of, 2-3, 99 ff., 106-8; proof of, 67-9, 79, 85-7, 105-6, 114, 127-8, 136 ff.; presupposed in the synthesis of imagination, 91 ff.; their extension beyond appearances, 121-2, 187-90; the individual categories, ch. IV passim;] [forms of judgment, 134-44; application to particular appearances, 109 ff., 130, 147-8; application or non-application to self as appearance, 148, 151, 164-6, 170, 174-5, 202, 227; schematisation of, 132 ff., 145-7

Causality, influence of Hume, 3; proof of, 79, 157-66; application to particular appear-

271

ances, 109 ff., 130, 161, 207;
application to appearance self,
164-6, 174-5; and substance,
152,157;] [community, 166 ff.;
regularity view of, 133-4, 163;
application to things-in-themselves, 179, 187 ff.; ground
and cause, 2, 133-4, 138, 146,
150, 189-90, 218;] [mechan-
ism, 260; causality and freedom, 227-40; Kant's *Treatment of Causality*, my previous work, 1 n., 89, 94, 126 n.,
164 n.

Certainty, claimed by Kant for
his work, 14-5, 220-1

Change, 60, 150, 159

Christianity, 249

Cogito, ergo sum, 126

Coherence, theory of truth, 69,
78, 80, 170

Common-sense propositions, 180

Community, meaning of, 133,
166-7; proof of, 79, 166-70;
non-application to self, 174-5,
207-8; derivation from disjunctive judgment, 144

Composition of *Critique*, 3-9,
95-105

Concepts, and intuitions, 36-7,
39, 55, 57, 62, 71-2, 93, 106-7,
116, 128-30; and judgments,
136, 142, *V. A priori*

Conservation of matter, 151, 156

Consistency, of Kant, 5 ff., 96 ff.

Constitutive,] [regulative principles, 148, 245

Contingency, 219

Continuity of time, 159; of
change, 173-4; of species, 258;
in psychology, 125

Contradiction, law of, 191, 196

Copernican revolution, 16

Cosmological argument, 242-4

Criterion of truth, 141

Critique of Judgment, 90 n., 92,
140, 227, 244-5, 252, 253, 255,
259-60

Critique of Practical Reason,
229, 234, 239, 244, 255

Descartes, 21, 126

Design, argument from, 244-5

Dialectic, Transcendental, meaning of term, 200; aim of *Dialectic*, 9, 24, 141

Disjunctive judgment, 142, 144,
201

Dissertation, Kant's Inaugural
of 1770, 2-3, 50, 54, 61, 62,
213

Dynamical principles, 148; dynamical antinomies, 225-6

Editions, second] [first, 67, 70,
114-5

Einstein, 46

Emotions, 85, 124

Empirical *v.* Experience

Ens realissimum, 201, 254

Epigenesis, 130, 131

Ethics, 220-1, 249, 250-2

Euclidean and non-Euclidean
geometry, 41-6, 48-9

Experience, meaning of term,
16 n., 68; proof of categories
by reference to experience, 26,
67-9, 85-7; no knowledge beyond experience, 64, 121; but
not all arises out of experience, 16-7; doctrine that there
is only one experience, 112-3.
V. Sense-perception

Form,] [matter or content, 149,
197, 244; forms of intuition *v.*
Space and Time; form in
logic, 143; forms of judgment,
134 ff.

Freedom, 218, 227-40, 246,
254-5

*Fundamental Principles of the
Metaphysic of Morals*, 234

Generatio æquivoca, 130

Geometry, 39-49

God, arguments for existence of,
10, 241-5; idea of God, 122,
188 n., 194, 201, 246-50,
252-4; difficulties solved by
Kant's view, 55, 239; relation
to morality, 249, 265-6

Ground, and cause, 2, 133-4, 138,
146, 150, 189-90, 218

Hegel, 140
Homogeneity, principle of, 257
Hume, influence on Kant, 2-3, 108; Kant's refutation of, 72 ff.
Hypothesis, when permissible, 172, 248

Idealism, Kant's, 151-2, 164, 176-87; transcendental] [empirical, 84, 181-2 ; problematic, 176, 204; Kemp Smith's sense of " idealist ", 262-3; *Idealism, my book*, V. 22 n., 185 n.
Ideals of Reason, 260
Ideas of Reason, 170, 195, 245-63
Identity of indiscernibles, 196
Illusions, 93, 165-6
Images, 80, 91, 94
Imagination, 90 n., 145;] [understanding, 91-5, 113, 114, 116
Immortality, 202-3, 205-6, 246 ff.
Incongruous Counterparts, argument from, 53
Inference, 20 ff., 47 ff.
Infinite judgments, 142
Infinity, problems of, 37-9, 209-26
Innate ideas, 31, 131
Inner Sense, 58 ff., 62, 123 ff.
Interaction between body and mind, 207. *V.* Community
Intuition, meaning of term, 17-8, 28, 36; pure intuitions, 28 ff., 35 ff., 54-5, 63 ff., 77, 116; intuitions and concepts, 36-7, 39, 55, 57, 62, 71-2, 93, 106-7, 116, 128-30;] [perception, 18, 63; non-sensuous, 121, 193, 250

Johnson, W. E., 45 n.
Joseph, H. W. B., 146 n.
Judgment, Kant's definition of, 119; analytic and synthetic, 18 ff.; how synthetic *a priori* judgments are possible, 26, 30, 40 ff., 47 ff., 58, 251-2; relation of forms of judgment to categories, 134 ff.; judgments and concepts, 136, 142;

judgment as faculty, 137 n., 144-5

Keynes, J. M., 253

Leibniz, 1, 10, 21, 53, 60, 61, 171, 175 n., 195 ff., 214, 217
Limitation, category of, 134, 138, 142
Limiting concept, 193
Lindsay, A. D., 1 n., 93, 194 n.
Locke, 18 n., 268
Logic,] [sensuous element in appearances, 146, 195 ff.; laws of, 69; formal logic and Kant's categories, 136-9; distinction between general and transcendental, 141; modern mathematical, 142-3

Manifold, given, 72, 75, 109-11, 117-8, 123-4, 145, 161, 179; pure, 77. *V.* Sensation
Mathematics *v.* Geometry and Arithmetic
Matter *v.* physical things
Meaning, sense in which metaphysical statements are held to have no meaning, 122, 190
Mechanism, 260, 261
Memory, 75, 77, 114
Mendelssohn, M., 204
Metaphysical First Principles of Natural Science, 24, 33 n., 57, 64, 161, 217
Metaphysics, use of term, 25; pre-critical view of, 2-3; rejection of, 12-3, 73, 171, 199, 209; as a natural disposition, 245; metaphysical deduction of the categories, 66, 135-44
Method, Kant's, 8, 25-7; *Transcendental Doctrine of Method*, 263-8
Modality, 135, 139, 142, 170 ff.
Monadologia Physica, Kant's work, 217
Monads, 197, 214-5
Moore, G. E., 180, 237.
Morality, connection with freedom, 228-9, 233-6, 237, 255; as ground for belief in God

and immortality, 206, 246 ff.,
    255, 265-6
Motion, science of, 57
Multiple theory of composition
    of *Critique*, 4-9, 95-105

Necessity, of *a priori* judgments,
    17; of causality, 134, 160, 163,
    173; necessary being, 219,
    226-7, 242-4
Newton, 11, 53, 60
Noumena, positive sense] [nega-
    tive sense, 193. *V.* Self, as
    real; Things-in-themselves
Number, as schema of quantity,
    147, 148

Objects, Kant's use of term, 84;
    concept of, 71, 79-80, 118;
    transcendental, 99-102; em-
    pirical, relation to self, 83 ff.,
    118, 177 ff.; objects and objec-
    tive order as basis of argu-
    ment for categories, 85-7, 119,
    159 ff., 166, 168
Ontological argument, 241, 243,
    244
Opinions, Kant admits none in
    philosophy, 14, 248-9
Organisms, causation in, 140,
    260
Outer sense,] [inner, 51, 58-60,
    123-4

Paralogisms, 201-8, 259
Patchwork theory *v.* Multiple
    theory
Paton, H. J., VI; criticism of
    multiple theory of composition
    of *Critique*, 4 n., 96, 101, 103;
    on space and time, 29 n.,
    31 n., 34 n., 38 n., 39 n.; on
    transcendental deduction, 76,
    89-91, 93, 105, 128; on meta-
    physical deduction, 138-9,
    142-3; on schematism, 132-3;
    on analogies, 155, 156, 159;
    on things-in-themselves, 193
Phenomenalist tendency in Kant,
    182-3
Philosophy, general function of,
    266-8

Physical things, 112-3, 152,
    161-3, 177 ff., 221; relation to
    self, 80 ff., 84, 204, 206
Politics, 260
Positivism, present-day, 74, 122
Possibility, 170-2, 173
Posthumous Work, Kant's, 90,
    170, 179, 240
Postulates of Empirical Thought,
    170-4
Pragmatism, 246
Pre-cognition, 172
Pre-critical views of Kant, 1-3;
    pre-critical passages in *Cri-
    tique*, 9, 31-2, 62, 99 ff.
Pre-formation theory, 130
Prichard, H. A., 163
Primary,] [secondary qualities,
    51-2, 61, 197
Probability, 140
*Prolegomena to Every Future
    Metaphysic*, 3 n., 40, 54, 92,
    105, 150, 190, 247
Propositions *v.* Judgments
Psychology, not a science in the
    full sense, 125, 266; Kant's
    psychology, 70; rational psy-
    chology, 201 ff.
Pure, use of term, 17

Quality, 134, 142; and degree,
    149
Quantity, 58, 79, 134, 142, 148,
    174; as schematised, 147; ex-
    tensive] [intensive, 149

Rationalist school, 1-2, 268
Realism, 164, 176 ff., 184 ff.,
    222; empirical or material] [
    transcendental, 51, 84, 181-2
Reason, functions of, 200, 210,
    250-1, 262, 264-5
Reciprocity, *v.* Community
Recognition, synthesis of, 75
Regressus in indefinitum,] [*re-
    gressus in infinitum*, 224-5
Regulative, analogies described
    as, 148;] [constitutive, 245.
    V. Ideas of Reason
Relations, 61-2, 95
Religion, 8, 249-50

Religion within the Bounds of Mere Reason, Kant's work, 228, 249 n.

Representation, use of term, 28

Representative perception, theory of, 183-4

Reproduction, synthesis of, 75, 90-1 n., 104, 109 ff.

Responsibility, 227 ff., 235

Riehl, A., 187 n.

Rousseau, 10

Scepticism, 68-9, 264-5

Schematism, 128, 132, 145-7

Schopenhauer, 161

Schulze, 136

Science, *Critique* as providing a philosophical basis for this, 11, 67-8; regulative principles useful for, 252-3, 255 ff., 260-1

Secondary qualities, 51-2

Self, as appearance, 60, 84, 123-7, 151, 164-6; as real, 60, 126-7, 203, 229 ff., 236; relation between real and appearance self, 59, 230 ff., 238, 239-40; unity of, 81 ff., 112, 117, 118, 126-7, 201-3, 259; relation to physical objects, 80 ff., 84, 204, 206

Self-evidence, rejection of this outside mathematics, 67, 69

Sensation, 34, 71-2, 94-5. *V.* Manifold

Sense-perception,][intuition, 18, 63; its function in knowledge, 22-3, 26, 61, 62; representative theory of, 183-4

Simple substances, 203, 204, 214-5

Smith, N. Kemp, VI, on composition of *Critique*, 4 ff., 95 ff.; on meaning of experience, 16 n.; on *Æsthetic*, 28 n., 31, 34, 42 n., 49; on transcendental deduction, 82, 88, 90, 93-4, 96-105, 107, 118; on metaphysical deduction, 142; on community, 170; on refutation of idealism, 179; on phenomenalism and subjectiv-ism, 182-3; on ideas of reason, 195; on paralogisms, 207; on antinomies, 221; on Ideas of Reason, 262-3

Space, argument that this is an *a priori* intuition, 28 ff.; separate intuition of space, 31-2, 54-5, 116, 128-9; space as whole][particular spaces, 29, 31, 34, 36-7, 54-5, 65, 170; subjective character of, 30, 49 ff.; empty space, 35, 55, 149, 169, 174, 213, 2¹4; and geometry, 39 ff.; absolute view of, 53-5, 60, 63-5, 214; relation to time, 56, 59-60; relation to categories, 62, 127-30, 169-70, 174-5; treatment in *Analytic*, 62-5, 77; antino-mies of, 212-3, 213-8

Specification, principle of, 257-8

Spinoza, 21, 175 n.

Subject, logical, 138, 201-2; that all judgments are reducible to subject - predicate form as-sumed, 18, 143

Subjective,][objective deduc-tion, 69-70, 74

Subjectivist tendency in Kant, 100, 182-3, 221

Substance, 133 n., 150-3, 225; its proof, 79, 153-7; rejection of view that self is substance, 150-1, 201-2; derivation from categorical judgment, 143-4, 201;][causality, 152, 157; application to reality, 188

Succession, relation to substance, 150, 153 ff.; doctrine that our apprehension is always succes-sive, 76-7, 154-5, 159-60; ob-jective][subjective succession, 160 ff.

Syllogism, Kant's use of this in his architectonic, 200-1

Synthesis, as necessary for all knowledge, 74 ff., 114, 115-6, 123-4, 136-7, 149; nature of, 88-91; as threefold, 75-8, 108, 113; empirical][transcen-dental, 90-1; synthesis of im-agination][synthesis of understanding, 91-5; different accounts of, 103-4; synthesis of pure intuitions, 65, 128 ff.

Synthetic] [analytic judgments, 18 ff.; how synthetic *a priori* judgments are possible, 26, 30, 40 ff., 47 ff., 58, 251-2; synthetic method, 40

System, 78 ff., 141, 144, 252, 256 n.

Teleology, 140, 205-6, 253-4, 259
Telepathy, 172
Things-in-themselves, consistency of Kant's belief in them, 187-95; application of categories to them, 99 ff., 121-2, 187-90; their unknowability, 61, 185-6, 187 ff.;] [transcendental object, 100 ff.; relation to appearances, 33, 194, 230 ff.
Thinking,] [knowing, 121-2, 188, 247
Time, argument that this is an *a priori* intuition, 28 ff., 55 ff.; unreality of, 60-1, 224; separate intuition of, 31-2, 54-5, 116, 128-9; time as a whole] [particular times, 29, 31, 56, 65; absolute] [relative view of, 53-5, 63-5; relation to space, 56, 59-60, 126, 177, 185; time and inner sense, 58 ff., 62; consciousness of time as premiss of argument of transcendental deduction, 26, 72; subjective and objective order in time, 154-5, 160 ff.; continuity and unity of, 157, 159; treatment of time in *Analytic*, 62-5, 77; relation to the categories, 62, 121, 127-30, 132-3, 145-7, 153-4, 158-60; antinomies of time, 211-2, 221 ff.; freedom impossible if we really are in time, 227 ff.

Totality, category of, 134, 138
Transcendent,] [transcendental, 25. *V.* Metaphysics
Transcendental, meaning of term, 25; idealism, 51; object, 99-102; proof, 105; unity of apperception, 81 ff., 112, 113, 114, 117, 118, 124, 126-7
Transcendental Deduction of the Categories, main argument of, 66-95; composition of, 95-105; first edition deduction, 105-14; second edition deduction, 114-31; relation to metaphysical deduction, 135-6
Truth, criterion of, 141

Understanding, 74 n., 141;] [imagination, 91-5, 113, 114, 116;] [reason, 210, 262; intuitive understanding, 194
Unity, of experience, objects and self quâ cognitive, 78-87, 112 ff., 128 ff., 157, 169-70
Universal concepts, 36-7, 77, 138, 145-6, 147, 195 ff.; universality as criterion of *a priori*, 17

Vaihinger, H., his theory of composition of *Critique*, 4 ff., 95 ff.; on refutations of idealism, 178, 179
Vleeschauwer, H. J. de, 104, 116, 127

Ward, J., 7 n., 58 n.
Will, 10, 62
Wilson, J. Cook, 142 n.
Wolff, 1, 21

Yates, B. Lund, 96 n.

Zeno, 216

INDEX OF COMMENTS ON PARTICULAR PASSAGES

Page in Text.	Page in Commentary.	Page in Text.	Page in Commentary.
A XIII	14	B 122 = A 89	106-8
A XVI	70	B 124 = A 92	70
A XX	14	A 94	108
B XVI	16	A 99	72, 74, 76, 104
B XXX	9	A 100	109 ff.
B 1	16	A 103	75
B 2	17	A 104 ff.	78 ff., 99 ff.
B 3	17	A 105	80
B 10 ff. = A 6 ff.	19 ff.	A 107 ff.	81 ff.
B 14	23	A 108 ff.	83 ff.
B 17	24	A 110	112
B 25 = A 11	25	A 111 ff.	85 ff.
B 33 = A 19	28	A 113	109 ff.
B 38 = A 23-4	33 ff.	A 115	104, 113
B 39 = A 25	36	A 119 ff.	85 ff.
B 40 = A 25	37	A 121 ff.	109 ff.
B 41	40	B 128	108
B 44 = A 28	51	B 130	115
B 45 = A 29	51	B 132	117
B 46 = A 30-1	56	B 135	117
B 47 = A 31-2	56	B 136	118
B 48	56 ff.	B 141	119
B 49 = A 33	49, 53, 57, 59	B 143	135
B 50 = A 34	60	B 144	120
B 53 = A 37	60	B 146	120, 121-2
B 56 = A 39	60	B 148	121
B 57 = A 40	60	B 151-2	91
B 61 = A 43	61	B 153	123
B 66	61	B 157	126
B 85 = A 61	141	B 160	127
B 92 = A 67	141	B 167	130
B 93 = A 68	142	B 171 = A 132	144
B 96 = A 71	142	B 176 = A 137	145
B 97 = A 72	142	B 182 = A 142	147
B 99 = A 73	142	B 195 = A 156	64
B 100 = A 74	142	B 199 = A 160	148
B 106 = A 80	143	B 202 = A 162	148
B 110	144	B 207 = A 166	149
B 112	144	B 222 = A 179-80	150
B 113	144	B 225	153
B 117 = A 85	105-6	B 225 = A 182	154

Page in Text.	Page in Commentary.	Page in Text.	Page in Commentary.
B 226 = A 182-3	156	B 453 = A 425	251
B 229 = A 186	157	B 454 = A 426	211
B 230 = A 187	150	B 455 = A 427	213
B 232	151	B 456 = A 428	212
B 234 = A 189 ff.	159 ff.	B 462 = A 434	215
B 243 = A 198	159	B 463 = A 435	216
B 244 = A 199	159	B 466 = A 438	215
B 246 = A 201	159	B 470 = A 442	217
B 257 ff.	167 ff.	B 472 = A 444	218
B 266 = A 218-9 ff.	170 ff.	B 480 = A 452	219
B 273 = A 226	172	B 481 = A 453	219
B 274	181	B 487 = A 459	221
B 275	177 ff.	B 488 = A 460	219
B 280-1 = A 228	173	B 525 = A 497	221
B 291	174	B 540 = A 512	224
B 310 = A 254-5	193	B 559 = A 531	225
B 327 = A 271	196	B 564 = A 536	227
B 329 = A 273	196	B 600 ff. = A 572 ff.	254
B 330 = A 274	197	B 620 ff. = A 592 ff.	241
B 332 = A 276	197	B 622 = A 594	242
B 335 = A 279	193 n.	B 631 ff. = A 603 ff.	242
B 344 = A 288	192	B 649 ff. = A 621 ff.	244
B 373 = A 316	260	B 674 = A 646	258
B 379-80 = A 323	201	B 676 = A 648	259
A 348	201-2	B 679 = A 651	262
A 351	202-3	B 680 = A 652	257
A 361	203	B 682 = A 654	257
A 363 n.	203	B 686 = A 658	258
A 370	177 ff.	B 700 = A 672	259
A 390	207	B 735 = A 707	264
A 402	202 n.	B 789 = A 761	265
B 408	202-3	B 839 = A 811	265
B 409	204	B 850 = A 822	249
B 410	201-2	B 855 = A 827	248
B 413	204	B 866 = A 838	266
B 424	206	B 868 = A 840	266
B 450 = A 422	210	B 883 = A 855	268